S0-DBB-216

Small Scale Bibliographic Databases

LIBRARY AND INFORMATION SCIENCE

Small Scale Bibliographic Databases

Edited by
Peter Judge
Central Information Library and Editorial Section
CSIRO, Canberra, Australia

Brenda Gerrie
Patent Trademark and Design Office
Canberra, Australia

ACADEMIC PRESS
(Harcourt Brace Jovanovich, Publishers)
Sydney Orlando San Diego New York
London Toronto Montreal Tokyo

ACADEMIC PRESS AUSTRALIA
Centrecourt, 25–27 Paul Street North
North Ryde, N.S.W. 2113 Australia

United States Edition published by
ACADEMIC PRESS INC.
Orlando, Florida 32887

United Kingdom Edition published by
ACADEMIC PRESS, INC. (LONDON) LTD.
24/28 Oval Road, London NW1 7DX

Printed in Australia

National Library of Australia Cataloguing-in-Publication Data

---

Small Scale Databases.
Bibliography.
Includes index.
ISBN 0 12 391970 3.

1. Data base management. 2. Electronic data processing.
3. Information storage and retrieval systems. I. Judge, P. J. (Peter John), date. II. Gerrie, Brenda, date.
(Series: Library and information science).

001.6

Library of Congress Catalog Card Number: 85-73034

Contents

Preface ix

List of Contributors x

1. Small scale databases 1

Brenda Gerrie

1. Introduction 1
2. Database concepts 2
3. Sequential versus linked databases 2
4. Why create a database? 5
5. Database processing 6
6. Composition of a database 8
7. Choice of computer hardware and software 10
8. Quality control 11
9. Management considerations 13
10. Trade-offs in the database design process 13
11. Conclusion 15

Further reading 15

2. General overview of a database system 17

John D. Shortridge

1. Introduction 17
2. The database 17
3. Database management 19
4. Cost implications and trade-offs 33
5. Conclusion 34

Further reading 35

3. Software options 37

Cathie Jilovsky

1. Introduction: the role of software 38
2. Characteristics of textual databases 41
3. Desirable characteristics of suitable software 43
4. Other software required 43
5. File organisation methods 45
6. Software options 47
7. Evaluation of software 51
8. 'Hybrid' options: some warnings 54
9. Training software 55
10. Microcomputers 55
11. Cost considerations 56
12. Conclusion 56

References 56

4. Hardware options 59

Kerry Webb

1. Introduction 59
2. Processors 60
3. Input devices 62
4. Storage units 64
5. Output devices 66
6. Online versus offline storage 67
7. Shared versus dedicated stystems 68
8. Environmental considerations 70
9. Conclusion 70

Further reading 71

5. Management, control and cost benefit 73

D. A. Tellis

1. Introduction 73
2. The management approach 74
3. Main elements for a bibliographic database 77
4. Costs 81

5. Cost effectiveness benefit 89
6. Conclusion 96
Acknowledgement 96
References 97

6. Staffing and other management questions 99

Peter Judge

1. Introduction 99
2. Staffing questions 99
3. Marketing and other output considerations 111
4. Copyright 114
5. Legal responsibilities 115
6. Conclusion 116
Further reading 116

7. Management with a DBMS 117

Ian S. McCallum

1. Introduction 117
2. Information retrieval 118
3. A 4GL DBMS 120
4. Building the database 122
5. Searching the database 128
6. Conclusion 131
Acknowledgement 132
References 137

8. Input processing and editorial responsibilities 139

George Levick

1. Introduction 139
2. Primary document handling 140
3. Maintenance of data standards 142
Further reading 145

9. Subject control 147

Brenda Gerrie

1. Introduction 147
2. Terminology 148
3. Current issues in subject control 150
4. The power of online retrieval 151
5. The role of a controlled vocabulary 152
6. Vocabulary control in a total system 155
7. Recall devices 157
8. Precision devices 159
9. Design of a total system 161
10. Conclusion 163

References 164

10. Document acquisition and selection criteria 167

Sherrey Quinn
Margaret A. Findlay

1. Introduction 168
2. Identification 169
3. Acquisition 170
4. Selection 173
5. Cooperative acquisition arrangements 177
6. Research in progress and directory information 178
7. Conclusion 179

References 179

11. The future 181

Peter Judge

1. Introduction 181
2. Technical developments 183
3. The future market 190
4. Conclusion 193

Further reading 193

Glossary 195

Index 197

Preface

This book examines principles and asks the kind of questions which its readers may wish to ask themselves when considering whether to develop a database. These are not only technical questions. For example, the simple marketing approach described later in the book may save you time and frustration: if your database is not to be solely for your own purposes, who are you hoping will use it? What do those potential users really want? Discuss it with them: it may prevent a lot of disappointment.

The book had its origins in a Workshop held in Australia. Many of the participants came from developing countries in the region, but as soon as the news of the topic was released, the Workshop was heavily oversubscribed with Australian participants. It seems that everybody is interested in databases, and for this reason it is hoped that this book will be not only timely but timeless.

Quite deliberately, it has not been tied to particular hardware or software. There is such a variety of these products available now, that to be too explicit would limit the usefulness of this book.

Because of its Australian origins, the prices and costs quoted in this book are in Australian dollars, currently worth about 70¢ US (or 50p in the UK), but exchange rates are moving targets and the costs show little more than relativities: the whole pricing and costing structure may vary between countries just as much as the exchange rates.

Whatever your motives in setting up your database, we hope that it brings you both fun and profit. Good luck!

List of Contributors

Numbers in parentheses indicate the pages on which the author's contributions begin.

Margaret A. Findlay (167), Margaret Findlay and Associates, Vale House, Vale Road, Bowden, Attrincham, Cheshire, United Kingdom.

Brenda Gerrie (1, 147), C.O. Patent Trademark and Design Office, Scarborough House, P.O. Box 200, Woden ACT 2606, Australia.

Cathie Jilovsky (37), Library Systems Officer, The Borchardt Library, La Trobe University, Bundoora Vic. 3083, Australia.

Peter Judge (99, 181), Officer-in-charge, Central Information, Library and Editorial Section, CSIRO, P.O. Box 225, Dickson ACT 2602, Australia.

George Levick (139), Central Information, Library and Editorial Section, CSIRO, P.O. Box 89, East Melbourne, Vic. 3002, Australia.

Ian S. McCallum (117), Manager, Information Retrieval Systems, ACI Computer Services, P.O. Box 42, Clayton, Vic. 3168, Australia.

Sherrey Quinn (167), 25 Kanooka Avenue, Lower Templestowe, Vic. 3107, Australia.

John D. Shortridge (17), Central Information, Library and Editorial Section, CSIRO, P.O. Box 89, East Melbourne, Vic 3002, Australia.

D.A. Tellis (73), Australian Mineral Foundation Inc., P.O. Box 97, Glenside, SA 5065, Australia.

Kerry Webb (59), Assistant Director (Applications), ADP Systems Branch, National Library of Australia, Canberra ACT 2600, Australia.

1. Small scale databases

Brenda Gerrie

1. Introduction
2. Database concepts
3. Sequential versus linked databases
4. Why create a database?
5. Database processing
6. Composition of a database
   6.1 File size
   6.2 Record structure
   6.3 File update
   6.4 Information processing and retrieval
7. Choice of computer hardware and software
8. Quality control
9. Management considerations
10. Trade-offs in the database design process
11. Conclusion

Further reading

1. INTRODUCTION

The books published on the subject of databases in the field of library and information science tend to focus on the use of online search services and searching techniques. There is no clearly identifiable literature on the creation and management of text databases. This book moves to redress this imbalance by covering the procedural aspects of building and managing information packages consisting largely of text and/or bibliographic information. By way of an introduction to the subject this chapter outlines the concept of a database; issues related to the need for a database; database processing; logical composition; procedures associated with building databases; technical and quality control aspects; and some of the factors to be considered during the database design process.

SMALL SCALE DATABASES
ISBN 0 12 391970 3

2. DATABASE CONCEPTS

Within the field of library and information science a database is defined as an organised and generally unlinked set of machine readable bibliographic or information source records. Taken collectively these records constitute a growing file of information that can be used to obtain a variety of products for a range of purposes. These information files are defined according to scope and subject coverage in many ways. The large scale databases of the LC (LCMARC) or the NLA (AUSMARC) are inventory in essence and not limited by subject. The variety of database types has grown over the last decade and now includes a range of specialist and smaller scale databases usually limited in scope to particular subject areas. These information files contain bibliographic information, factual information reporting research in progress, biographic information, numeric information, or even entire texts as sources of information. Some databases are hybrids containing a mixture of this range of record types.

Databases are usually defined in terms of the type of information they contain and/or in terms of the attributes of the system(s) used to update, manage, analyse, retrieve and display information from these files. For example DBMS generate databases which have a logically consistent structure in that records are actually linked and the information is shared and integrated in a single file for particular retrieval purposes. This distinction between sequential databases (within library and information science) and linked databases (within DMBS) reflects important differences related to the purposes each database is intended to serve.

3. SEQUENTIAL VERSUS LINKED DATABASES

Sequential files of machine readable information comprise discrete logical records and each record is broken into fields of discretely accessible units of information. Each field of information is usually identified by a field name or tag and separated from the next field by a terminator mark. Fields may be further broken into subfields deemed the smallest logical element of information within a record which can be identified, manipulated or conveniently accessed.

This resolution of logical records into fields and subfields allows records to be typeset for display purposes. Resolution also enables merging and partitioning of the database for management purposes and adds a degree of precision to each record for retrieval purposes. Hence the structure of the logical record is related to the character of the information recorded and its intended purpose.

The structure of the bibliographic record often parallels the intellectual processes associated with its creation in terms of the order in which the fields occur. The record contents reflect its intended purpose in terms of field occurrences—fields may occur more than once in each record (subject descriptors for example) and perhaps logically there must be at least one occurrence of a given field (a subject or a title for example) and so on. The logical structure of each record therefore enables information to be stored as it is gathered, found as it is needed, and stipulates the conditions under which each field in a given record contributes to the overall quality control of the database.

The MARC format for transferring cataloguing data from one system to another is an example of how the character of the information gathered and its intended purpose can be interwoven by means of the record structure. The tag or field label is three digits; the first digit groups the fields according to bibliographic function (for example the 100 series of tags are allocated to main entry headings; the 200 series to information that forms the descriptive body of a bibliographic entry and so on); the second and third digits of a tag identify the formal relationship of data to the logical record (for example tags that end in '00' introduce personal names, those that end in '10' introduce corporate names and so on). In this way implicit information is carried economically through the tagging and both the character of the gathered information (formal relationships) and its intended purpose (functional relationships) are identified. The ascending order of tags in a MARC format reflects the intellectual process of cataloguing.

As it stands a sequential file has no linkages between records and direct information retrieval is limited to that single key that arranges the records in the file. In a sequential file each logical record is a discrete item and an element of data is repeatedly stored whenever and wherever it is needed. An element of information is repeated within a logical record when it serves different purposes (for example the name of an author stored as a main entry heading and also stored as part of the descriptive body of a bibliographic entry). Information redundancy between records is a natural consequence of having an unlinked file of information sources that share the same author or the same subject and so on. Information redundancy is reduced or removed by linking the data in a file through a pointer system whereby only the first occurrence of a data element is recorded and linked to subsequent occurrences of that data element. So a database may also take the form of a series of linked records managed by a database management system.

Functionally the difference between linked and unlinked databases is

DOC 1	AU	Breckwoldt, R	AU		TI	Wildlife in the home paddock
DOC 2	AU	Boyd, C	AU	Breckwoldt, R	TI	Wildlife refuges

(a) *Fixed field record structure*

001DOC 1>100Breckwoldt, R>245Wildlife in the home paddock=001DOC 2>100
Boyd, C>245Wildlife refuges>700Breckwoldt, R=

(b) *Simplified MARC record structure*

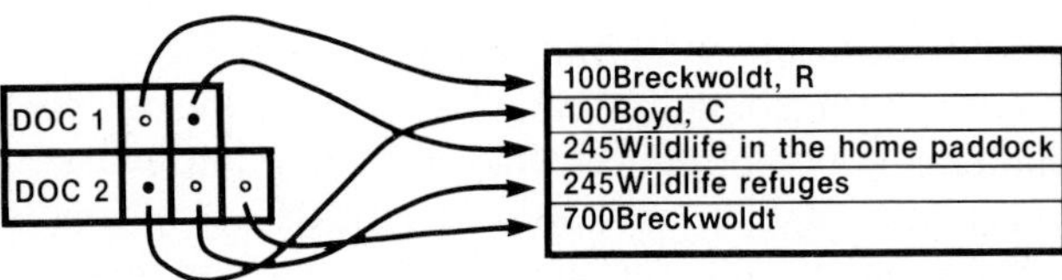

(c) *Functionally linked record structure*

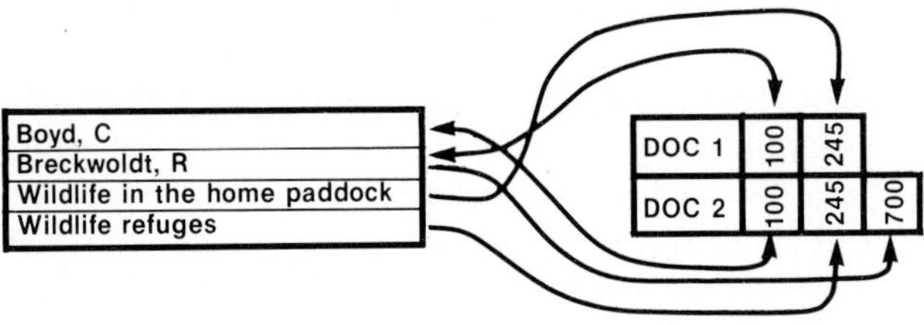

(d) *Formally linked record structure*

Fig. 1.1 Various representations of physical records.

marked. In Fig. 1.1 two simplified bibliographic records are stored in four different ways. The two records share a common author to illustrate how the need to repeat data elements can be eliminated using a pointer system.

The records shown in Fig. 1.1(a) are stored in a fixed field format and since the text information varies this format gives rise to wasted space when data does not fill the allocated storage and data may have to be truncated when it exceeds the available space. A MARC format accommodates the variability of the text data by using tags and delimiters to introduce and to end fields.

The simplified MARC records in Fig. 1.1(b) are divided into fields each introduced by a three digit tag and delimited from the next field by a field terminator (>). Each logical record is separated from the next by a record terminator (=). MARC record strucures are used as a vehicle for cooperative exchange of bibliographic records. This record structure is not designed for storage, management and retrieval of information because:

i. Storage space is wasted when many records share the same data elements.
ii. There are no linkages between records, and so retrieval of a field of information as an entity entails sequentially searching until each instance of that data element is located.
iii. The same information is recorded many times over and so increases the probability of error, can lead to problems associated with the integrity of data and makes authority control difficult.

These difficulties can largely be overcome by linking records.

Fig. 1.1(c) shows how the bibliographic records can be linked according to a given function which is shared by a data element and in this regard information redundancy between logical records is eliminated. The same data element must still be repeated in storage when a data element functions in different ways—in this example 'Breckwoldt, R' functions as a main entry heading in the first logical record and as an added entry heading in the second.

A totally flexible record structure is shown in Fig. 1.1(d). Each data element is stripped of its tagging information and integrated into a single list with a pointer system that can be used to construct a logical record for display or to directly access data elements. Information redundancy within and between records is eliminated, quality control is straightforward from a technical point of view, access to individual elements of data is enhanced and none of the original information is lost.

The unlinked MARC type representation depicted in Fig. 1.1(b) is typical of the textual database formats used for exchange purposes. The formal representation of data in Fig. 1.1(d) approaches one kind of data model in a DBMS for management of information. The distinction between these two types of databases is important for the creators and managers of small scale databases. The unlinked communications format must be converted to some kind of linked format for information retrieval or management purposes or otherwise manipulated to produce database products.

4. WHY CREATE A DATABASE?

This brief introduction to database concepts introduced the notion of a commodity that can be reformatted, augmented, customised, even merged with other databases and repackaged for subsequent marketing and distribution both directly and via communications networks. Historically there appear to be four reasons why textual databases are created:

i. Because machine readable data are a necessary component of computerised production for abstracting and indexing services and other publications.
ii. Because computerised typesetting is to be employed.
iii. To alleviate problems in a library when the ever-cumulating card catalogue becomes a managerial nightmare.
iv. To enhance and facilitate information service when a body of knowledge useful to a particular clientele can be readily identified and controlled.

The first two reasons have usually provided the real rationale for the creation of databases and information retrieval is a fortunate by-product. The managerial nightmare of a large and growing catalogue usually applies to large national or university libraries and the databases created to alleviate these problems are large scale databases (or will be with the passage of time).

During the mid 1960s and early 1970s databases were the by-product of some publishing activity. More recently databases created de novo are planned as total systems for the publication of by-products, information retrieval and also location of documents.

The variety of database types indicate practicality and resourcefulness in the rationale for creating the database. Database creators tend to avoid duplicating the coverage of a particular subject field and concentrate on developing an information package which is readily identified but hitherto not readily accessible to a clearly identifiable clientele. The database creation process may well analyse the information sources to reveal subject content to varying degrees and not simply record the existence of the information sources. Also existing database records can be exploited by merging and reformatting records from different databases to produce a new information package.

5. DATABASE PROCESSING

Databases are generally created for the dual purpose of:

i. Information control by means of the routine production of printed products.
ii. Information retrieval directly from the database online, interactively or in batch mode, or indirectly via the derived printed products.

The production of printed products has been revolutionised by the application of computers to the process. In principle a single indexing operation culminates in the creation of a logical record of information.

From the single records a variety of specialised indexes can be generated automatically by matching index terms against stored search strategies representing the profiles of particular products of interest to particular communities of users. The production of specialised indexes is efficient, economical and flexible enough to allow for a certain amount of tailoring to suit particular situations. The same logical record, because of certain attributes or characteristics, may qualify for inclusion in a number of different headings in each index. The computer can also store the thesaurus or list of subject headings so that the validity of indexer assigned headings may be checked. A controlled vocabulary stored in machine readable form can also be used to generate the 'see' and 'see also' references needed in a particular issue of an index to give it a syndetic structure making the index easier to use. Hence the computer is used to process information efficiently and accurately in the production of a printed product from a database file in the following ways.

a. Replicating and sorting. A logical record is replicated as many times as there will be entries in the printed product and then the entries are sorted by the heading under which they are to be printed. This may include subject and bibliographic headings designated as print headings by the indexers.
b. Checking validity. The variety of indexer assigned headings can be checked against authority files stored in machine readable form and the necessary cross references which apply to those headings interfiled into the systematically arranged list of entries derived from the sorting and replication operation.
c. Formatting. The computer can automatically transform each entry in the list into a standard print format, arrange the entries in columns if necessary and introduce page headings, column headings, page numbers and other niceties.

At another level the computer can be used to generate different forms of indexes which would be impossible to produce manually. KWIC, KWOC and permuterm subject indexing are good examples of this. A more sophisticated example is the PRECIS indexes to the British National Bibliography. In principle the computer takes a single logical input in the form of a title, a PRECIS string, or a string of index terms in a particular citation order, and decides on the basis of the input which index entries are to be generated and automatically derived the necessary entries for the index.

Direct computer-based searching on the database in batch mode can operate in much the same way as information processing for the production of the printed products. Searches can be batched and passed through a sequential search of the database file as it stands.

On the other hand, online information retrieval directly from the machine readable database requires that the database undergo a conversion to a suitable format for interactive and real time searching. The logical records must be linked, in much the same way as outlined in Fig. 1.1(d), through the creation of an alphabetical index to the database file maintained as a sequential file for print and display purposes. The computer software designed in the 1960s and 1970s for online interactive retrieval maximises the use of information in each logical record by breaking each record down into a series of access points not limited to the indexer's choice of print heading. The retrieval software normally provides a range of retrieval capabilities for matching and coordinating concepts, in ways that are not possible manually.

6. COMPOSITION OF A DATABASE

The database design process begins with a study of the general characteristics of the file to be built and maintained so that computer software and hardware requirements can be defined. Typically this file will be central to an information system concerned with the transfer of information between a source and a destination. The design decisions therefore relate to the content of the database and the information dissemination processes. Firstly the content of the database must be considered at two levels. At the first level the information to be included in the file is considered—this determines the scope of the database in terms of its subject coverage, language, type of material, chronological coverage, and so on. These decisions are closely tied to the specific objectives of the database system. At the second level the contents of each logical record in the database are considered. The composition of the logical records in terms of field descriptions and content is tied to the choice of computer processing system and the information dissemination processes. Consideration of these two points shapes the general character of the database in terms of file size, record structure, file updating demands, information processing and retrieval demands.

6.1 File size

The size of the database file and therefore the storage requirements is determined by how many logical records will be added to the file each year, month or week, and the size of each logical record. A modest database might, for example, be created as a prototype using 5000 logical records. Each record may vary in size from say 200–2000 characters. If an average of 3000 records are added to the base every year thereafter, then after two years the base will contain 11 000 records and require storage for 2.2M–22M characters for a sequential file.

Field characteristics	Options	Examples
Field name	Functional	
	Formal	
	A blend of both	Main entry
		Corporate author
		Descriptive added entry corporate author
Field identifier	Numeric	
	Mnemonic	
	Alphanumeric	100
		AU
		A10
Field occurrences	Mandatory	
	Optional	Title
		Series note
Field repetition	Once only	
	Repeatable	Abstract
		Subject index terms
Nature of allowable characters in fields	Numeric	
	Alphabetic	
	Alphanumeric	Accession number field
		Authorship fields
		Classification code fields
Number of allowable characters in fields	Fixed length	Langueage code, e.g. ENG
	Variable length	Title
Online searchable	Yes or No	Presumably most descriptive fields will be searchable but control information like who did the indexing may not be searchable
Source of information and standards used	Standard list of codes	Country codes, language codes etc.
	Standard thesaurus	ERIC thesaurus
	Anglo American Cataloguing Rules	Rules of description and choice of access points
	Precedence	A growing authority file of subject terms or authors names etc.

Fig. 1.2 Options for the composition of a logical database record.

6.2 Record structure

From the point of view of the data user and the database creator the record structure is usually taken to mean the fields into which each logical record is broken. Fig. 1.2 summarises the options and therefore the major decisions that relate to the composition of each logical record. The record structure in terms of number of fields, nature of the fields and so on is tied to the computer processing system (any system that does not allow flexibility in defining data is to be avoided), the nature of the data being handled and the database's intended purpose.

6.3 File update

The need to update files in terms of adding new records, deleting existing records, merging or amending records must also be considered in relation to the choice of computer system. Unlinked textual or bibliographic databases are relatively stable over time and individual records are not usually updated. If a new edition of a book is published a new bibliographic record is created and all the records of previous editions remain unchanged. A database that lists research projects may require existing records to be amended with them, and new records announcing new projects to be added. The update frequency is related to the type of data, the purpose of the database and to economics.

6.4 Information processing and retrieval

The information processing and retrieval demands affect decisions relating not only to the choice of computer system but to what information is stored and how it is stored within the machine. Certain fields of information become key fields for processing (usually sorting) and retrieval (information matching), and particular attention must be paid to the content of these retrieval and sort key fields. The database may be used to produce regular publications for routine distribution in some printed format. The information selected for inclusion in a publication must be processed, sorted and presented in a form suited to the publication's audience and purpose. A lack of quality control over the content of these fields will affect the usefulness of the publication.

The database may also be available for online interactive searching on demand. Access to the online database is by means of retrieval keys which are matched against the sought information. The retrieval keys may be keywords from titles or abstracts, assigned descriptors or identifiers, and so on. Consideration of the content of these fields in the database design phase will make subsequent searching and retrieval easier.

Routine reporting and on demand information retrieval require different computer facilities and influence the choice of computer software and hardware.

7. CHOICE OF COMPUTER HARDWARE AND SOFTWARE

Once the appropriate software and hardware support is chosen other database design decisions tend to fall into place. The producers of a database will in the first instance look to their own organisation for technical support. If the organisation already supports a computer facility then one option is to acquire standard software to build an in-house system. An organisation may be tempted to develop its own software, but the development cost of an adequate software package to create, manage and exploit even a small database must be measured in man years of effort. A third approach appropriate for database producers without technical support is to consider the services of a service bureau with an established expertise. This initial approach need not preclude moving to in-house processing when suitable capabilities and expertise are built up. Whether producers look within their own organisation or to a service bureau for technical support the same checklist of questions can be applied:

- Can planned objectives be met and if so what precisely will be involved? (Feasibility and pilot studies are often the only way that the true capabilities of technical support can be measured.)
- What flexibility is there in the choice of fields and access points? (Many systems cannot handle variable length textual records.)
- What assistance with quality control can be provided? (This can range from the storage of an authority file for automatically checking the validity of access points and for generating cross references in a printed product to the routine production of housekeeping tools for error checking.)
- To what extent will staff be involved in the day to day running of the system, in other words what services are really provided?
- What equipment will need to be bought (that is computer terminals, printers, modems and so on) and who will maintain it?
- What will the costs be in terms of staff resources and capital and recurring expenditure?

Activities can be discretely divided into database creation, the production of tools and printed products, online information retrieval and the different agencies used for each. One service bureau may provide facilities for database creation, that is data entry, error checking facilities and quality control mechanisms. Another bureau may specialise in computer typesetting, printing, computer output on microform and therefore used for the production of printed products. A third agency may manage a public access network on which the database may be mounted for online information retrieval. The transfer of data from one agency to another must be considered; if data cannot be transferred in a standard format then conversion programs will have to be written at some cost.

8. QUALITY CONTROL

High quality printed products and effective information retrieval demand a high quality database. Quality control is most often achieved through the combination of a trained editor and the application of a comprehensive input and indexing manual. The editor's responsibilities may include monitoring the input selection, maintaining authority files, checking for duplicate entries in the database, particularly when contributions to the database come from many sources, and generally overseeing the quality of the database. The input and indexing manual may include the precise details of the database contents in terms of fields, their characteristics, and rules for data entry including the system of indexing in use, its principles and the indexing policy and exact input specifications.

A list of subject headings, a thesaurus or a classification scheme may be used by indexers to select subject access points. Whether or not to use a controlled vocabulary and which vocabulary to use are significant decisions. A database producer has four options: choose an existing vocabulary with little or no modification; use several vocabularies in conjunction with each other; extensively modify an existing vocabulary to suit the local environment; develop a vocabulary from scratch or let one evolve as the database grows. Making use of an existing vocabulary with little or no modification is the cheapest option. Developing a vocabulary requires considerable resources to produce a first edition and the ongoing costs associated with publication updating and maintenance are not small. This option should only be considered after all possible existing vocabularies have been evaluated and deemed unsuitable.

A checklist for evaluating the suitability of an existing vocabulary may include:

- Assessment of availability and cost.
- Currency and prospects for updating.
- Subject coverage in relation to the databases content and purpose.
- Cross reference and hierarchical structure as an indexing and searching tool.
- Organisation and structure (whether it has an alphabetical arrangement, a permuted index, a relative index, a hierarchical display and so on).
- Size in terms of allowable terms in relation to the proposed size of the database.

The suitability of the vocabulary must be checked against its intended purpose:

- Is it to be used for pinpointing specific subjects?
- Is it to be used primarily to arrange a current awareness bulletin or for browsing?
- Is it to be used in online searching?
- Is it to be used for arranging a printed product and therefore for manual searching?

9. MANAGEMENT CONSIDERATIONS

The producer of a proposed database may well be engaged in providing information service but this new venture may stand apart in that a fee for service or by-product is proposed. This may mean that the parent organisation has to consider: lease or licence of the database to another party; collection of royalties for use of the database; and the sale of printed publications. If the database is to be managed on the basis of profit or cost recovery, marketing, publicity and user education programs must be planned and steps taken to measure the database's performance.

Evaluation of a database can be carried out at four levels. At the first level the retrieval effectiveness can be measured to gauge ability to provide answers regardless of cost. The traditional measures are recall (the measure of the system's ability to provide *all* relevant information) and precision (the measure of the system's ability to provide *only* relevant information). These measures taken together provide a crude objective measure of effectiveness because they rely on a subjective judgement that retrieved information is relevant to a given information need. At the next level a benefits evaluation ascertains the impact of an information system and is also, for similar reasons, subjective and difficult to quantify. In this regard it is easier to compare systems and to say that system A is of greater benefit than system B. At the third level the level of performance in terms of recall and precision can be related to the cost of achieving it. Apart from the difficulties of measuring recall and precision there are also the issues associated with providing the minimum information to solve a given problem and ascertaining the minimum requirement. At the fourth level cost benefit studies relate the cost of providing a service to the benefit of having that service available. It may well be straightforward to ascertain the savings made through the use of an information serviced as compared with the cost of obtaining documents or information from another source. But it is another matter to calculate the loss of productivity that might result if the information were not readily available, to assess the improved productivity and decision making that results from having timely information available in the right form, or to assess the avoidable duplication of research effort brought about by a lack of knowledge of previous research. Table 1.1 relates these four levels of evaluation.

10. TRADE-OFFS IN THE DATABASE DESIGN PROCESS

To this point all the aspects of the database design process have been identified and with the possible design options available the different

Table 1.1 Evaluation of a database.

	Efficiency (worth relative to cost)	*Effectiveness* (ability to provide answers regardless of cost)
Output (direct from the system)	Cost effectiveness	Relevance (to a search strategy)
Outcome (use of output)	Cost benefit	Utility (to an information need)

permutations of design are considerable. The difficulties of evaluating a given information system are also considerable and it may be prudent to consider the early months of operation as a pilot investigation to explore various processes, calculate cost comparisons, compare trade-offs and determine the most suitable combination of processes. Trade-offs are largely independent of choice of hardware and software when they are made between input and output. In general terms, if great care and expense is invested in the input or database creation process there will be resulting economy in output effort or searching and therefore a cost benefit. Conversely, economies in input and database creation processes will increase output costs for the same level of performance. Changes in database processing will likely cause change elsewhere in the database use chain, for example errors in input not only damage the credibility of the database producers but make their products more difficult to use. The brunt of errors introduced in the database use chain are borne by searchers and users who must spend extra time circumventing errors and offsetting retrieval losses whenever necessary. To illustrate the issues associated with trade-offs in the database design process consider two characteristically different databases that could be processed on the same system.

Database A uses a large, dynamic but carefully controlled vocabulary. Indexers are highly trained and index exhaustively (for example 10 or more index terms per item) and there is an indexing review process that monitors quality and candidate index terms for inclusion in the vocabulary. Input productivity will be relatively low and input costs relatively high and there may well be long delays between data capture and the availability of that information in a printed publication or an online database. As a consequence rapid, accurate retrieval is probably possible, the burden on the searcher is minimal for effective retrieval, no screening or editing of output is needed and search costs are low.

Database B uses a small and relatively static vocabulary supplemented by textual information. Indexers have little or no training, assign only two to four terms per item and there is no indexing review process. Input productivity could potentially be high, input costs low with the minimum of delay between data capture and the availability of the information online or in a published product. As a consequence greater skill is needed to search the database comprehensively, screening and editing of output is required to produce a high quality tailored product and search costs are relatively high.

Database A could be characteristic of a highly centralised information facility that disseminates information widely to a range of audiences with a range of information seeking skills. Database B could be characteristic of a small information facility reliant on a variety of decentralised stores for its information sources and disseminating its database information to other information centres that offer services as third parties to their clients. But neither is *wrong*; they suit different circumstances, and these have to be recognised in the initial design stages.

11. CONCLUSION

In the following chapters we try to identify some of these factors in more detail, and show how the database designer can make sense of these trade-offs and compromises to accommodate the constraints, and take advantage of the opportunities in a particular situation.

FURTHER READING

ACI Computer Services. 1984. *Information Retrieval Systems Newsletter* 30 (January).

Ashford, J.H. and Matkin, D.I. 1980. 'Report of a study of the potential users and application areas for free text information storage and retrieval systems in Britain, 1979-1981.' *Program* 14(1): 14–23.

Borko, H. and Bernier, C.L. 1978. *Indexing concepts and methods.* New York, Academic Press.

Foskett, A.C. 1982. *Subject approach to information* 4th ed. London, Bingley.

Goodman, F. 1977. *Thesaurus of ERIC descriptors.* 7th ed. London, Macmillan Information.

Harrod, L.M. (Ed.) 1978. *Indexers on indexing: a selection of articles published in the Indexer.* New York, Bowker.

Lancaster, F.W. 1978. 'Trends in indexing from 1957 to 2000.' In *New Trends in documentation and information. Proceedings of the 39th FID Congress*, University of Edinburgh, 25–28 September, 1978. pp. 223–233.

MacCafferty, M. (compiler) 1977. *Thesaurus and thesaurus construction: ASLIB bibliography No. 7.* London, Aslib.

Riatt, D.I. 1980. 'Recall and precision devises in interactive bibliographic search and retrieval systems.' *ASLIB Proceedings* 32(7/8): 281–301.

Svenonius, E. and Schmierer, H.F. 1977. 'Current issues in the subject control of information.' *Library Quarterly.* 47(3), 1977: 326–346.

Wellisch, H. and Wilson, T.D. (Eds.) 1972. *Subject retrieval in the seventies: new directions.* Westport, Conn., Greenwood.

2. General overview of a database system

John D. Shortridge

1. Introduction
2. The database
3. Database management
   3.1 Database update
   3.2 Selective retrieval
   3.3 Hard copy products
4. Cost implications and trade-offs
5. Conclusion

1. INTRODUCTION

In this chapter I will provide an overview of the various components of a system for handling bibliographical databases. I will do this by describing, in both abstract and practical computer orientated terms, a typical database and the various operations which are carried out on that database.

2. THE DATABASE

The database used as an example is based on a real database and contains information on research in progress within Australia in the field of marine science. The database has been set up for two main reasons: firstly to facilitate production of a biennial hard copy Directory of Australian Marine Research in Progress; and secondly to support online searches by users who wish to query the database in order to answer specific questions about Australian marine research. The database consists of some 700 records, with

SMALL SCALE DATABASES
ISBN 0 12 391970 3

each record corresponding to a research product.[1] Each record, in turn, contains a number of items or fields which together describe the research project.

The complete list of items which follows is rather long, but aspects of many different terms will be used later in this chapter for illustrative purposes, so it is worth going into some detail.

i. A unique 'file key' which is used internally to unambiguously identify the particular record.
ii. The title of the research project.
iii. The organisations involved in the research project.
iv. The addresses of those organisations.
v. The names of the leader(s) of the project.
vi. The name of the 'contact officer', to whom enquiries about the project should be addressed.
vii. Telephone numbers of the project leader(s) and contact officer.
ix. A statement of the project's methodology.
x. A statement of the project's status.
xi. A statement on any cooperation with other Australian marine research projects.
xii. One or more descriptors (that is, words or phrases which describe the content of the project). These are assigned by a professional indexer.
xiii. One or more four-letter classification codes. A classification scheme is used in which each project is assigned by the database editor to one or more of the total of 49 subject classes. These classes are grouped under nine broad headings, and each subject class has an associated four-letter code.
xiv. One or more single-letter geographic codes. The waters around Australia have been divided into 21 areas for the purposes of this database, and each area is represented by a single-letter code.
xv. One or more specific locality names, indicating particular geographic localities (for example rivers, bays) associated with the research project.
xvi. Information on organisations which may be assisting by sponsoring the research project.
xvii. The value of grants associated with the sponsorship.

The items may vary in many ways in the degree to which their formats can be controlled, the processing required for the items, and so on.

The output operations performed on the database are briefly described below to provide a background for the more detailed description of all the operations which follows.

[1] By 1985 the database contained some 1400 records, three hard-copy directories had been produced and the database was available for searching via an Australia-wide computer network.

The first reason for establishment of the database was as a part of the process of producing the directory *Australian Marine Research in Progress.* The directory, some 550 pages in total, comprises various introductory sections, a list of all projects ordered according to their subject classification, and five indexes of various types.

Fig. 2.1 shows a sample page from the Project Summaries section of the directory, illustrating most of the items described above. Fig. 2.2 shows a sample page from the Subject Index. This is a permuted index. That is to say, for each project summary in the database one subject index entry is generated for each descriptor, and within the subject index each descriptor is followed by the other descriptors assigned to the project summary, cyclically permuted. For example on the sample page shown in Fig. 2.2, entries for project summary number 94 occur associated with Tidal Amplitude: Numerical Analysis..., Tidal Current: Tidal Amplitude... and Tides: Tidal Currents... Fig. 2.3 shows a sample page from the Organisation Index. Here, because many of the index entries have a large number of associated projects, the project titles are included in the index to facilitate index browsing. Fig. 2.4 shows a page of the Project Leader/ Contact Officer Index. Fig. 2.5 shows a page of the Geographic Area Index. As with the Organisation Index, project summary titles are included in the index. Finally, Fig. 2.6 shows a page of the Locality Index.

The second reason for establishing the database is to support an online query facility. In conventional online information retrieval systems the online query process typically involves the 'searcher' entering various words or phrases, being told how many items occur in the subsets in various logical combinations so as to eventually build up a set of records corresponding, as well as possible, to the searcher's current area of interest. Fig. 2.7 shows a simple stylised online search.

3. DATABASE MANAGEMENT

I will now consider in some detail the component processes involved in database management. Before a system such as our example is set up its scope must be defined, and mechanisms for reaching all potential contributors must be organised. Mailing lists will need to be produced, and data collection forms sent out. Once these forms have been returned they will need to be edited and indexed by an appropriately qualified person, after which they will be ready for conversion to computer readable form and entry into the database. Thereafter, there are three processes that are fundamental to most databases: addition of data, selective retrieval of information in response to ad hoc queries, and the generation of various hard copy products (indexes, directories and so on) from the database.

Physical sciences - Geology (cont.)

STATUS

The workshop was held in March 1981 and a report prepared.
P.J. Cook has attended the planning committee meeting of IPOD and a report has been written on that meeting.
A submission has been made to AMSTAC-FAP to support further involvement in IPOD.

GEOGRAPHIC REGION: A

MAJOR DESCRIPTORS: Geological surveys/Deep sea drilling/Proposed research/Conferences/Long term planning/

[COGS--001]

---

150 **Lagoonal sedimentation at One Tree Reef.**

PERIOD: February 1981 - December 1981

ORGANIZATIONS: Great Barrier Reef Marine Park Authority
P.O. Box 1379
Townsville, Qld 4810

University of Sydney (Subcontract)
Sydney, N.S.W. 2000

PROJECT LEADERS: Mr R. Kenchington (077) 712191 (GBRMPA)
Mr W. Kiene (02) 6921122 (Sydney Univ.)

CONTACT OFFICER: Mr W. Kiene

OBJECTIVES

1. To define the 3-d facies geometry of lagoonal sediments of One Tree Reef.
2. To develop the relationship between the temporal variation in flora and fauna remains in sediment, and variation in environmental and ecological parameters.
3. To estimate contribution of patch reef sediment to lagoonal infill.

METHODOLOGY

Samples of substrate taken in lagoon and analysed to determine vertical granulometry.
Samples to be taken progressively further away from patch reefs to determine contribution of patch reef sediment to lagoonal infill.

LOCALITY: One Tree Island

GEOGRAPHIC REGION: R

MAJOR DESCRIPTORS: Coral reefs/Sedimentation/Environmental factors/Hydroclimate/Geological history/

[GBRMPA002]

---

151 **Sedimentation between the Herbert Delta and Orpheus Island.**

PERIOD: January 1981 - October 1981

ORGANIZATIONS: Great Barrier Reef Marine Park Authority
P.O. Box 1379
Townsville, Qld 4810

James Cook University of North Queensland
Post Office
Townsville, Qld 4811

PROJECT LEADERS: Mr R. Kenchington (077) 712191
Dr D.P. Johnson (077) 814111

CONTACT OFFICER: Mr R. Kenchington

OBJECTIVES

1. To detail terrigenous carbonate transition between Herbert Delta and fringing reefs and Orpheus Island.
2. To quantify sediment inputs to reefs.
3. To investigate geochemical record in coral skeletons.

Fig. 2.1 Sample page from Project Summaries section.

SUBJECT INDEX

Thermal stratification
Tidal currents, Predictions, Density stratification, Seasonal variations 47
Thermocline
Isotherms, Mathematical models, Diurnal variations 78
Thermohaline circulation
Water mixing, Air-water interface, Flushing, Estuaries 51
Thunnidae
Pelagic fisheries, Fishery management, Fishery development, *Thunnus maccoyii* 447
Thunnus maccoyii
Thunnidae, Pelagic fisheries, Fishery management, Fishery development 447
Tidal amplitude
Numerical analysis, Mathematical models, Tides, Tidal currents 94
Tidal constants
Data acquisition, Sea level variations, Meteorological data, Time series analysis 52
Tidal currents
Bottom friction, Estuaries, Channels 69
Flushing, Hydrodynamics, Hydraulic models, Estuaries 91
Instrumentation, Estuaries 22
Mathematical models, Hydrodynamics 96
Predictions, Density stratification, Seasonal variations, Thermal stratification 47
Tidal amplitude, Numerical analysis, Mathematical models, Tides 94
Tidal range, Mathematical models, Coral reefs 95
Turbulence 64
Wind-driven currents, Coral reefs, Ocean circulation, Water currents 37
Wind-driven currents, Numerical analysis, Continental shelf 76
Tidal range
Mathematical models, Coral reefs, Tidal currents 95
Tides
Sea level, Resonances, Seasonal variations 53
Storm surges, Wave setup, Flood forecasting 73
Tidal currents, Tidal amplitude, Numerical analysis, Mathematical models 94
Water waves action, Water currents, Sediment transport 31
Time series analysis
Aeolian transport, Coastal erosion, Long term changes, Photogrammetry 164
Beach erosion, Long term changes, Aerial surveys 165
Sediment transport, Construction, Wave climate, Data acquisition 75
Tidal constants, Data acquisition, Sea level variations, Meteorological data 52

Fig. 2.2 Sample page from Subject Index.

ORGANIZATION INDEX

University of Melbourne
Taxonomy, distribution and phylogeny of marine algae from eastern Australian islands and the Great Barrier Reef. 221
The taxonomy and ecology of Lord Howe Island benthic marine algae. 222
Ecology and distribution of zooplankton. 270
Amino acid biosynthesis in marine siphonous algae. 324
Ecology and physiology of Antarctic sea-ice microalgae. 325
Tolerance of cadmium in marine bacteria. 326
Trace metals and radionuclides in squid and other organisms from Bass Strait. 327
Factors controlling sessile communities of kelp beds. 409
Investigation of the structure of food chains in seagrass communities with associated aspects of nutritional physiology of herbivorous animals. 410
History of marine botany in Australia. 430
Application of side-scan sonar to mapping deep-water rough-bottom fishing grounds. 492
Island breakwaters to protect bulk unloading terminals. 496
Analysis of multi-leg mooring systems. 499
Development of wave research facility (WR1). 500
Dynamics of mooring lines. 501
Floating breakwaters. 502
Hydrodynamic damping of flexibly mounted cylinders in waves. 503
Motions of moored vessels. 504
New concept of breakwater. 505
Optimum design of mooring systems. 506
Random wave forces on simple ocean structures. 507
Iceberg utilization. 511
Hydrocarbons in seawater and the effects of crude oil on ice algae. 550

University of New England
Biology and taxonomy of the Indo-Pacific Gerreidae. 290
Ecology of intertidal Littorinids. 411
Ecology of marine parasites. 412
Studies on Southern Ocean marine invertebrates: 1. Metal contents in sub-antarctic holothuroids. 2. Reproductive condition in (a) littoral vertebrates, (b) *Euphausia superba* 551

University of New England (Subcontract)
Study of reef top sediments on Wreck Reef. 152

University of New South Wales
Breaking of internal waves. 90
Hydraulic behaviour of tidal inlets. 91
Ocean dynamics of the south-central Great Barrier Reef Lagoon. 92
Theoretical studies of waves on a Continental Shelf. 93
Tides of the southern Great Barrier Reef. 94
Myoglobin of Cartilaginous fishes. 123
Nonlinear diffraction of water waves. 124
Bedrock topography and acoustic stratigraphy of selected areas of the New South Wales Continental Shelf. 186
Foraminiferal ecology of New South Wales Continental Shelf. 187
Pelagic foraminifera in sediments of the continental shelf of eastern Australia. 188
Resolution of problems of foraminiferal zonation, correlation and palaeoceanography in the marine Cainozoic sediments of the Australian region. 189
Structure and physiology of mycorrhizas of plants of coral islands. 210
Oysters of the Indo-West Pacific region (Bivalvia : Ostreidae and Gryphaeidae). 276
Salinity adaptations in blue-green algae. 322

Fig. 2.3 Sample page from Organisation Index.

PROJECT LEADER/CONTACT OFFICER INDEX

Lanzing, W.J.R. 331
Larkum, A.W.D. 333, 334, 335, 553
Lassig, B. 355
Law, J. 362
Lawler, J. 75
Lawrence, M.W. 172
Lawson, J.D. 174, 496, 502
Laxton, J.H. 61, 62, 364, 536, 538, 565
Leis, J. 386
Lenanton, R.C. 391
Lennon, G.W. 51, 52, 53
LeProvost, I. 561
Lewis, J. 352, 353
Lewis, R.K. 482
Leyendekkers, J. 111
Lilley, R.McC. 333
Limpus, C. 397
Ling, J.K. 239, 401
Lleonart, G.T. 66
Loch, R.G. 35, 106
Lockwood, K. 138, 145
Logan, B.W. 25, 196, 198, 199, 200
Lord, D. 68
Lorimer, P. 489
Lorimer, P.D. 458
Lu, C.C. 256, 257, 392, 427
Lucas, J.S. 247
Luong-Van, T. 311, 383
Lyons, T.J. 131
MacDonald, H.B. 169, 569, 570, 571, 572, 573, 574, 575, 576, 577
MacIntyre, R.J. 522
Mackay, M. 322
Mackey, D.J. 113
Magryn, T. 167
Maher, W.A. 118
Majkowski, J. 447
Major, G.A. 18
Marsden, M. 519
Marsden, M.A.H. 3
Marsh, H. 230, 463
Marsh, J.A. 329
Marsh, L.M. 277, 279, 280
Marshall, A.T. 315, 317
Marshall, J.F. 140
Martin, K.R. 116
Mather (Kott), P. 265
Mather, P.B. 363
Maxwell, G. 445
May, V. 393
Maynard, C.A. 495
McColl, G. 438, 579
McConchie, C. 209
McDonald, G. 432, 440, 441
McDonald, T.J. 395
McElligott, K.V. 497
McEwan, A.D. 40
McGinnity, P. 563
McKay, T.R. 516, 517, 518, 519, 520, 521, 522, 523
McKee, W.D. 94, 124
McKenzie, G.H. 324
McKenzie, K.G. 171, 266, 267
McLaren, N. 354
McMahon, P.K. 443
McMonagle, G.J. 67
McNamara, P. 498
Meagher, T.D. 422, 560
Meek, S.D. 307
Melloy, C.R. 13
Mercer, G.W. 461
Merrick, J.R. 284
Middleton, J.H. 92, 94
Miller, G.J. 530, 531
Millis, N.F. 205, 326
Milward, N.E. 229, 233, 234, 366, 462, 464, 465
Misconi, L.Y. 117
Mitchell, H.L. 23
Mitchell, W.R. 82
Moriarty, D.J.W. 298
Moss, J. 566
Muir, F. 155
Mulhearn, P.J. 81, 100
Munro, I.S.R. 283, 446
Murphy, G.I. 447
Murray-Smith, S. 5
Murray, C.G. 170
Murray, J.C. 422
Murray, M.D. 407
Nash, W 245
Nash, W. 245, 247, 466
Nicholas, E. 145
Nicholas, W.L. 336
Nichols, P.D. 410
Nielsen, A. 71
Nielsen, L. 163
Nielsen, P. 194
Nilsson, C.S. 80
Nix, H.A. 128
Norman, N.E. 513

Fig. 2.4 Sample page from Project Leader/Contact Officer Index.

GEOGRAPHIC AREA INDEX

Great Barrier Reef

Study of Australian coastal water turbidity. 48
Tides of Torres Strait. 53
Drift card study of Great Barrier Reef surface currents. 54
Man made noise in the ocean. 55
Hydrodynamic studies of water movements within the Great Barrier Reef region. 59
Ocean dynamics of the south-central Great Barrier Reef Lagoon. 92
Theoretical studies of waves on a Continental Shelf. 93
Tides of the southern Great Barrier Reef. 94
The isolation of novel compounds from marine invertebrates. 114
Sedimentation and trace element geochemistry - Fitzroy Reef, Capricorn-Bunker Group. 116
To investigate the structure, metabolic pathway, nutritional and clinical use of marine compounds and to obtain an understanding of the processes involved in their ecology and evolution. 117
Aromatic hydrocarbons in the marine environment. 119
Behaviour of heavy metals in marine and estuarine systems. 120
Study of the halogens, especially iodine, in the marine environment. 122
Environmental geochemistry and climatic reponse of sediments and corals. 10°-20°S. 128
Stable-isotope study of palaeoclimate and environmental geochemistry of the Great Barrier Reef. 129
Rates of sediment accumulation and coastal progradation along the Great Barrier Reef Province. 134
Rates of sediment accumulation and coastal progradation along the Great Barrier Reef province. 135
Factors affecting growth and maintenance of reefs in the central Great Barrier Reef. 139
Inter-reefal studies to investigate the geological development of the central Great Barrier Reef. 141
Lagoonal sedimentation at One Tree Reef. 150
Sedimentation between the Herbert Delta and Orpheus Island. 151
Study of reef top sediments on Wreck Reef. 152
Study of the fringing reef at Orpheus Island. 153
Geomorphology of the Great Barrier Reef. 155
Queensland marine geology and geophysics. 170
Ostracoda : Banks Strait, South Pacific. 171
Pelagic foraminifera in sediments of the continental shelf of eastern Australia. 188
Effect of sediment characteristics on beach profiles and surf-zone hydraulics. 190
Impact of coastal engineering works upon coral cays. 191
Eastern shelf stratigraphy and heavy-mineral sands. West German/Australian cooperative survey using R/V Sonne. 201
Coral Reef Survey; manta tow data analysis. 202
Bacterial degradation of aromatic hydrocarbons, including polynuclear aromatic hydrocarbons, in a coral reef system. 205
Biology and systematics of Articulate Coralline algae in north Queensland with particular reference to genus *Jania* Lamouroux (1816). 206
The genus *Sonneratia* (Sonneratiaceae) in Australia 207
Structure and physiology of mycorrhizas of plants of coral islands. 210
Salt and water relations of higher plants of islands of the Great Barrier Reef. 212
Systematics and Ecology of phytobenthos of Swain Reefs 214
Systematic survey of the turf algal flora of coral reefs in NE Queensland. 215
Systematics and ecology of tropical Australian benthic algae. 216
Taxonomy, distribution and phylogeny of marine algae from eastern Australian islands and the Great Barrier Reef. 221

Fig. 2.5 Sample page from Geographic Area Index.

LOCALITY INDEX

Abbot Point 372
Adelaide 545
Admiralty Gulf 274
Aldinga Bay 399
Alligator Creek 378
Anderson Inlet 184, 427
Anna Bay 164
Arafura Sea 7
Auckland Creek 255
Auckland Islands 426
Avon River 391
Barwon Heads 204, 526
Batemans Bay 295
Belmont Bay 165
Black Rock 32
Botany Bay 71, 337, 541, 552, 553
Bountiful Islands 474
Bowen 569
Bramble Bay 30
Bribie Island 96
Brisbane 395
Brisbane River 529
Brisbane Water 566
Broad Sound 59, 94
Broken Bay 161, 166
Broome 101
Bundaberg 570, 572
Bunker Group 12, 59, 228, 359, 531
Burdekin River 20
Burrill Lake 27, 345
Byron Bay 159
Cairns 573
Calliope River 255, 543
Caloundra 576
Campbell Islands 426
Cape Cleveland 295
Cape Ferguson 206
Cape Naturaliste 144
Cape Paterson 427
Cape Schanck 535
Capricorn Group 12, 59, 210, 221, 228, 359, 361, 531
Carter Reef 531
Christmas Island 352
Clarence River 162
Cleveland Bay 234, 308, 312
Clyde River 27, 336, 345
Cockle Bay 367
Coffs Harbour 68, 159, 221
Coomera Island 362
Coomera River 362
Corio Bay 250
Corner Inlet 158, 410
Cowan Cowan 498
Cowell 477
Cronulla 516
Crookhaven River 27, 345
Dampier 104, 109
Dampier Archipelago 274, 277, 421, 422, 517
Darwin 33
Dee Why Lagoon 565
Devonport 32
East Alligator River 203
Edithburgh 323, 405
Elizabeth Reef 193
Embley River 340
Exmouth Gulf 199, 460
Fitzroy Reef 116
Fremantle 277
Fullerton Cove 161
Geoffrey Bay 206, 365
Geographe Bay 277
Gosford 61, 62, 566
Great Barrier Reef Marine Park 439, 579
Great Barrier Reef Marine Park - Cairns Section 11, 431, 432, 510
Great Barrier Reef Marine Park - Capricorn Section 12
Great Barrier Reef Marine Park - Capricornia Section 11, 228, 424, 440, 461, 562
Great Palm Island 129
Green Island 10, 527
Gulf St Vincent 323, 354, 400, 403, 404, 405, 545
Harbord Lagoon 565
Harvey estuary 419
Harvey River 391
Hastings Point 159
Heard Island 142
Herbert River 151
Heron Island 10, 190, 191, 212, 271, 295, 309, 423, 528
Hervey Bay 238, 572
Hopkins River 107
Houtman Abrolhos 197, 198, 274, 277, 300, 421
Hunter River 336
Inverloch 427
Karumba 469
Kent Group 251
Keppel Isles 429

Fig. 2.6 Sample page from Locality Index.

(In this highly stylised example commands entered by the user are shown in upper-case, responses from the computer are shown in lower-case, explanatory comments are in *italics.*)
[*The searcher wishes to search the Australian Marine Research in Progress database for information on research on lagoonal sedimentation in the area of the Great Barrier Reef*]
specify database:

AMRIP

enter command(s)

LAGOON$ ADJ SEDIMENT$

[*identify all records in the database which contain any word beginning with the characters 'LAGOON' adjacent to any word beginning with the character 'SEDIMENT'*]
1 25 records
[*the system has identified 25 such records and has formed them into a "set", to be known as set 1*]
enter command(s)

REGION = R

[*identify all records in which the geographic region code has the value 'R'*]
2 377 records
enter command(s)

1 AND 2

[*identify all records which occur in both of the sets so far established*]
3 1 record
[*a third set is formed, containing 1 record*]
enter command(s)

DISPLAY 3

[*at this stage the record satisfying the search will be displayed on the terminal*]

Fig. 2.7 Stylised example of a simple online search.

3.1 Database update

The first major process in the management of a database is update of the data. This process of adding data to a database can itself be regarded as consisting of three separate component processes: conversion of the data to machine readable form, validation of the data, and then incorporation of the data in the database. In practice, these processes can be carried out sequentially and separately, or they can be performed more or less simultaneously in a system which does not permit any one process to be performed in isolation.

Conversion of data to machine readable form normally, though not always, involves a keyboard operation, in which the data entry operator enters the contents of each record (in our case, each form containing details of a marine research project) onto some appropriate medium. Validation of the data involves checking the data as entered against criteria for the data's correctness specified in some appropriate fashion (details are given below). Incorporation of the data in the database involves adding the text of the records as entered into the database while also updating any indexes or directories that may be relevant.

Data are normally entered onto some magnetic medium, although this is not always the case. When data are entered thus there is still a wide range of possible machine configurations. The computer which drives the operation may be a simple dedicated micro- or minicomputer, or a general purpose minicomputer or mainframe. In both these cases the computer which manages the data entry is likely to be carrying out other tasks simultaneously. However, in the first case (dedicated micro- or minicomputer) these other tasks will be similar data entry operations, while in the second case they could be any other tasks which the computer is capable of undertaking.

There are other options for data entry. In the past, data have been transcribed by keypunch operators onto paper tape or cards, which have then been transcribed onto magnetic media, but this approach is now of historical interest only. OCR devices may also be used to transfer data from paper to magnetic form, and some work is being done on developing touch sensitive pads on which editors of documents (for example) could write.

The second component of the process of adding new data to a database is that of data validation. Computer processing, if its potential is fully exploited, allows detection of a very large proportion of potential errors. In our database the edit checks can be classified in various ways. At the broadest level, they can be divided into checks on the acceptability of entire records and checks on the validity of individual items, although, as I will show below these two types of checks do interact.

The checks at the record level are the most important and for these checks each record must contain a 'file key' item which unambiguously identifies the record. Consequently, each transaction applied to the database must contain precisely one legitimately-formed file key. Further, if the transaction is claimed to be a 'new record' the associated file key must be one which is not already present in the database; conversely if the transaction is claimed to be an 'amendment' the file key must refer to a record already in the database. If these criteria are not met the record will not be accepted.

Each record is made up of a number of items and the checks on these items are also very important. Each item is identified by some sort of item identifier. Clearly, there will be a limited range of legitimate item identifiers for the database, and any items with unknown (that is illegal) item identifiers will be rejected by the validation software.

In most databases of this type certain items must occur in a record for the record to 'make sense', while others are optional. In our example every project should have a title, and therefore a record which did not contain a title item should be rejected. On the other hand, many projects may be unrelated to any specific locality, so the locality item is optional and its absence does not reflect on the legitimacy of the record. There may also be relationships between the presence or absence of one item and the presence or absence of another item which must be satisfied for the record to be consistent. For example for each organisation that is listed there must be a corresponding organisational address, and likewise for each address there must be a corresponding organisation. Also every 'project leader's telephone number' item must have a corresponding project leader item, while the reverse relationship here would not necessarily hold. In all these cases records violating these conditions should not be permitted in the database and the editing software should allow us to check and detect illegalities of this type.

The number of checks that can be done at the record level are however, small compared to the number that can be done at the item level. The item-level checks that are applied to the various items outlined can be divided into two broad groups: checks that can be specified in a relatively general fashion and checks that require specially developed software for their implementation. Checks of the first type can be effected by invoking standard facilities of the data entry system, and include simple tests such as checking that the length of the data item lies within legal limits; that the individual characters of the data item are legitimate (some items may necessarily be all numeric, others all alphabetic, and so on); and that the item supplied matches an 'authority list', known to the system, of values which the item may take. For all items in our database (in fact for all items in any database) limits on lengths must be specified, although some items will have rigid restrictions and other, textual, items will be allowed a wide range of possible lengths. Other edit checks which correspond to the items of the Australian Marine Research in Progress database are:

i. The file key specified must be unique and must be in a particular format.

ii–iv. No special edit checks apply to the project title, the organisation names or addresses.

v–vi. Project leader and contact officer names are checked to see that they contain a special character (underline), used to indicate the start of the portion of the field to be used for indexing. For example, a project leader's name may be entered in the form 'Prof. A. B._Smith'. The software (described below) which produces the hard copy publication will change this to 'Prof. A. B. Smith' for inclusion in the body of the directory, and to 'Smith, Prof. A. B.' for inclusion in the project leader/contact officer index.

vii–xi. No special edit checks apply to the telephone number items or to the essentially textual statements of objectives, methodology, status and cooperation.

xii. Descriptors are separated by 'slash' characters. By counting the number of slashes, the editing software verifies that there are between one and five descriptors.

xiii. The four-letter classification codes entered are checked against a stored list of all the legal classification codes to ensure that only known codes occur in the database.

xiv. The single-letter geographic codes are checked for legality.

xv–xvi. No special edit checks apply to locality names or 'assisting organisation' names.

xvii. Information on the value of grants is checked to see that its format is plausible.

It should also be noted that some of these edit checks give rise to 'informative' error messages, while some give rise to 'fatal' error messages. An informative message merely draws the attention of the database producer to an apparent anomaly in the format of an item of the database, while a fatal message informs the database producer that an item has been rejected from the transaction. Further, the effect of a fatal error at the item level on the entire record transaction is variable. In some cases the item is rejected, and there are no further ramifications; but if the item is one that must occur for the overall record to be acceptable then the record itself will be rejected. In our example, a 'value of grant' item of '$12P45' would be rejected as meaningless without effect on the rest of the record, whereas an illegal classification code would result in rejection of the entire record.

After all this, the process of checking to ensure the quality of the database is still not finished. In textual data many errors can only be detected by proofreading, and even the most conscientious proofreader is unlikely to pick up all potential problems. In this type of application, one of the problems that can detract from the quality of the database is that of minor inconsistencies in terms used for indexing. An expert proofreader may detect all spelling errors, but inconsistent usage of indexing terms in documents that may be widely separated in terms of their entry into the database is almost impossible to detect unaided. For example, one descriptor used several times in our database is 'Long term planning'. Given that it has been used several times in this form, there are clear aesthetic reasons why a new descriptor 'Long-term planning', should be discouraged (it will make the index look strange), but the proofreader cannot be expected to pick up this sort of inconsistency when considering the record in isolation.

In general, inconsistencies of this type can only be detected by looking at the relevant index. Consequently, it is necessary to produce a 'draft index' to be proofread. This sort of index is similar to a normal index except that associated with each index term is a list of file keys, as opposed to page or document numbers. This enables amendments arising from the proof-reading to be simply prepared, as amendments to each record are specified in terms of the record's unique keys.

Index maintenance is also important as it is involved not only in the building and update of a database but also in the information retrieval process. Most interactive information retrieval is supported by machine readable indexes (although this is not always the case), and these indexes may either be updated and maintained as a by-product of the database building process or be specifically manipulated at a later stage.

Before leaving the topic of database building, the question of software availability needs to be considered. Generally, it is undesirable to develop software 'in-house' when it can be acquired commercially. On the other hand, most databases, like ours, have quite rigid and specific rules which can be stated about the format of various items, and these cannot be expected to be incorporated in 'packaged' software. If complete development of software in-house is undesirable there are two alternatives. Firstly, it may be possible to develop a software module which effects the required in-house quality control and somehow incorporate this in the sequence of operations involved in building the database. This could be done either as a program run independently of the packaged software or as a series of routines invoked by one of the packaged programs. Alternatively, it may be preferable to accept the commercial packaged software with whatever limitations it has and attempt to compensate for these with exhaustive and detailed proofreading. The cost of developing in-house software will be independent of the size of the database, whereas the cost of proofreading will be directly related to the size of the database. For smaller databases the second alternative may well be preferred.

3.2 Selective retrieval

The second major process to be considered is selective retrieval of data from the database in response to ad hoc queries. At the broadest level the retrieval process involves a user who needs information putting a query to the database, either directly or via a 'search intermediary', who would be an information professional. The query would presumably be initially expressed as a statement in natural language of the user's interest, and the first component of the search process is the translation of the query into a form acceptable to the particular software system.

At this stage, it is important to recall our concern with 'small scale' databases, as retrieval may be an area where options available for small scale operation differ significantly from those available for 'average' and 'large scale' databases. I will consider an average database first. In general, the statement above regarding the initial step of a search is slightly misleading. Where the user has access to a general purpose information retrieval system, the process of translating the original query from natural language to the form demanded by the system is not a discrete first stage of the system but rather a process of successive refinement, in which the desired query statement is built up more or less simultaneously with the retrieval of the desired hits. Details of the process vary with the specific package being used, but generally the process of retrieval from an average database using a commercially available retrieval package can be described as follows.

The end user or the search intermediary translates the original natural language query statement into a logical expression comprising various logical combinations of search terms. These terms can then be entered into the retrieval system and the numbers of associated documents noted. Likewise, various logical combinations of the terms can be tentatively produced, and in this way the ideal formulation of the query can be iteratively approached.

In the case of small scale databases there are other options. The database may well be prepared on some in-house system of the user's which does not support any of the commercially available retrieval packages. Similarly, irrespective of the computer system on which the database is set up, the cost of acquiring a commercial retrieval package may be unacceptable for a small scale operation. On the other hand, the fact that the database is small scale may mean that it is possible to access it using simpler but less powerful software techniques. For instance, the process described above whereby a powerful software package enables iterative development of a query has great economic advantages when dealing with a large database, but if the database is sufficiently small it may not be a problem to develop the query via a series of complete searches.

The essential components of this system, taking a broad overall view, are the computer hardware required to store and process the data, the software systems required to support the desired user's view of the data and, of course, the data. The last raises the question of just how the data are translated into the form required by the retrieval software. Any retrieval system (be it a common package or an in-house operation) is going to require the data in a specific format. It is possible that the database creation and retrieval software will be two facets of an integrated package, in which case the question of manipulating the data into the format required for retrieval becomes moot, but this need not necessarily be the case. For instance, many databases are formed by combining various subsets of other databases, and these may have been prepared at remote sites by other organisations using different software or hardware systems. Another significant point is that many databases which are of national importance will be stored to allow availability via a nationwide information retrieval network (or, possibly, a network permitting international access). These databases have to be stored on a host computer that permits access for retrieval by many users simultaneously. On the other hand, there may be economic incentives to perform as much as possible of the data entry and validation on small local systems, so again the database creation process may not leave the data in the form required by the retrieval software. In any case, some special purpose but fairly simple, software may be needed to translate the original database into the form required for input into the retrieval system. Thereafter, the data can be translated into the retrieval system's required format (data and indexes) as a batch operation.

3.3 Hard copy products

The third major process in the management of our database is the preparation of hard copy output. However before I describe this process in detail some broad considerations should be discussed.

Firstly, hard copy output will not be fundamental to every database management operation as some databases are used only for online access. Many small scale databases are of this type, however many will contain information which justifies the production of printed copy. Also, of course, many existing databases came about originally as a by-product of an automated system for producing hard copy products.

Secondly, the exhaustive (and, possibly exhausting!) quality control procedures incorporated in the data validation software described earlier are justified if production of hard copy is required. Some of the errors which may mar the quality of a database may not be too serious when dealing with online ad hoc access to the database, but all errors tend to appear embarrassingly obvious in print, particularly errors involving slightly misspelled indexing terms. These errors will also be obvious during online retrieval provided that the online retrieval package allows searchers to look at contiguous sections of the indexes, but even so the errors will be seen only by the proportion of searchers who look at that particular subsection of the relevant index.

Thirdly, where the finished hard copy product is to be generated using phototypesetting techniques to produce camera-ready copy, there are implications for the overall database management operation. The phototypesetting operation will provide a number of different fonts, the use of boldface and italic and, most importantly, will allow a far wider range of special characters than would normally be available in an interactive information retrieval system. Typical special characters available on a phototypesetter but not elsewhere are Greek characters and various special mathematical symbols; accenting of letters is also usually possible, as is the use of super- and subscript characters. However, for these characters to be produced the phototypesetting software has to be presented with special predefined sequences of standard characters. Example might be '^alpha^' to produce 'α' or "Schro^umlaut^der' to produce 'Schröder'. The significance of all this is that the database designer is faced with three options. He can ignore all possibilities which the phototypesetting process provides, thus reducing the 'quality' of the final hard copy product; he can maintain the special sequences needed to produce special characters thus complicating both the online search process and marring the appearance of online output' or he can produce what is, in effect, a slightly reduced subset of the database for searching, with consequent cost increases.

The production of hard copy begins with the existing master file of records stored in the database. The first step is to sort these into the order in which they are to appear in the final printed product. In the case of our example database, the records are sorted in accordance with the classification scheme used to assign the four-letter codes to each record, and, within this classification, the records are sorted alphabetically by the project titles. When the file is in this order the indexes are assembled from the various items within the records for which indexes are required. This file can then be processed by another program which produces the index on the printer, or, for a higher quality product, it can be passed to further programs which exploit the possibilities offered by computerised typesetting.

4. COST IMPLICATIONS AND TRADE-OFFS

The prospective database owner will be faced with a multitude of trade-offs in considering the detailed design of a proposed system. It is only possible here to discuss them in general terms, but it is hoped that the following gives some feeling for the questions that must be considered.

Probably the most significant decision from the cost viewpoint is the decision on the nature and extent of human editing to be applied to the data. At one extreme, textual databases can be set up with no human editing and only minimal machine editing, and it should be appreciated that this may be appropriate for some databases, particularly those containing information of a relatively ephemeral nature. At the other extreme, the detailed machine edits described earlier for our sample database would only be appropriate when associated with relatively deep involvement by one or more rigorous human editors. Between these two extremes there are various intermediate possibilities and the trade-off is between cost and quality.

The prospective database administrator will also have several related choices to make regarding the software and hardware required to support the database system. The choice of hardware may be determined by organisational considerations. If this is not the case the choices available will include buying the services of a bureau or acquiring a micro- or mini-computer for in-house processing. Microcomputers, and associated software described as 'database management' are proliferating at such a rate that any specific statement of options here would be outmoded by the time this book is in print. In any case, the would-be database producer should carefully study the facilities offered by the packages under consideration and check that the packages actually provide the facilities claimed by the vendor.

The degree of quality to be provided in the output is also a consideration. If typeset products are required the cost of these should be carefully assessed. It is likely that for small scale database producers economics will dictate that the typesetting component of their operation will always be carried out by a service bureau, as the associated hardware and software are both expensive and complicated. If complex editing facilities are required there will almost certainly be a need for special purpose software development for the particular database application. The cost of this development will also need to be considered by the prospective database owner.

Where a service bureau is not used it is vital to evaluate the performance of the hardware and software chosen, to ensure that the hardware is sufficiently powerful to handle the expected load. This can be done by benchmarking techniques, where a series of runs is carried out to simulate the load which will occur in practice. From the viewpoint of the small scale operator, however, setting up these tests is itself time consuming, and if possible it may be preferable to find a comparable existing operation and obtain performance data from them. If this is not possible, however, some sort of benchmarking should be carried out to ensure that the proposed configuration is technically feasible.

5. CONCLUSION

It can be seen from the above that the process of establishing even a simple database is necessarily quite complicated if a database of good quality is to be produced, and that a significant systems analysis exercise is required.

FURTHER READING

Australian Environment Council. 1985. *Report no. 15: Australian environment and conservation database feasibility study.* Canberra, Australian Government Publishing Service.

Davis, C. H. and Rush, J. E. 1979. *Guide to information science.* Westport, Conn., Greenwood Press.

3. Software options

Cathie Jilovsky

1. Introduction: the role of software
   1.1 Qualitative aspects
   1.2 Quantitative aspects
2. Characteristics of textual databases
   2.1 Comparison of database characteristics
   2.2 Characteristics of textual data
3. Desirable characteristics of suitable software
4. Other software required
   4.1 Operating system
   4.2 System utilities
   4.3 Programming languages
   4.4 DBMS
5. File organisation methods
   5.1 Sequential files
   5.2 Chained files
   5.3 Inverted files
   5.4 Computed access files
   5.5 Clustered files
   5.6 Indexed sequential access
6. Software options
   6.1 Turnkey systems
   6.2 Software packages
   6.3 Development of an in-house system
      6.3.1 Development by a software house or group
      6.3.2 Development within the library
   6.4 Use of a service bureau
7. Evaluation of software
   7.1 Assessment of needs
   7.2 Vendor or producer
   7.3 System output
   7.4 System input
   7.5 Searching
   7.6 Security

SMALL SCALE DATABASES
ISBN 0 12 391970 3

7.7 Training
7.8 General considerations
8. 'Hybrid' options: some warnings
9. Training software
10. Microcomputers
11. Cost considerations
12. Conclusion
References

1. INTRODUCTION: THE ROLE OF SOFTWARE

Software can be defined as 'all those programs which in some way can assist all users of a computer to make the best use of the machine', and a computer program as a 'set of instructions to a computer'. The importance of software is such that investment in its production and maintenance is a major (possibly *the* major) item in the development, marketing and application of computers.

A computer cannot reason, but is entirely dependent on instructions supplied to it by its all too human users. Hence it cannot be expected to perform any task adequately unless the problem it is required to solve has been specified correctly in every detail and the instructions it is asked to obey define in complete detail each step of the solution.

So where does a potential user of a bibliographic or textual database begin? The value of the data is dependent on how easily it may be used. No matter how complete and accurate the data in a database is, there is no point in having it on computer if it cannot be used.

1.1 Qualitative aspects

The qualitative aspects of handling textual databases are basically human intellectual activities and are generally not easily imitated by computer software. The computer has been described as a 'very fast moron', and this is a useful definition to remember when considering what a computer can and cannot do. When searching textual data, the computer avoids completely one of the problems faced by the human searcher of a document system in manual form—the difficulty of manipulating long lists of words—however it cannot contribute directly to solving the intellectual problems of natural language searching.

In many existing computerised retrieval systems most, if not all, of the intellectual processing is conducted by humans, and the computer merely acts as a giant matching device. However more fully 'automatic' retrieval systems are developing and the amount of human intellectual processing is being reduced. Computer software can, in fact, be used to index documents; prepare abstracts or at least extracts of documents; automatically elaborate on a search strategy; or develop links among semantically related terms, thereby creating a form of searching aid (a kind of machine constructed thesaurus). A fully automatic system would index, generate a thesaurus, and develop search strategies automatically from a natural language statement of information needed (Lancaster, 1979).

A natural language search is interrogation of a file by means of an English sentence request. This is particularly appealing for online systems being used by non-librarians, for example scientists, research workers and other professionals. However the success of this form of system is heavily dependent not only on the efficiency of the controlling software, but also on the quality of the request statement which needs to be a complete and accurate description of the user's information need.

It is possible to imagine the 'perfect' retrieval situation where a store of information contains all the documents required to answer a particular information request. To obtain the required information the user could read *all* the documents in the store, retain the relevant ones and discard all the others. This solution is obviously impractical. A user either does not have the time or the inclination to read the entire document collection, apart from the fact that it may be physically impossible to do so. When high-speed computers first became available for non-numerical work, it was thought that a computer would be able to 'read' an entire document collection to extract the relevant documents. Unfortunately, it soon became apparent that using the natural language text of a document not only caused input and storage problems (it still does), but also left unsolved the intellectual problem of characterising the document content and matching the need to the document. The difficulty is not only knowing how to extract the information but also how to use it to decide relevance (Van Rijsbergen, 1979).

The principle of 'relevance' is of prime importance. An automatic retrieval strategy should retrieve all relevant documents at the same time as retrieving as few of the non-relevant as possible. The characterisation should be such that when a document it represents is relevant to a query, it enables the document to be retrieved in response to that query. Human indexers traditionally characterise documents in this way when assigning index terms and attempt to anticipate the index terms a user would employ to retrieve these documents. Implicitly the user is constructing queries for which the document is relevant.

Intellectually it is possible for a human to establish the relevance of a document to a query. For computer software to do this a model is required within which relevance decisions can be quantified. Much of the research that has been done in the information retrieval field has been concerned with different aspects of such a model.

At this time most computer-based retrieval systems store only a representation of a document based upon intellectually assigned index terms. The searcher uses the retrieval software to match and compare indexes to the database against selected search terms and strategies and the success of a search is dependent on these terms and strategies.

1.2 Quantitative aspects

The quantitative aspects of handling a database are activities which computer software can perform extremely well. Some of these tasks which are important for information retrieval are:

a. Validation of data. For numerical data validation is simple, for example upper and lower range of valid values. The textual data validation is possible within certain limits depending on the structure of the data, for example the presence/absence of upper or lower case characters or numeric digits is easily checked.

   A check on spelling is possible on large computer systems (this involves storage of and subsequent reference to a comprehensive dictionary). This option is becoming more economically feasible with the advent of sophisticated word processing packages for microcomputers.

   If the data is stored in some predetermined format (for example MARC format), then more validation is possible, for example coded data fields against a table containing the complete range of values, presence or absence of tags or subfields and their dependency on others.

   Record control numbers (for example ISBNs, LCs) can be checked for correct format and check digits.

   Punctuation can be checked for formatted data or even automatically inserted.

b. Duplicate checking. In almost all computerised systems textual data will be stored in such a way that the representation of each document will have some unique number associated with it. This may be a system specific number or some other number associated with the document, for example ISBN or ISSN. The computer software can easily notify users of duplicated index numbers, and some systems will not allow input of a document under a duplicate number.

c. Data integrity (authority control). For data that is formatted (for example MARC) the integrity of the data can be crosschecked during input by keeping indexes of the authority fields.

d. Reporting. Software can easily be programmed to produce a wide variety of reports on the database, for example routine reports such as listings of new documents added to the database; ad hoc reports such as a printout of the answer to a particular search query; comprehensive reports such as a printed index for the database. It is worth noting that it makes no difference whether the report is produced on paper, on a catalogue card, as an instantaneous display on a computer terminal or on microfiche. The format of reports can be handled well by software (for example headings, page numbers) (Rowley, 1980).

2. CHARACTERISTICS OF TEXTUAL DATABASES

There is an innate difference in the composition of a body of data (or database) that contains textual material and is likely to be used for information retrieval, as compared to a database that contains 'traditional' computer data. For example a typical commercial system might contain a few textual fields containing names and addresses but the bulk of the data would consist of numerical data—amounts of money. For such a system the computer is used to perform complex arithmetic computations very rapidly. In the information retrieval situation the processing is much more concerned with identification, storage, rearrangement, and sorting of alphabetical data.

Computerised information retrieval systems must be economical as well as feasible. In the same manner that economic considerations have led to more critical and hence more mathematically sophisticated design of engineering structures and chemical engineering processes, it is the economic considerations that are leading to a requirement for more precise mathematical formulation of the principles of information retrieval to ensure that computers and computer accessible storage devices are used in an economic manner. Since computer hardware is continually being improved, operational retrieval systems will continue to be subject to constant revision and expansion. This presents less difficulty than might be expected at first, since although computer hardware and programs may change, the vast quantities of stored information may remain unchanged or be converted within the computer.

2.1 Comparison of database characteristics

Before considering in detail the nature of textual data, the following comparison of bibliographic and commercial databases (Table 3.1) gives some idea of their rather different characteristics.

Table 3.1 Comparison of bibliographic and commercial databases.

Bibliographic	Commercial
Ad hoc retrieval is a vital part of the system.	Ad hoc retrieval is absent, or rare.
Basic application is almost completely standard, i.e.: information retrieval.	Applications are very diverse, e.g.: payroll, stores, orders etc.
Most operations in the system are initiated by librarians or users.	The Data Processing Dept runs the system, and user staff are 'cogs' within it.
Data structure is of a particular structure, i.e.: there is one main file of data, with various associated files of thesaurus, indexes etc.	Data structure in general consists of many files, which may have relationships between them.
Text data is very important.	Text data is incidental, and is often treated as variable, unsearchable comment fields.

(After Tagg, 1982)

2.2 Characteristics of textual data

The important characteristics of textual data which have a bearing on the capabilities of the software include:

- Matches. In information retrieval generally those items which only *partially* match a request are required, and then a few of the *best* matches are selected.
- Incomplete queries. A query may often be incomplete as the search is for relevant documents rather than just matches. This means that matching errors are insignificant for information retrieval.
- Alteration of data. Deletion and update are unimportant in the overall context of the database.
- Variable length data, which itself contains variable length fields. If variable length information is compressed into a fixed field format data will be truncated (long items) or empty space will be left (short items). Variable field formats guarantee compact storage, but need more complicated software routines.
- Amount of data. Many bibliographic files contain extensive amounts of data. Although this book is concentrating deliberately on small scale databases, the more general case has an effect on the available software.
- Occurrence. Fields may be single occurrences or multiple occurrences, and in some records may be absent altogether.
- Truncated search items. A question term should be searchable for its appearance as a fragment of a larger term. This truncation may occur on the left, on the right, or on both sides of the term.

(Lancaster and Fayen, 1973; Van Rijsbergen, 1976; Heaps, 1978; Salton, 1975).

3. DESIRABLE CHARACTERISTICS OF SUITABLE SOFTWARE

As a consequence the software should have the following capabilities:

- Ability to handle variable length data, which in itself contains variable length fields.
- Ability to communicate with different types of users, ranging from casual users, those who are concerned with extracting an endless variety of specified subsets of data, to users who want to execute complex functions on the data.
- Ability to accommodate change.
- Ability to cope with other than 'normal' computer filing sequences. This generally means that specific sorting software is required which may be extremely complex.
- Ability to cope with the ad hoc nature of subject information retrieval.
- Ability to respond to queries rapidly, that is a good response time.
- Provision of browsing facilities.
- Search facilities which include truncation of terms.
- Ability to recover from aborted searches and to cancel search terms.
- Validation of input terms, including display of unacceptable terms.
- Administration capabilities, that is collection of statistics, administration of time usage and costs, control of security and backup facilities, provision of an audit trail.
- Output display, that is a selection of options as to detail and format, display of vocabulary, synonym availability and thesaurus features.
- Ability to handle data which may include elements which are often absent, but which, when they do occur, may be in multiples and vary dramatically in size (Salton, 1975; Van Rijsbergen, 1976; Atkinson, 1979).
- Query languages which ideally should be simple enough for a novice user but complex enough to allow for retrieval for complicated searches. Capability at a minimum should handle Boolean searches, ranging up to more sophisticated systems with controlled vocabularies and/or free text searching.
- Ability to operate in an online interactive mode (Salton, 1975; Bell and Jones, 1979; Lancaster, 1979).

4. OTHER SOFTWARE REQUIRED

All computers, regardless of their application, require a certain basic amount of software which controls the actual physical operation of the machine and acts as a backbone for the rest of the system activities. A brief description of this controlling software follows.

4.1 Operating system

The operating system is a program which controls the central processor, memory and peripheral equipment of a computer system. Other terms commonly used are the monitor, the Executive or the Supervisor (usually depending on which computer manufacturer you are referring to). The operating system generally has various facilities available to users depending on the specific job. These facilities include compilers and assemblers (to translate programs written in high level languages into machine language), debuggers (a tool to assist programmers to find program errors), text editors (to enable the creation and modification of software), and linkers (to link together all the various modules required for a particular program). Multi-user operating systems allow a number of users to simultaneously share the resources of the computer.

4.2 System utilities

Depending on the sophistication of the operating system available, there may be a selection of useful utility programs available, for example data copying programs, sort/merge utilities (Grosch, 1979; Rowley, 1980; Fosdick, 1981).

4.3 Programming languages

As bibliographic data processing has specific and rather unusual software needs, the programming languages available are especially important.

There are several available papers on the relative merits of common and uncommon programming languages for textual data processing (Fosdick, 1979, 1981). The requirements that are considered necessary include the handling of character format and variable length data, and string manipulation facilities.

Some common languages are COBOL, FORTRAN, PL/1, SNOBOL, COMIT, ALGOL, PASCAL, BASIC.

4.4 DBMS

DBMS software is available nowadays for many sizes and types of computer. The majority of installed systems are in the traditional commercial world of data processing. The basic task of a DBMS system is to convert and control the use of data on a storage medium into a view of a database which individual users wish to see (programs and/queries), and vice versa. The user does not need to know what is happening at the physical level, and should be insulated from changes made at that level, or from the requirements of other users (Tagg, 1982). The DBMS communicates with the operating system. Various utility functions are generally also included, for example backup and recovery facilities, reorganisation of data, input and editing of data.

There is no intrinsic reason why a DBMS cannot be used for a bibliographic database, however the pecularities of textual data (as discussed earlier) make many of the commercially available DBMS systems unsuitable, the main problem being handling of variable length data (Tidswell, 1980a, b; Wagner, 1980). Some have been used successfully as the backbone of an information retrieval system, for example ADABAS, BASIS. Note that even with a bibliographically oriented DBMS system, applications programming will still be required to produce an operational system.

Some of the advantages of a DBMS over a traditional file-structured system include the control of data redundancy and data consistency. In a DBMS system changes in physical organisation or storage medium should not affect the operation of application programs, which access only logical data structures.

Many DBMS software packages require a large computer to run on, which generally implies more than a small scale database. However the development of DBMS software is very much an on-going phase at present, and already some DBMSs are available in micro- or minicomputer versions (Floam, 1976; Huffenberger and Wigington, 1979).

5. FILE ORGANISATION METHODS

In a traditional file environment, as opposed to a DBMS environment, data is organised and stored for single applications. The design of the application programs is dependent upon the structure of the data. This is why much of the literature on information retrieval systems covers various file structures in detail. For the sake of completeness a brief description of each of the major file organisation types follows.

5.1 Sequential files

A sequential file is the most primitive of all file structures. Records are simply a serial accumulation of data with new items added at the end. Any search must process the entire file, from start to end. Sequential files are the only file type that can be stored on magnetic tape. They are cost effective where the nature of the job means that the complete file must be checked and the file is small. Obviously sequential files make the most efficient use of space, since there are no storage overhead requirements (that is pointers, links, redundant items).

5.2 Chained files

In chained files the stored items are separated into sets in such a way that all items within a given set are identified by a common keyword or keyword set. The elements within each set are connected by pointers (chained) and a directory is used to obtain access to the first item in each chain. Search times are shorter than for serial files. The chains can be updated by adding new data to the top of the chains. However there are some disadvantages in that search times will be slow if the chains become excessively long, storage space for pointers will produce some overheads, and the directory must be stored, searched and maintained.

5.3 Inverted files

An inverted file is a chained file where each chain contains only one item, and the directory consists of as many entries for each keyword as there are items characterised by that keyword. The main advantage of inverted files is the short search time produced by eliminating all pointers from the main file and by performing most of the search in the directory alone. Some of the limitations include tedious directory updating, storage overheads as the directory size increases, and a search time that is proportional to query length.

5.4 Computed access files

Computed access files are characterised by files that are partitioned into groups of items with key word sets related in some mathematical manner ('hashing'), that is the search procedure for an item consists of a computational process that manipulates the key words to obtain the storage address of corresponding records. The main advantage of this method is fast file access, and also in many cases no directory is required. However, for bibliographic and textual keys the selection of a hashing function that gives a desirable scattering of the records on the storage medium may be difficult. File maintenance problems arise when the indexing is allowed to change.

5.5 Clustered files

This type of file is clustered into groups of related items. An association coefficient is used to estimate the relationship between pairs of items, and then classes are set up containing all items thought to be sufficiently similar. If each class is identified by a class profile, then searching is carried out by matching the search requests first with class profiles and then examining the matching classes in detail. Fast searches are possible since only a few classes need to be handled for each search. It is easy to modify query and document indexing since full key word sets are available for all items. The disadvantages in using clustered files are mainly in the clustering itself because most known clustering methods tend to be expensive when carried out for large bodies of data, such as bibliographic documents. Also a fair amount of storage overhead may arise because the 'class profile' or 'centroid' file must be stored and maintained.

5.6 Indexed sequential access

The indexed sequential access is often used for disc files of data and is a compromise between a sequential scanning process in which each memory position is scanned in order to find a desired record, and a direct-access process in which a directory look-up or hashing procedure directly locates the desired addresses.

For practical purposes the serial file organisation and chained organisations produce response times that are too slow to be worthwhile. Many of the computed access file arrangements present problems. Clustered files are not currently used because of the expense of the clustering process. This means that most practical implementations of large query and document files use either the inverted or indexed file organisations (Lancaster, 1973; Salton, 1975; Van Rijsbergen, 1976, 1979).

6. SOFTWARE OPTIONS

The functional aspects of the generation and management of small scale databases can be broken down into three basic activities: database creation and updating, production of printed products, and online searching.

The following sections discuss in some detail the four major options available for each of these activities. There is no reason why each of these basic activities could not each make use of a different option, provided that adequate safeguards are provided to ensure data compatability across systems.

6.1 Turnkey systems

A turnkey system is designed, marketed and maintained by a vendor who supplies a complete system of software and hardware to perform a defined application. In addition, turnkey system vendors may offer assistance in converting procedures to their system and training users. Hardware maintenance may be performed by the turnkey vendor, the original computer supplier or a third party. Software maintenance support varies among vendors. To be sure that a turnkey system will perform the desired application and realistically meet the needs of the purchaser, a written list of requirements (a specification) needs to be prepared.

Some advantages of purchasing a turnkey system are:

- There is no need to acquire permanent specialised data processing staff.
- Existing library staff can be trained to operate the system and provide liaison with the vendor.
- Both software and hardware maintenance are usually provided by the vendor.
- Benefit can be obtained from a vendor experienced in other installations of the same system.
- System acquisition cost is known, and operating costs can be reasonably accurately estimated.
- Enhancements to the system can be bought from the original vendor when they become available.

Some possible disadvantages are:

- Dependence on one firm for all maintenance, both hardware and software. There is no fall back if the vendor goes out of business during the life of the system.
- There is generally not much flexibility in the degree of customisation of a turnkey system, that is more compromise may be necessary on the part of the purchasing library to conform to the requirements of the turnkey system as offered.
- Varying responsiveness on the part of the vendor to problems, particularly when these are software errors.
- Varying responsiveness on the part of the vendor to customer proposed system enhancements.

Careful evaluation of a turnkey system must include investigation of other installations, including the vendor's record of customer support and response to suggested system enhancements. This approach to software selection is likely to appeal to libraries with more restricted budgets (Grosch, 1979).

6.2 Software packages

This option includes purchase of a software package to run on existing hardware or alternatively purchase of both software package and the appropriate hardware. This approach is likely to be more expensive than a turnkey system, but cheaper than developing a new system (either by contract or in-house).

It is unlikely than an existing package will meet all requirements. Either compromises must be made on the list of requirements or negotiations can be made for modifications to the package. However extensive modifications can be expensive and there is a danger that extensive modification of an existing system will produce a bastard that may have lost many of the advantages of the original design without supplying the needs of the new system in the most appropriate way.

Advantages of purchasing a software package are:

- The package has presumably been tested out and run successfully over a number of months or even years.
- The purchase includes the experience and expertise of the organisation who developed the package, plus experience from current users of the system. Users of various commercial packages often join together to form 'User Groups', which offer existing and potential funds of operating experience.
- Using an existing package creates compatability or at least easy convertibility, which may well be important for participating in any information networks.

Some possible disadvantages are:

- The selection of software may be severely restricted by pre-existing hardware. Generally software packages are designed for use with a particular series of computers and are not easily converted for different equipment.
- Unless the vendor is prepared to make (and maintain) alterations to the package to customise it, compromises are likely to be necessary on some aspects.

Library and information oriented packages have been produced and marketed by computer manufactures, software houses, academic and research institutions, national bodies and other libraries. A good software package is likely to be cheaper, more readily available and possibly easier to implement than a tailor made system (Lancaster, 1973; Grosch, 1979; Rowley, 1980; Williams and Goldsmith, 1981; International Directory of Software, 1982/3).

6.3 Development of an in-house system

Development of an in-house system will probably (but not necessarily) produce the best software system for a particular set of requirements, but the cost in terms of money and manpower will be great. The development of suitable flexible software to generate and manage even a small scale database must be measured in man years of effort. This approach is unlikely to be viable unless the organisation has considerable resources and a long term plan to create a range of databases and products on a commercial basis.

However if an organisation wishes to consider this option further there are two possibilities.

6.3.1 Development by a software house or group

The actual software development can be contracted to a software house or software development group.

Some advantages of this approach are:

- The organisation need not maintain its own in-house development staff.
- System development costs are set under contract according to specifications.
- The software house is likely to have a range of expertise in all aspects of system development.
- Installation and operating dates can be incorporated into a contract.
- The software house may have produced similar systems for other customers, the use of parts of these can reduce costs.

Some disadvantages are:

- A separate contract will probably be required for software maintenance.
- The organisation will need staff to liaise closely with the contracting firm on technical development.
- Conversion from an existing system will be the library's own responsibility.

6.3.2 Development within the library

The software may also be developed within the library or the library's parent organisation. This approach provides the greatest prospect for a system to meet exact requirements, however it also has the greatest prospect of failure. The key seems to be to secure competent management for this type of activity.

Some advantages of this approach are:

- Complete responsibility and control over the project from initiation to completion.
- Complete control over modifications.
- Ability to respond to needed system changes as national or regional developments occur.
- Control over hardware.
- Potential to contribute to the state-of-the-art Library Systems development.
- Potential to make software available to other organisations.

Among the disadvantages are:

- The difficulty of controlling costs. A longer than expected development time will automatically increase costs.

- Problem in attracting and retaining component managerial and technical staff.
- Direct and indirect costs will become a significant continuing portion of the organisation's budget.
  (Lancaster and Fayen, 1973; Grosch, 1979.)

6.4 Use of a service bureau

For a first venture into computerised systems the use of a Service Bureau which can provide expert advice on a consulting basis, is a sensible alternative approach.

Some of the factors which need to be considered are:

- Can the bureau meet the system specification, and if not what compromises will be required?
- What flexibility is available?
- What is provided in the way of quality control?
- To what extent is the database creator involved in the day-to-day operation of the system? That is what staff involvement will be required?
- What equipment will need to be purchased? For example computer terminals, printers, modems, or can it be leased?
- Break down of costs, in terms of capital and ongoing expenditure.

Some advantages of this approach are:

- The cost is continuous and ongoing, with a minimum capital expenditure.
- Competition in the operation of such bureaus is increasing.
- Present firms, especially those specialising in library and information systems have large and strong customer bases.
- New functions are likely to be added to existing systems as the need arises.
- Connections with other bibliographic systems are moving towards direct online computer to computer interaction, so that one bureau with many customers may be able to organise such communications easily.

Some disadvantages are:

- It may not be possible to customise requirements without incurring a heavy cost.
- For an organisation that only requires a simple system, the offered service may have too many 'bells and whistles'.
  (Grosch, 1979.)

7. EVALUATION OF SOFTWARE

Before any evaluation of software products can take place, a complete specification of the requirements of the software system is recommended. The exercise of identifying the library's needs and determining specifications to meet these needs is the best way to formulate specific questions to be asked, to communicate needs to prospective vendors, and to ensure that the software will be able to perform all the expected functions.

Some of the questions to be considered are listed below; these are taken from Tenopir (1980), see also Lancaster (1979).

7.1 Assessment of needs

- Why is a new system desired and/or needed?
- If an old system exists, how will the new system replace or interact with it?
- Detailed and specific formulation of what the new system will be required to do.
- Any special compatibility requirements? For example, is there a need for MARC compatibility.
- Rank all desired features, that is some are necessary, and some would be nice, but not vital.
- How do you envisage the system operating in five or ten years time?
- Who will be the primary users of the system? Will a librarian act as an interface?
- Where will the access points be? In one or multiple locations?
- What is the expected size of the database and what is its expected growth rate?
- What management, personnel and data processing support will there be for the system?
- What is an acceptable price range?
- Is hardware currently available in-house? If so, what is its capacity and its future in the organisation?
- If there are data processing staff available, have they worked with the library before? How will your project fit in with their priorities?

7.2 Vendor or producer

- What is the reputation of the creator or marketing agency of a product? Especially as regards reliability, responsiveness and quality?
- Is it a general software concern, or do they specialise in library/information applications?
- Investigate some of their other products and if possible talk to people who are still using them.
- What kind of support services are offered? For example installation, conversion of data, converting of existing systems.

- Is their geographic location close enough so that a quick response can be made to any problems or questions?
- Are the sales staff helpful? Do they seem to genuinely try and understand your needs?

7.3 System output

- Online display formats: are these easy to understand and read?
- Printed lists and reports: are these well set out and do they cover the information required?
- What about statistical reports?
- Can the system generate magnetic tape output? For example for transfer of data to other systems.

7.4 System input

- Can data on magnetic tape be used for input? (Both for the initial database creation and as an ongoing procedure.)
- What other input methods are there? Can several methods be used if desired?
- Does the system prompt for input? Are the commands easy to remember?
- What about error checking? Are input errors displayed on the screen when they are found?
- What about deletion of records? Can both entire records and parts of records be deleted? Can existing records be easily edited if necessary?

7.5 Searching

- Is the query language easy to learn and easy to use?
- Is help available online for inexperienced users? For example detailed explanations of commands.
- What sort of response is received if erroneous commands are entered? Is it understandable?
- Can a thesaurus be examined online? Can it be printed?
- What sort of searching logic is available? For example 'AND', 'OR', 'NOT'.

7.6 Security

- Can different levels of passwords be set up for different classes of users?
- Is it impossible for unauthorised users to alter the contents of the database?

- What sort of backup systems exist?
- Is it possible to create an audit trail? That is a record of usage of the database.

7.7 Training

- What training is provided by the vendor?
- Does the query language include 'help' messages if required?
- What are the system manuals and documentation like? Are they clear and understandable for all classes of user?
- What sort of training will you need to provide for new users? Can it be done online or will detailed lessons be needed?

7.8 General considerations

- What is the maximum size database that the system can handle? What sizes are operating now?
- Do you have information on all cost factors?
- Compare cost analyses of existing systems with the new system in five or ten years time (remembering that the new automated system is likely to be performing services not presently available).

8. 'HYBRID' OPTIONS: SOME WARNINGS

As mentioned earlier, there is no reason why logically distinct parts of the system cannot be controlled by different software systems running on either the same computer or several different computers. For example one system could be used for data entry and validation, another could be used for online searching, and a third could be used for the production of printed products.

When considering any 'hybrid' the following points need to be borne in mind.

- The method(s) of transfer of data between systems. If the data is not stored in identical format, a conversion program may be necessary. If the computers are not identical (even though they may both be made by the same manufacturer) then a magnetic tape written on one machine cannot *necessarily* be read on the other machine without some conversion process.
- The standards used in each system. Even if the systems use the same format, standards may vary. For example a record containing the minimum 'compulsory' fields on one system may not be accepted as a complete record on the second.

- No part of a 'hybrid' system should be accepted as operational until it has been proved that its inputs and/or outputs are useable by other parts of the 'hybrid'.

9. TRAINING SOFTWARE

A critical factor affecting the success or failure of an online retrieval system is the effectiveness of procedures employed to teach people how to use the facilities. Of the several possible methods, the use of software to provide online instruction on the terminal is one that merits investigation if it is available or can be made available.

Some of the possibilities include:

- Use of the terminal to display a set of instructions that could equally well be presented in conventional printed form.
- Use of CAI techniques, either to give the user a one-time introduction to the system or to lead him by the hand in the conduct of a demonstration search.
- Incorporation of explanations of specific commands or system features that the user can call up when he needs them (that is a 'HELP' feature).

Lancaster and Fayen (1973) discuss training in some detail.

10. MICROCOMPUTERS

In the relatively young world of microcomputers, software is much more likely to distinguish systems than hardware. The indisputable advantage of microcomputers is their cost and it is appropriate, in a work pertaining to small scale databases, to mention suitable software available for microcomputers. There is no software capable of performing complicated information retrieval tasks, however Griffiths (1980), Falk (1981), Fosdick (1981), Lankford (1981) and Williams and Goldsmith (1981) give details of what is available.

Many microcomputers have communication facilities and can serve as intelligent terminals to larger systems or can communicate with other microcomputers. They can also be useful in online searching, for example they can be programmed to handle dial-up procedures, communications protocols and log-on procedures for various host systems. This makes the user's task of connecting to a system easy, and can substantially reduce online time and thus save on search costs. Searches can be prepared offline on the microcomputer and checked for typing and syntax errors. Similarly the results of online searches can be stored and sorted, reformatted or printed locally as required.

11. COST CONSIDERATIONS

Whichever software option, or combination of options, is selected the following list gives an indication of costs likely to be associated with the project.

- Contracts with a software house or a service bureau will include some sort of lease or licence agreement.
- Both software and hardware maintenance are likely to be covered by maintenance contracts, which will be regular, on-going costs.
- Manuals and documentation, especially extra copies are likely to be a separate cost.
- Training of staff.
- System conversion.
- Installation and testing of the system.
- The actual size of the database, and the expected growth rate.

Putnam and Fitzsimmons (1979) and Ashford (1976) give details on the estimation of software costs from the point of view of controlling software development.

12. CONCLUSION

This chapter has attempted to show that in spite of the bewildering range of software options, it is possible to make a reasonable and rational choice to suit one's particular requirements. The choice of software is vital to the existence and operation of any system, for without software there would be no usable system. However, the choice of software cannot be made in isolation from the other essential system components i.e. hardware to run it on and a database to run it with.

REFERENCES

Atkinson, M.P. 1979. 'Progress in documentation—database systems'. *Journal of Documentation* 35: (1): 49–91.

Ashford, J. 1976. 'Software cost: making or buying it?'. *Program* 10: (1): 1–6.

Bell, C. L. M. and Jones, K. P. 1979. 'Towards everyday language information retrieval systems via minicomputers?'. *American Society for Information Science Journal* 30: 334–339.

Falk, H. 1981. 'Computer software and equipment considerations'. *School Library Journal* 28: (Nov): 29–32.

Floam, G. 1976. 'Putting a data base on a mini'. *Datamation* June: 97–100.

Fosdick, H. 1981. *Computer Basics for Librarians and Information Specialists.* Arlington, Va, Information Resources Press.

Fosdick, H. 1981. *Computer basics for librarians and information specialists.* Arlington, Va. Information Resources Press.

Griffiths, J.-M. 1980. 'Applications of mini and micro computers to information handling'. In Benenfeld, A. and Kazlauskas, E. *Communicating information: proceedings of the ASIS 43rd annual meeting, 1980.* White Plains, NY, Knowledge Industry Publications.

Grosch, A. N. 1979. *Minicomputers in libraries 1979–1980.* White Plains, NY, Knowledge Industry Publications.

Heaps, H. S. 1978. *Information retrieval: computational and theoretical aspects.* Library and Information Science Series, New York, Academic Press.

Huffenberger, M. A. and Wigington, R. L. 1979. 'Database management systems'. *Annual Review of Information Science and Technology* 14: 153–190.

International directory of software. 1982/83. London, CUYB Publications Ltd.

Lancaster, F. W. 1979. *Information retrieval systems: characteristics, testing and evaluation.* 2nd ed. New York, Wiley.

Lancaster, F. W. and Fayner, E.G. 1973. *Information retrieval on-line.* Los Angeles, Melville (Wiley).

Lankford, M. D. (compiler). 1981/1982. 'Micro-computers: software evaluations and print resources'. *Booklist* 78 (Oct. 1): 242–4 (Apr. 1, 1982): 1028–2.

Putnam, L. and Fitzsimmons, A. 1979. 'Estimating software costs'. *Datamation* September: 189–198 October: 171–177 November: 137–139.

Rowley, J. 1980. *Computers for libraries.* Saur/Bingley, New York.

Salton, G. 1975. *Dynamic information and library processing.* Englewood Cliffs, NJ, Prentice-Hall.

Tagg, R. M. 1982. 'Bibliographic and commercial databases—contrasting approaches to data management with special reference to DBMS'. *Program* 16 (4): 191–199.

Tenopir, C. 1980. 'Evaluation of library retrieval software'. In Benenfeld, A. and Kazlauskas, E. *Communicating information: proceedings of the ASIS 43rd annual meeting, 1980.* White Plains, NY, Knowledge Industry Publications.

Tidswell, A. 1980. 'Data base software evaluation methodology'. *Australian Computer Society (ACS) Bulletin* March: 7–11 (a) April: 5–7 (b).

Van Rijsbergen, C. J. 1979. *Information retrieval* 2nd Ed. London, Butterworths.

Van Rijsbergen, C. J. 1976. 'Progress in documentation—file organization in library automation and information retrieval'. *Journal of Documentation* 32 (4): 294–317.

Wagner, J. B. 1980. 'Data base management system design for library automation'. *Journal of Library Automation* 13:56–61.

Williams, P. W. and Goldsmith, G. 1981. 'Information retrieval on mini- and micro-computers'. *Annual Review of Information Science and Technology* 16: 85–111.

4. Hardware options

Kerry Webb

1. Introduction
2. Processors
3. Input devices
4. Storage units
5. Output devices
6. Online versus offline storage
7. Shared versus dedicated systems
8. Environmental considerations
9. Conclusion
Further reading

1. INTRODUCTION

Small scale databases can be run on a wide range of computers, from small personal or business computers through minicomputers to large mainframes. Since all computers have some easy-to-use forms of input and output devices the only special factor is the storage unit. Thus, while a programmable calculator is a basic form of computer, unless some form of extra storage is attached to it, there is little chance of operating any sort of database on it.

In the past, the lines of demarcation between microcomputers, minicomputers and mainframe computers were easily drawn. One could set indicators of physical size, or processor capacity, or types of peripheral devices which could be attached to the computer, and any of these criteria were sufficient to categorise a particular machine. Once it was even possible to determine the 'size' of a computer merely by the manufacturer—IBM made only mainframes, Digital made minicomputers, and so on. The situation at present is that most manufacturers make and sell a complete

SMALL SCALE DATABASES
ISBN 0 12 391970 3

range of machines—from personal computers to very large mainframes—and the extent of the range blurs distinctions.

The most powerful microcomputers can now outperform what would recently have been a very respectable minicomputer, and for several years the 'superminis' have been encroaching on the territory of the smaller mainframes. However, for the purposes of this consideration of small scale databases, a clear distinction between categories is not necessary. Certainly, some factors apply to mainframes and not to smaller computers, but these will be clearly indicated as they occur.

From the system user's point of view, the important aspect is that a smaller computer generally provides (and calls for) more control by that user. The operator of a small scale database on a small computer—whether creating, maintaining or accessing—is likely to be required to perform more organisational tasks than if using a mainframe. Note that this does not refer to those tasks involved in the interaction with the computer system as such. The log-on procedures and the command language of a microcomputer will most likely be as sophisticated and user friendly as on a mainframe. It is the 'housekeeping' tasks associated with the computer, such as turning the machine on and off, loading the software system, making sure that copies of the database and other files are taken regularly and kept in a safe place, which the microcomputer user will probably be called upon to perform. A small database on a mainframe will be one of many systems and the organisation supporting the mainframe and its users will take care of most of these tasks.

In considering hardware options for small scale databases, there are four main classes of equipment: processors, input devices, storage units, and output devices. With some computers, it is possible to acquire an integrated system with all this equipment already connected, perhaps even in the one physical box. Nevertheless, it is important to be aware of the features of the different types of devices so that the correct system for the application can be selected. These considerations are not only important when a small computer is being investigated. It is vital to check any potential computer system to determine that the equipment on offer can perform as required. If a user is being steered towards operating a database on his organisation's mainframe system and the input or output devices are unsuitable, even though there may be sufficient processing capacity and storage, other alternatives must be considered.

2. PROCESSORS

The computer processor performs the work of the computer: controlling input, output and storage devices; accepting commands and input data;

searching the database; assembling retrieved data; and despatching data to the output device. It must have the power to perform these functions reliably and at an acceptable response rate. Reliability is generally not a concern, especially with modern computers, but needs to be investigated if the system on offer is a few years old. The rate of response is more critical in both small and large computers. Sitting at a computer can be very boring if you have nothing to look at but an empty screen while waiting many seconds (or even minutes) for the answer to what you believed was a simple request. Some small computers do not handle file searching quickly and it is highly advisable to test such a machine on a typical problem before you buy it.

The problem of slow response will often occur in a large computer for a different reason. The small database user will probably be one of many users of the machine and in that case can not expect to have high priority among those on the machine at the time. This means that even though the database system is online, the computer will be spending a large proportion of its time servicing other people's needs. Again, the solution to this problem is to test your system on the computer before you contract to use it (if you can) and if the results are not acceptable, alternative systems should be explored.

Another problem with processors (now mercifully rare) is that they sometimes cannot handle the data required of them. This is not a problem of capacity or processing speed, but one related to the internal architecture of the system. Most databases of concern to libraries are textual and in most cases a mixture of upper and lower case characters is required. (This is compounded if foreign language characters must also be accommodated.) Some older computers are so constructed that they can only handle upper-case text, numerals and some punctuation characters. There are ways to extend this capability on such computers, but their performance is necessarily degraded.

It is also necessary to consider the capacity of the system, both present and projected. A system based on a small computer may be adequate now, but could the computer accommodate the storage devices needed as the size of the database grows? A user may find use of a mainframe system acceptable, but could another one or two concurrent users of the database be connected to the system if required? It is a certainty that databases grow bigger and successful systems attract increased usage. Rates of growth can be extremely unpredictable, but there must be some allowance for increase in size of the system and its storage and terminal capacity.

The purchase price of a processor will vary greatly depending on size, range of devices which can be connected, and the range of functions which can be performed. A complete microcomputer system for a small database application could be purchased for as little as $2000 of which the processor may account for half. Mainframe computers usually cost hundreds of thousands of dollars at least, and the small user of such a system may expect to pay hundreds of dollars per month for use of the system.

3. INPUT DEVICES

The purpose of an input device is to convey information to the computer. The simplest devices of this sort are those based on a typewriter keyboard, with the information being entered also displayed upon a cathode ray tube (generally referred to as a VDU) or on paper (similar to a teletype machine). Although these are by far the most common input equipment, there are a number of variations worth noting. Light pens can be used in connection with a VDU screen to enter commands or data already indicated on the screen. Similarly some systems use VDUs with various touch sensitive areas on the screen which register to the computer when touched. (These are used in some public-access catalogue systems.)

Another type of device is the joystick or 'mouse' where movements of an apparatus attached to a VDU cause a cursor on the screen to move. When the cursor reaches the required point on the screen, the user pushes a button or key (on the apparatus or the keyboard) which indicates the information for input. Speech recognition devices are also being developed, where a word or words from a vocabulary (and particular speaker) recognised by the device can be entered. These non-keyboard devices indicate a trend in the development of equipment which will be more usable by people without keyboard skills, and such devices can be expected to become more common in the systems of the future.

This is of course not the extent of the development of input devices. Optical character recognition, recognition of handwriting, bar codes or characters printed in special fonts, is used for some computer input, although rarely in the field of small databases.

For the present though, the usual device is the VDU. Keyboard layouts are more or less standard in the QWERTY format, although some models are available in the Dvořák configuration. (It is interesting to see that most VDUs currently being manufactured can accommodate changes to keyboard layouts readily. With microprocessor control replacing discrete wiring of keyboard circuits, a simple software modification is all that is needed to change what the device recognises at a particular key position.) In addition to the text characters, the keyboard provides for various control keys to assist in insertion or deletion of characters or lines on the screen, to position the screen cursor up, down, or sideways or to a designated position, or possibly to print the contents of the screen on an attached printer. A numeric keypad is now standard on most models.

The screen can come in a variety of sizes and shapes, but is generally square with a diagonal measurement of about 30 cm. A screen this size will display about 24 lines with 80 characters per line (although some micro-computer screens will only produce 40 characters per line). Screen displays are usually monochromatic (white on black, green on black, amber on brown) with multicolour capability becoming more popular, especially when graphical output is required. These generally are more expensive than single-colour screens.

Terminals communicate with processors using a range of communications protocols (software to control the flow of information) and depending on which protocol is used, a simple and reliable VDU can cost less than $1000. Others using more complicated communications software, and capable of many extra operations can cost $5000 and more. These may have internal microprocessors to perform the more complex activities, and when the terminal is not being used as an online device to the computer, it may be employed as a stand-alone microcomputer to perform other tasks. Terminals may have integrated cassette or disc drives (used for offline data entry) or internal communications controllers which enable a number of other VDUs or printers to be attached to them or through them to the main computer.

Printing terminals, although less flexible in their operation than VDUs may provide an adequate service in some applications. They have the appearance of an electric typewriter, with some of the function keys which are present on the VDU keyboard. A benefit of this type of device is that a printed record of all activity on the terminal is automatically retained, and prices are significantly lower than for VDUs. However their operating speeds are lower than VDUs, and are noisier, and as they contain more mechanical parts they are more liable to break down.

One interesting example of a printing terminal is the type which packs into a briefcase-sized package and has an attached acoustic coupler, which enables communication with a remote computer via a standard telephone handset. This highly portable arrangement allows an extremely flexible approach, for example, interrogation of a database from many different locations.

In determining the specific features desirable for handling small scale databases, it is necessary to examine what the data consists of, who will enter it and interrogate the database, and where these operators will be located. Nearly all terminals can handle upper and lower case characters but, as with processors, if foreign language text is involved, special devices may be necessary. In creating and interrogating the database, if records consist of a large number of characters, savings in staff time and telecommunications charges can be achieved by using the most efficient telecommunications protocol available.

Where a database is searched on behalf of clients (especially if they are paying directly for the service) the appearance of the printed output could be a factor in choosing equipment. It may be possible to interrogate a database on a main computer using a microcomputer as the 'terminal' and to use the microcomputer offline to reformat the results of the search in order to make them more presentable to the client. If the user of the database will not be operating from a fixed location, a portable will be needed. This may take the form of the printing terminal described above or one of the range of portable microcomputers currently available.

4. STORAGE UNITS

All computers have available to their processors a certain amount of storage capacity physically and logically contained in their system. The data contained in this internal storage ranges from as little as 1000 characters or bytes (referred to as 1K bytes) in very small microcomputers to more than 32 million bytes in large mainframes, and the data in this storage is erased when the computer's power is turned off. Therefore there is a need for another means of storing the contents of a database in a non-volatile manner (that is, a manner which does not require power to be continually supplied to the storage unit).

Disc media are used for the storage of databases because they (in their many forms) provide fast and random access to information in their files. Information may also be held on magnetic tape, but this must be read serially, and locating the desired record on a tape may require passing an entire tape through the tape drive. Because of the way that the recording of data on discs is organised, searching time is greatly reduced.

Through the history of computing, various magnetic media have been used for random access storage—banks of magnetic cards, magnetic drums, and removable discs. Although this last type is widely used on medium and large computers, the industry is concentrating on fixed discs and floppy discs.

A big problem with disc processing has traditionally been that, with the unit's read/write heads travelling at high speed in very close proximity to the surface of the disc, any impurities such as dust or smoke particles (which are much larger than the gap between head and surface) can cause errors or damage to the disc surface. Whereas removable discs are exposed to the atmosphere (and therefore may be contaminated) when they are mounted and demounted, fixed discs are sealed inside the drive units and are never removed. Floppy discs are less susceptible to this problem because the heads in their drives travel further away from the disc surface.

Fixed discs consist of a stack of platters of rigid material which have a magnetic recording substance deposited upon each surface. Each platter is separated from the next by a space sufficient to allow an arm containing read/write heads to move forward and backward along the radius of the disc. The recording surfaces consist of a number of concentric tracks upon which thousands of characters may be stored. It can be seen then how a read/write head may be positioned to a location on a disc pack in a fraction of a second as the pack rotates at high speed. Compare this with the much longer time taken to access data on a magnetic tape. Fixed disc units on mainframe computers consist of one or more stacks of platters within one physical box and can contain from 300 million bytes to more than one billion bytes in the unit. The cost of the larger units is in excess of $100 000. On microcomputers, fixed disc units with a capacity of ten million bytes in one stack of platters will cost only a thousand dollars.

Floppy discs (of which there are two standard sizes, 5.25 inch and 8 inch, although smaller discs are available) are single flexible discs which are also coated with magnetic material and use the concentric recording track layout. Their flexibility means that they need not be handled with such extreme care as other disc media—they may be sent through the post with little protective packing. Both the discs and disc drives are relatively cheap—a few dollars for the discs and drive units start at a few hundred dollars.

Floppy discs are rarely used with larger computers, but they are the prime storage media for microcomputers. The main concern on microcomputers however, is the lack of compatibility in different disc formats. Even with discs of the same size, different computers will often record at different densities (more or less characters per centimetre along the recording track) and with different numbers of tracks on the disc. So it cannot be assumed that a disc written on one computer can be read by another brand of computer.

The most important operational consideration with disc files (and indeed any other storage medium) is the need to provide regular backup storage for the data. This means that if there is a failure of the online file (in the case of fixed disc) or if a floppy disc is lost or damaged, a copy of the data can be used to recreate the file or files to their status at the time that the copy was made. On larger systems, disc files are usually backed up to magnetic tapes and saved in a secure location, perhaps in a fireproof safe or at another computer site.

On smaller systems, it was previously the practice to back up to floppy discs from fixed disc files, but as fixed disc capacity grows, it becomes necessary to improve this facility. Some computers use floppy disc magazines which can hold a number of discs to be loaded into the unit automatically as required. Another method is to use large capacity cassette tapes, which operate at high speed—a useful feature in backup processing.

In setting up a system, it is necessary to decide not only how but when to perform backup processing. The crucial dependency is how often the file is changed, because when a file is re-created from a copy, all changes which occurred between the time of the copy and the re-creation are lost. Therefore a file which changes often needs to be copied more regularly than one which is more stable. Of course, one way to ensure that no data is lost is to keep a journal file of all changes between copies and to apply this to any re-created file. This will require extra processing every time the main file is changed, and it might be decided that the extra cost is not worth the trouble.

5. OUTPUT DEVICES

As indicated above, VDUs and typewriter terminals, as well as being used for input, are quite often the units by which output from the computer system is displayed. Other output devices of interest to users of small database systems are printers and, to a lesser extent, plotters.

Printers come in several types. Those associated with microcomputers and small business computers are character printers (with one character being printed at a time) and include dot matrix, golfball/thimble and daisy wheel printers. The last two types are used where letter-quality print is required. Dot matrix printers are cheaper with less attractive output. Such printers can be used on larger computers, but on small machines they are the primary output devices. On minicomputers and mainframes, printers of the band or train/chain variety will more often be found. Another type becoming more popular on large computers is the laser printer which uses electrostatic technology similar to that employed by photocopy machines. These printers can produce many different text and graphic symbols in a variety of sizes.

Apart from the quality of the output produced, the main factor in determining the printer to be used for a particular application is speed. Golfball printers can print about 15 characters per second; line printers using train/chain technology will print at speeds of between 300 and 2000 lines per minute; laser printers can print at 20 000 lines per minute and above. The prices of these printers increase with the rated speed. Character printers may be purchased for a few hundred dollars while the fastest laser printers cost hundreds of thousands of dollars.

For graphic output, produced from numeric databases or as a product of business systems, plotters may be used. Some rudimentary plotting can be done with conventional printers of all types, although such output is limited by the restriction of the paper travelling only in one direction and the manipulation of text characters to approximate graphical output. A true plotter can move paper back and forward and this, together with the travelling span of the printing head, provides flexible plotting capacity in two axes. Plotters usually employ inked pens (some devices have a multicolour facility) but there is development in thermal and electrostatic technology.

Unlike most computer equipment, printers (and to a lesser extent plotters) are dirty and noisy. In the printing process, paper particles are scattered through the air and this debris provides potential hazards for magnetic recording devices. For this reason, printing equipment is often located in a separate room from processors, disc and tapes drives, and is often (like VDUs) remote from the central computer in a location convenient to the end user. Because excess noise is unwelcome in an office environment, there is a range of acoustic hoods and other attachments which serve to muffle much of this noise.

In addition, printers require the provision of special paper, mostly with sprocket holes along each side to allow for fast and accurate feeding into the printer. This paper can be a standard product or may be overprinted by the paper manufacturer with letterheads and overlays of various designs, in the interest of providing a more attractive and useful product. Printers also require ink, ribbons and for laser printers, processing chemicals. These are inherently messy products, although the trend is for manufacturers to make their handling simpler and cleaner.

Having discussed the physical devices which make up the hardware in a computer system, it is appropriate to pay attention to some operational aspects of the system: advantages and disadvantages of online and offline storage; advantages and disadvantages of shared and dedicated computer systems; and environmental considerations.

6. ONLINE VERSUS OFFLINE STORAGE

When planning a database system for storage and retrieval, online data storage is obviously preferable, because of the speed at which online can be accessed. In fact, most databases of any size are held online with the only offline component being the backup copies stored in some other medium in another location. In some cases though, the requirements of an installation may be such that the amount of available online storage is less than the amount of data which comprises the databases and general files required by users of the system. Such an example would be a service bureau offering a number of applications systems to a number of clients.

In this case, one solution would be to offer access to different databases at different times. This practice is known as 'windowing'. For example, during a week, one database (the most in demand) would be available each day all day, another would be mounted only each morning, and others less popular would be only available for a couple of hours each week. It may be that a segment of a database (perhaps the most recent entries) may be required more than the rest. Then, providing that the software was flexible enough to cope with only a partially available database, that segment alone could be mounted.

When windowing is used, there is both user inconvenience and extra cost associated in loading the database from offline storage to the online device at the start of the period, and if the database is changed during the period, the database must be copied at the end of the window. This situation is less cumbersome if media other than fixed disc are used. A removable disc or floppy disc is merely removed from the drive at the end of the period and the next database to be made available is mounted.

The increased use of microcomputers may in fact bring a significant change in the way small databases are processed. It is now feasible to consider whether a database comprising about 300 000 characters may be duplicated and disseminated on a floppy disc to a number of users with the same kind of microcomputer. An example may be a network of school libraries with a union catalogue or union list of serials distributed to their members. Perhaps other database providers could consider making their products available in this manner, in much the same way as microfiche catalogues and publications are distributed now.

This sort of development would depend on the size of the database and the capacity of the floppy disc. It is certain that the discs currently on the market will be improved and will one day contain more than the present limit of around 500 000 characters on one side of a disc. Even so, there are alternatives to waiting for technology to come to our aid. It may be acceptable to store the indexes to the database on one disc and the actual data on another. If the computer has more than one disc drive, there will be little decrease in performance by splitting the database in this way (it is possible that performance will be increased). If only one drive is available, it may still be reasonably efficient for the retrieval program to direct the operator to load another disc to retrieve the desired record, after its location has been found in the indexes.

7. SHARED VERSUS DEDICATED SYSTEMS

With any computer system, it is necessary to investigate the best method of acquisition, either by sharing the system with other users or by having a system dedicated to one particular application. With any acquisition, there will be a considerable cost involved either initially by purchase or by ongoing payment for services in a shared environment.

A user who is part of a larger organisation which already has some computing facilities may be expected to accommodate his needs on that system. For instance, a university computer centre running administration, payroll and library acquisitions systems may have the spare capacity to also support a database application. For this type of operation, charges may be levied on the basis of storage costs of the database, and usage charges in terms of connect time, processor time, and input/output operations. The same sort of charging schedule would be applicable to customers of a commercial service bureau.

The advantages of this approach are that the capital costs of establishing the system are divided between all the users and that obvious economies of scale are achieved. Fewer operations staff are required in a shared environment than in a number of discrete systems. Another benefit is that the central site operation handles the relations with the vendors of hardware, software and communications facilities.

Disadvantages include the loss of control over the ultimate operation of the application. For instance, towards the end of the financial year, a user may find that processing is interrupted so that the payroll group may complete the processing of the employees' taxation group certificates. There is also the possibility that the user will not be permitted to develop the system as she wants it, because the extra processing capacity is not present at the time or in the future.

Using a shared computer system will often mean that the programming staff of the organisation are allocated between the various users. The difficulty in this case is that such staff are rarely under the ultimate control of the user and may be called away at an inopportune time to do some other high priority job. With this type of arrangement it can be difficult to maintain the continuity of skills associated with the system, as programmers attached to the central facility come and go.

A dedicated computer for a small database application will usually be a small minicomputer or microcomputer. While this will give the user much control over many aspects of the operation, there are also responsibilities. These include the management of operating staff, administration of the computer site, ordering of supplies (paper, discs and so on), liaison with suppliers and so on. It is possible that the equipment may have surplus capacity (at least in the beginning) and this capacity may be sold to other users. On a small system, the overheads of site, staff and supplier liaison may not be significant—especially if vendor supplied software is used extensively.

A variant of the dedicated system is the duplicated system. This is applicable to the use of microcomputers in an organisation, with databases distributed on floppy discs, according to the examples outlined above. In such cases, the software and hardware used by the different machines would be the same. This would mean that liaison with suppliers and maintenance would be much simpler.

8. ENVIRONMENTAL CONSIDERATIONS

If the computer system to be used is a mainframe, the devices for which a user is responsible will be no more than terminals and printers. For a small minicomputer or microcomputer, all of the equipment may be in the hands of the user. Either way, some attention must be paid to the location where the devices are to be installed.

Generally speaking, this type of equipment will operate wherever humans are comfortable. Large computers need special air-conditioned sites and high voltage power circuits, but terminals and small computers need no more than the average office environment and the standard domestic power supply. The problem of noisy printers and possible solutions were referred to above. Terminals and microcomputers make little noise and are unlikely to disturb the surrounding area.

The lighting environment for screen-based equipment deserves careful attention. Manufacturers are becoming more aware of these matters and provide installation information for siting devices in such a manner that potential sources of eye injury are minimised. Attachments to VDUs such as hoods and mesh screens designed to reduce reflection of ambient light are also available. Tables and chairs provided for screen operators should allow sufficient adjustment that a comfortable yet correct posture may be achieved.

The arteries of any computer system are the communication cables. In a fully integrated microcomputer, these may be completely enclosed within the basic unit, but in other cases the provision of cabling is a factor sometimes given little attention in the planning phase. This is more important in areas where telecommunications are involved and the responsible authority provides the service, or when the internal cabling in a building must be installed by an external agency such as the electricity authority. Careful attention to these matters is important, not only because of scheduling such work (often associated with tight deadlines) but also because of the installation requirements of these authorities which may be more demanding than one might assume.

Finally, ancillary storage associated with the equipment should be provided for. This will be needed for operating manuals, log books, backup copies of disc files, and spare paper and ribbons for printers.

9. CONCLUSION

This chapter provides a broad description of the components and operational matters associated with computer equipment used to run a small scale database. The hardware and procedures must be appropriate for the operation, they must be adequate for current processing loads, and they should be flexible enough to support future growth. The equipment must be reliable, safe, and comfortable to operate. These criteria should be listed fully before the acquisition process is started, and any system under consideration should be evaluated against each point. The best solution may not be the cheapest, but it must meet any criteria which have been declared as essential.

FURTHER READING

Grosch, A. M. 1980. *Minicomputers in libraries 1979–1980.* White Plains, NY, Knowledge Industry Publications.

Journals

AUERBACH Data World
Australian Microcomputer Handbook
Byte
Rydge's Data Trend EDP Manual

5. Management, control and cost benefit

D. A. Tellis

1. Introduction
2. The management approach
    2.1 Analysis and decision making
    2.2 The decision making process
3. Main elements for a bibliographic database
    3.1 Resolution of prerequisite major factors
    3.2 Resolution of elements
    3.3 Resolution of activities and events
4. Costs
    4.1 Cost elements: AESIS and ESRISAT
        4.1.1 Development costs
        4.1.2 Processing costs
        4.1.3 Cost of products
        4.1.4 Management and support services
        4.1.5 Unit costs
5. Cost effectiveness and benefit
    5.1 Cost effectiveness and benefit: AESIS and ESRISAT
        5.1.1 Cost benefit
6. Conclusion
Acknowledgement
References

1. INTRODUCTION

In other chapters there have been underlying elements of management and control. This is because the question of management and control is inherent in any undertaking or operational system. It is possible therefore that this paper will impinge on topics already covered; however there will be a

SMALL SCALE DATABASES
ISBN 0 12 391970 3

difference in emphasis. I shall endeavour to reiterate some basic principles and methods that are considered essential for the effective utilisation of resources in the creation and operation of small scale databases, as against analysing the methods themselves.

2. THE MANAGEMENT APPROACH

It is axiomatic that any system is affected by all factors that are involved in the creation and operation of the system. The first principle that comes into focus therefore is: *effective utilisation of resources is not possible without consideration of all factors that affect both the whole system and the system as a whole.* That is, we must consider and analyse the internal factors that constitute the operating system and the interaction of these factors, and the external factors that affect the system in the environment in which it functions—technical, economic, sociological and political.

Whilst it may seem rather overpowering to consider all these elements when talking about small scale databases, there are three important reasons which prompt such considerations. First, many factors are applicable irrespective of scale. Second, 'small scale' is a relative term and in Australia many of the national and regional specialised databases with inputs ranging from 2500 to 5000 citations per year are 'small scale'. Third, and this especially is the reason for giving consideration to a wider range of factors, small scale databases more often than not tend to grow faster than anticipated and become, in surprisingly short spaces of time, large scale systems. If design considerations have by default neglected provisions for growth and some degree of flexibility, experience shows that major remedial measures become necessary. Such measures are usually costly, irksome and possibly too difficult to implement economically. The database is then scrapped or endured as the next best thing, much to the dissatisfaction of all concerned.

This notwithstanding, inevitably there are always better things around the corner and one has to freeze options and decide on a path of action, within prevailing constraints. The point I wish to make is: better by decision than default.

2.1 Analysis and decision making

The approach advocated in the first principle covers the full spectrum of factors involved, from macro-elements on the one hand to micro-elements on the other. This brings into focus another well known and perhaps dominant principle: *the resolution of a problem or analysis of a system is best achieved through the resolution of the factors that constitute the problem or system.* The universal applicability of this principle makes it all pervasive and is the underlying thesis for the rest of this discussion.

Implicit in the analysis process is the reason for making the analysis.

Almost invariably the reason is to help make some decisions, be they technical, economic, budgetary or otherwise. If we can identify through progressive iterations in increasing depth the constituent elements of a system and its subsystems we have a sound basis for making decisions. Decisions so made enable the development of functions and controls that ensure a system that has been obtained through conscious design rather than through a mixture of design, intuition and a degree of luck. In the real world, of course, one tends to punt on also having fortune on side but in the management process it has little place unless one can see 'risk analysis' or the use of 'statistical probability' and other such processes as a means of quantifying the luck factor.

So it is quite justified when selling information services to extol the value of information by saying a decision is only as good as the information upon which it is based. The corollary should also hold good. An information system, or the database on which it largely relies, is no better than the decisions that go into its creation.

The importance of good decisions in the creation and management of databases, be they small or large—much the same as in any successful enterprise—is imperative.

2.2 The decision making process

Park (1981) examines group decision making in non-routine decisions. In discussing the advantages of group decision making she says it gives 'greater knowledge or information about the problem, more alternatives to consider, better comprehension of the decision', and so on. In this I find reinforcement for the fact that, accepting the plus and minus characteristics of group dynamics and the inherent benefit of the synergism (Park's word) that can result from group interaction, it is the contribution of greater information which makes the group approach valuable. Further, Park says that there is now a trend with some researchers to give more attention to the process of decision making. Her emphasis on this phenomenon also appeals to me, for it is in the 'processes' that I see more universal application for problem solving.

Overall Park bases her discussion on Harrison's (1975) model for group decision making and identifies the following six major steps or phases in the decision making process:

i. Setting objectives.
ii. Searching for alternatives.
iii. Comparing and evaluating alternatives.
iv. Choosing among alternatives (making decisions).
v. Implementing the decision.
vi. Monitoring and controlling.

These steps satisfy the progressive resolution of the constituent elements process advocated in my two basic principles. As Park states: 'it reduces the complexity of the decision making process by partitioning it into manageable pieces addressed in logical sequence'. Now the partitioned set gives us a framework within which to proceed. Let us examine the first step, that is setting objectives.

All ventures start with a proposition to do something. In the context of this particular book it is probably to create a database. Let us state this as an overall objective: *to create and sustain a database in the field of XYZ as a viable proposition*. This is a broad statement and as we have to start somewhere, perhaps it is acceptable for a first intent. However, setting objectives takes more than just expressing an intent. It needs a further breakdown into subobjectives and sub-subobjectives, the partitioning process, the resolution of the elements involved. But to do this and set meaningful objectives some appreciation of the expected actions and functions to follow is essential. This is not as anomalous as it first appears. Given an adequate basis the human mind is particularly good at making projections.

In another study, Townley (1978) looked at a Systems Analysis approach and identified four elements in her initial system study:

- Statement of goals.
- Statement of requirements.
- System study: input.
- System study: output.

In dealing with these concepts she makes a very significant point when she says:

> The statement of goals must come first. However, if the impression has been given that the four elements ... are sequential, please correct it now. Apart from the initial study of goals, they are simultaneous.

Without distorting Townley's intentions in this statement, I see her method as reflecting the need for prior appreciation of what could be involved and what I call the need to conceptualise and identify the entity with which we are concerned, so that we can proceed with the partitioning process.

Townley, as an example, breaks down her 'Statement of Goals' (or Objectives) into:

- What are the goals of the system?
- What are our objectives in providing a system of this kind?
- How do they rank in order of importance to the organization?
- How do they fit into the system which is the organization?

She similarly effectively breaks down the other three elements as well.

To answer these series of questions, to use the decision making process to its full potential we have to go back to my two basic principles—looking both inwards and outwards in increasing resolution in both dimensions. To do this we need to project dimensions and resolve the proposition into identifiable parameters.

In the context of a reference database how may we conceptualise in such a way as to give dimension to the proposition we have mooted.

3. MAIN ELEMENTS FOR A BIBLIOGRAPHIC DATABASE

In a previous paper (Tellis, 1979) I have attempted to create such a model by identifying what I termed obvious but inescapable prerequisites for a viable reference database system. Figs 5.1 and 5.2 show the main elements considered necessary, which are:

i. A sizeable and growing area of information which is useful but not readily accessible—TARGET INFORMATION.
ii. A relatively large population of users who would use this information if it were accessible—CLIENTELE.
iii. A system through which the two could meet; a storage and switching mechanism—DATABASE.
iv. Resources to sustain the operation—FUNDS, REVENUE, COOPERATIVE FUNCTIONING.
v. Management—CONTROL and COORDINATION.

The database itself is only a part of the overall functioning system. Importantly, we have managed to identify some of those external factors concerned with the environment in which the database will operate. The effect these have on the viability of a database cannot be minimised.

We can now proceed to resolve each of these parameters and their subparameters to identify all the constituent elements that should be considered. When they are identified we can commence looking for and evaluating alternatives through to making a final choice for implementation.

3.1 Resolution of prerequisite major factors

In analysing the potential external environment, amongst other considerations specific to the particular exercise, we need to identify and establish:

i. Key sources and groups concerned with the generation and use of the target information. Their participation must be sought and acknowledged in the development and implementation stage. Lancaster (1979)

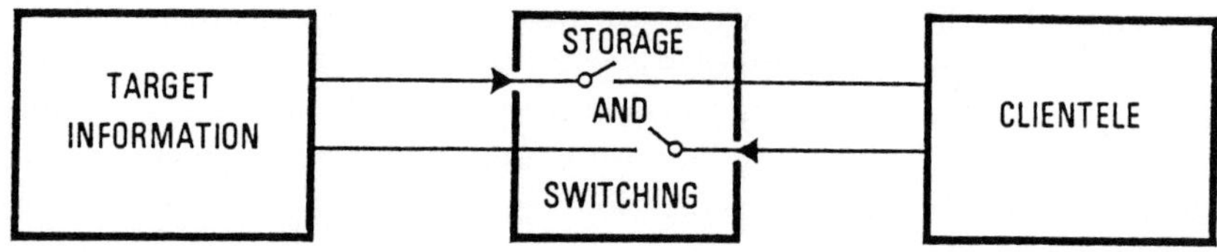

Fig. 5.1 Simplified main elements in information transfer.

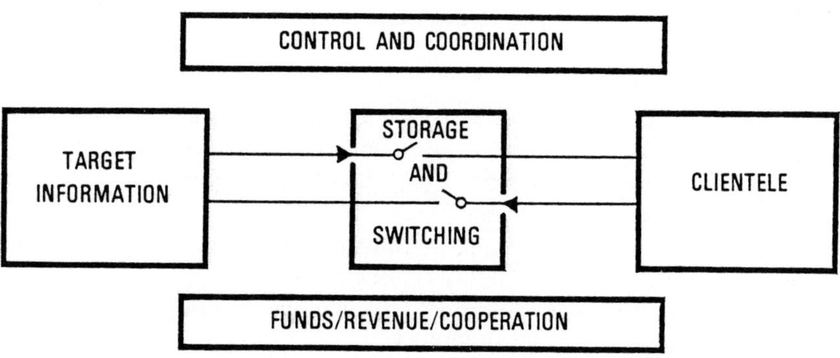

Fig. 5.2 Simplified main elements in overall functioning system.

says: 'There is one cardinal principle that must be borne in mind from the very beginning. An information system is more likely to be accepted and adopted by a user community if the community has been actively involved in the design of the system from the very beginning'.

ii. A controlling agency that has close working affiliation with the particular user population. This is implied in i. above and Barwise (1980) makes similar observations when he discusses improving the climate for the information industry in the context of the EEC.

iii. An early feel for the size of the proposition in terms of size and implementation time. This is very helpful in canvassing viability and seeking cooperation and collaboration.

3.2 Resolution of elements

Let us examine this aspect through the AESIS model, with which I am most familiar, as shown in Fig. 5.3 and the AWRC version where the AESIS model has been adapted in a paper (AWRC, 1982) dealing with the Australian Water Data Base (Fig. 5.4). The database (STREAMLINE) is now operational and mounted on AUSINET as WATR.

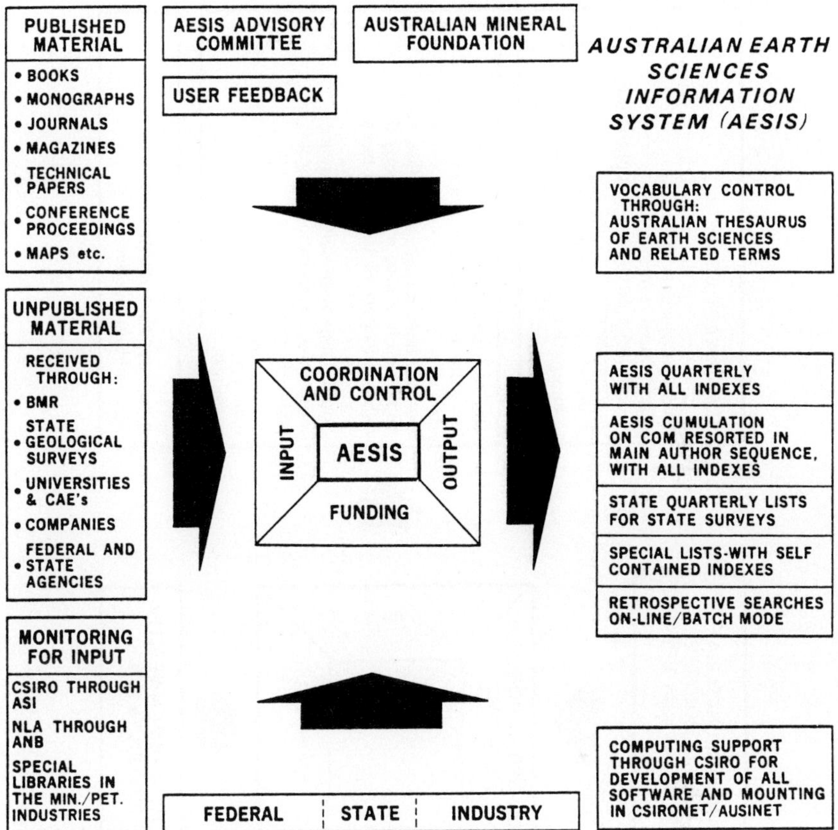

Fig. 5.3 AESIS. Overall functional format.

After identifying elements in greater detail, you will note the arrows show that there is a dynamic state as well! There is some movement expected in the system. This takes us back to identifying a fresh set of elements, but this time on a different plane. For optimum working we need to examine and chart the flow of elements through the system.

3.3 Resolution of activities and events

Still holding with the principle of progressive resolution of elements, we now transpose this resolution to identifying activities and events and the sequence in which they occur or should occur. Let us examine the sequence of events in Fig. 5.5 and note the progressive resolution of activities. The

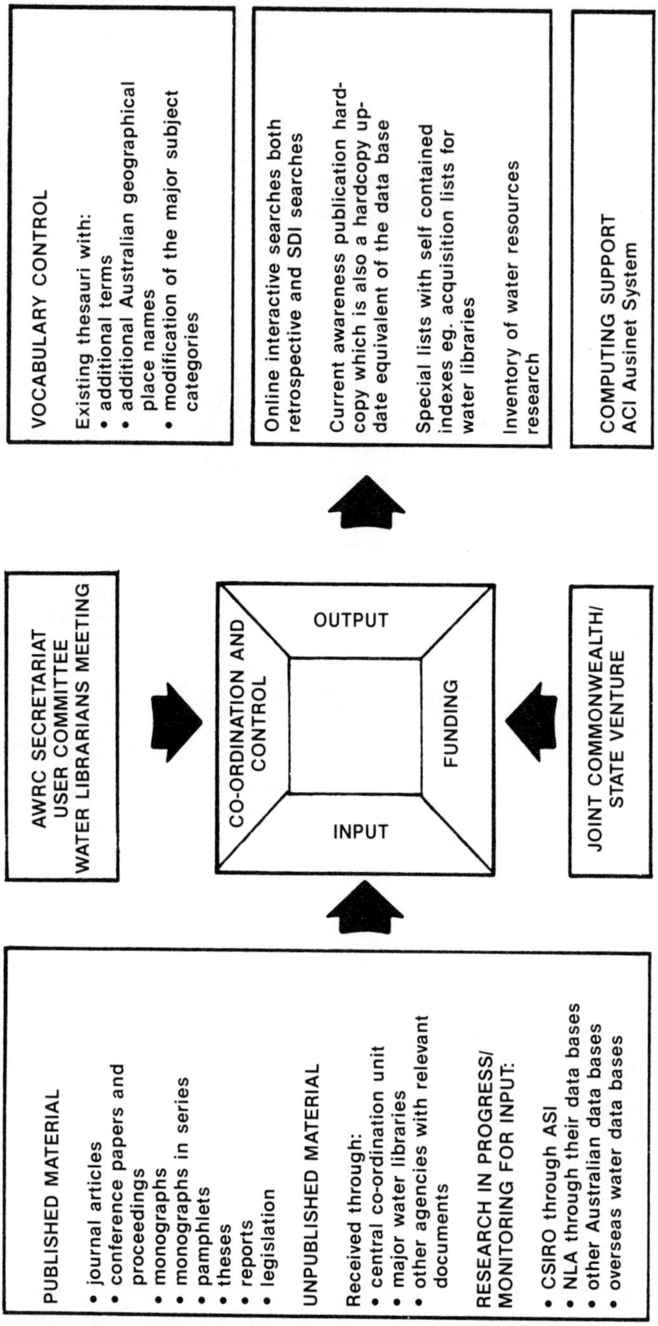

PUBLISHED MATERIAL

- journal articles
- conference papers and proceedings
- monographs
- monographs in series
- pamphlets
- theses
- reports
- legislation

UNPUBLISHED MATERIAL

Received through:
- central co-ordination unit
- major water libraries
- other agencies with relevant documents

RESEARCH IN PROGRESS/ MONITORING FOR INPUT:

- CSIRO through ASI
- NLA through their data bases
- other Australian data bases
- overseas water data bases

AWRC SECRETARIAT
USER COMMITTEE
WATER LIBRARIANS MEETING

CO-ORDINATION AND CONTROL

OUTPUT

INPUT

FUNDING

JOINT COMMONWEALTH/ STATE VENTURE

VOCABULARY CONTROL

Existing thesauri with:
- additional terms
- additional Australian geographical place names
- modification of the major subject categories

Online interactive searches both retrospective and SDI searches

Current awareness publication hard-copy which is also a hardcopy up-date equivalent of the data base

Special lists with self contained indexes eg. acquisition lists for water libraries

Inventory of water resources research

COMPUTING SUPPORT
ACI Ausinet System

Fig. 5.4 Summary of the major characteristics of an Australian water database.

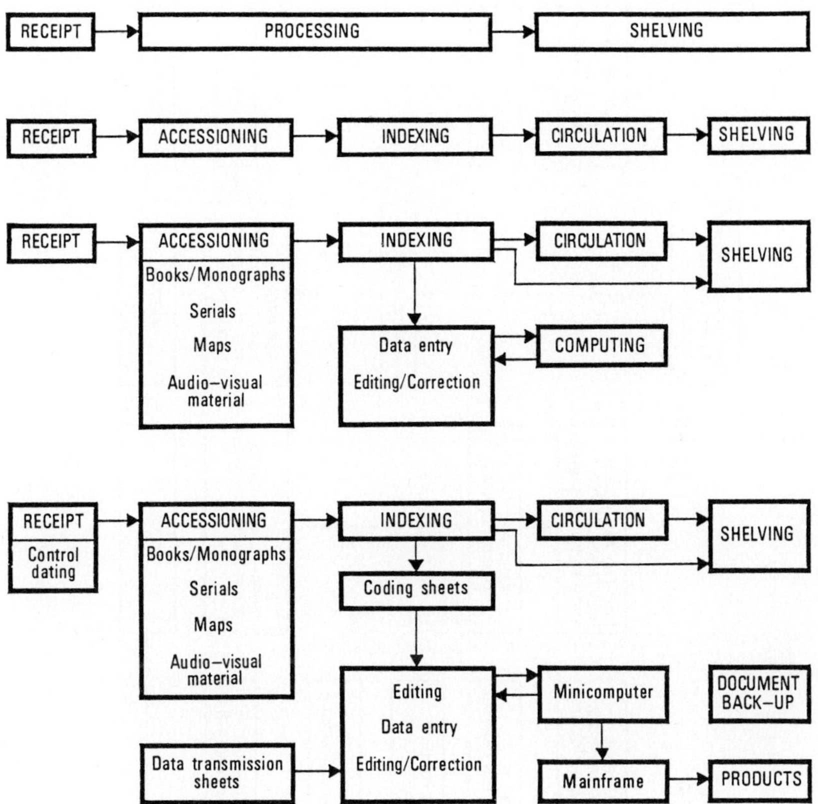

Fig. 5.5 Simplified progressive resolution of activities and events for library data processing.

analysis could continue to much greater detail. By progressive identification of the elements involved we determine the optimum path for material flow, optimum expected time scales, optimum staffing, resources required and other considerations. The process is illustrated in the outline schematic of the CRRERIS system shown in Fig. 5.6 (CSIRO, 1980).

The method is very familiar to the work study engineer and on a larger scale to those involved in scheduling through network systems such as CPM or PERT. There have been numerous publications on these methods over the last 20 years, for example Burch and Strater (1974).

4. COSTS

Everything costs—another fundamental and perhaps superfluous observation? In the field of databases, computerisation reduces manual effort,

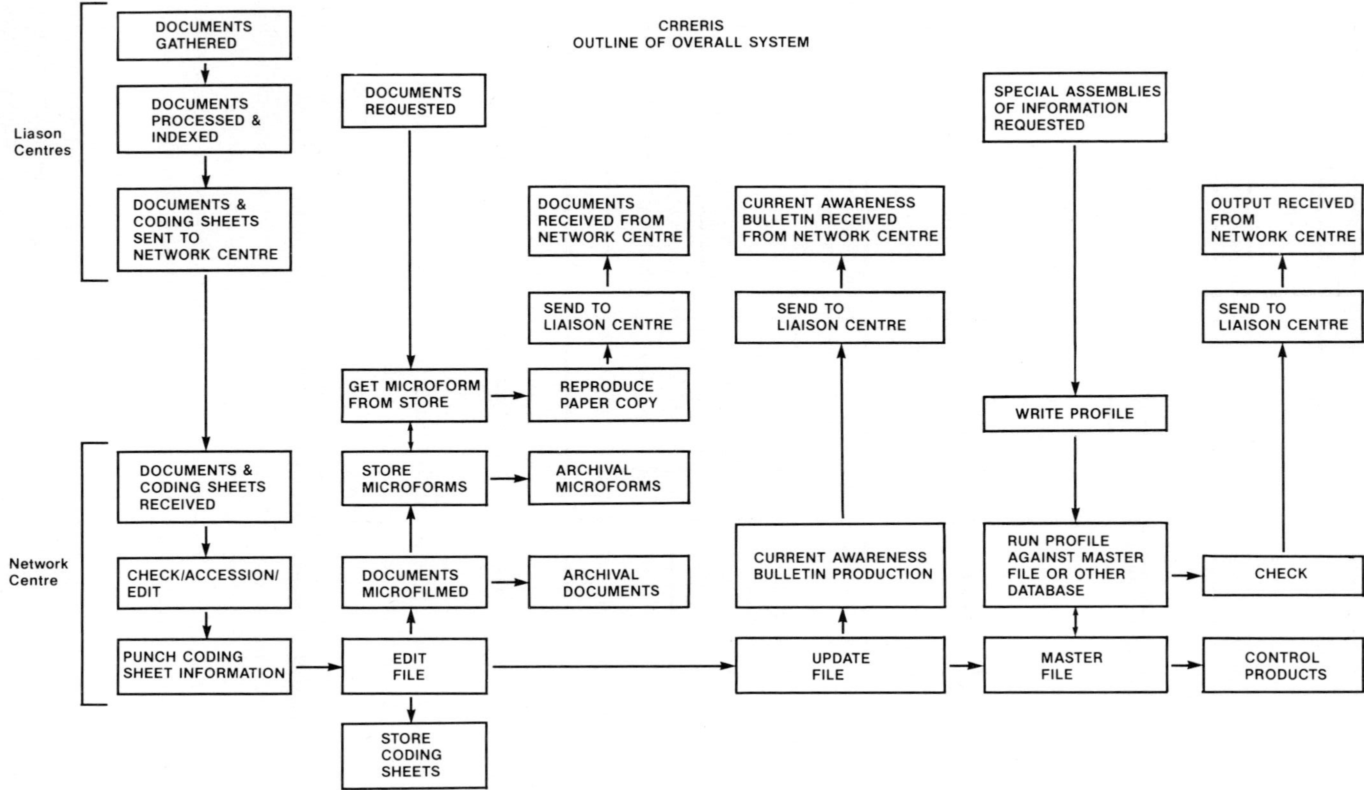

Fig. 5.6 CRRERIS. Outline of overall system.

which is a high cost element, and also increases the system's capabilities by orders of magnitude—yet another oft heard statement, and certainly one with due credibility. But computerisation has its own costs, and recurring ones at that, no matter what has been said to the contrary.

Costing and cost projections need to be looked at realistically. Most of us, in an endeavour to push a project, have a tendency to minimise costs and wrestle with the consequences later on. Perhaps there is no other way in some cases. Many projects and systems would never have got under way if people had baulked at the real projected costs. But here again there is no reason for not breaking down projected costs in detail before deciding on a course of action. Once again, proceeding by decision rather than default.

Costing in industry is a profession in itself. There is therefore more to it than simple arithmetic totals of equipment costs and staff salaries. In small scale systems, parameters are probably less complicated. Nevertheless in the light of my opening statements we ought to be as careful here as with any other consideration in the system, if not more so.

How do we proceed? Without recourse to all the principles of cost accounting let us again fall back on the old formula of breaking down the proposition into constituent elements.

In another paper (Tellis, 1981) I have endeavoured to do this in respect of two computer-based services developed and managed by AMF: AESIS, referred to earlier, and ESRISAT. The former is the national database for the earth sciences in Australia and the latter is a monthly current awareness bulletin produced for AMF member companies. To quote from my paper:

> Conventionally, it is customary to break down overall costs into direct and indirect costs in order to focus on those costs most closely related to the operation being examined. I propose to do this by examining the following cost facets:
>
> i. Development costs
> ii. Processing costs
> iii. Cost of products
> iv. Management and support services costs.
>
> Costs at i. and, to a lesser degree, at iv. above are considered to be more in the nature of indirect or fixed costs.

A further breakdown of these elements, and associated discussion, is reproduced in part in Section 4.1. To say the least the unit costs given are revealing if not alarming, depending on how new you are to the information scene. In retrospect, I should have added a qualifier to the basic 'direct costs' element and that is that there is in the region of a 25% to 30% leeway in these costs due to progressive human efficiency and other human operating norms. In section 4.1.4, Table 5.5, direct processing costs could therefore be seen as $8.00 to $9.00 and the other unit costs reduced by the same margin of $3.00 to $4.00. However in 1983, inflation would have restored the figures in terms of 1983 dollars.

In 1983 we had under implementation a software package (Formatext) for validation and other editing and input controls to assist faster throughput and better quality control, in addition to a minicomputer installed in 1982 as a work station on CSIRONET for all input processing. These moves should contain inflationary cost increases and cost increases due to growing volumes of material being processed. The production of printed products always places a greater burden on the need for good editorial practice and consistency in indexing terms used, format, typography, grammatical usage, word forms and similar considerations. Purchase of the software package introduced some non-anticipated 'capital' costs with recurring maintenance fees, but the immediate benefits and long-term cost savings made the acquisition very attractive if not inescapable.

It has always been difficult to get a perspective on costs or any feedback on the figures presented from time to time. From personal conversations in Australia, however, for reference (bibliographic) databases a unit cost in the region of $20.00 seems to have some credence, see Section 4.1.4, Table 5.5, Cost element 6.

Hans Zwillenberg, until recently Director (Technology) at the NLA, has done some work in this area and in a personal comment has said that he believes the figure of $20 is on the low side. Interestingly, in a talk presented to The Australasian Institute of Mining and Metallurgy, Australian Capital Territory Branch, Canberra, in August 1983—and on the basis of details in my paper (Tellis, 1981) he projects a unit cost in the region of $37, adding that the cost of creating an equivalent library catalogue card entry would be in the region of $24. Amortised development costs for the computer based system account for about half the cost of the difference. The observation is very interesting because of the light it sheds on estimated costs of manual card systems. Insomuch as the computer-based system has considerably greater potential he points out that the costs do not have meaning in representing the real value and benefits of the two processes. Obviously much depends on the basis on which costs are calculated. In Section 4.1.4, Table 5.5 goes as far as a unit cost of $42.70 at Cost element 5.

Nevertheless, these figures are presented more to give, first, an indication of the orders of magnitude involved in terms of cost, rather than to indicate absolute values. Second, to make the point that databases are, in the nature of libraries and research and development work, investments by organisations or nations for longer-term benefits rather than propositions for immediate commercial profits—that is, not in themselves or not yet anyway.

All the factors considered in my examination of costs are not appropriate in every case, but I believe the presentation of these various cost elements is illuminating as, in varying degrees, they have relevance to the viability of databases be they large or small.

4.1 Cost elements: AESIS and ESRISAT

As Lancaster (1979) and Marron (1969) have shown costing of information services is not an easy exercise, primarily because it is difficult to isolate costs directly attributable to such operations. In the case of AESIS and ESRISAT, besides the two services being produced within the general resources of AMF and cooperating agencies, many of the costs are common to both services and would therefore be very difficult to separate in any meaningful way.

4.1.1 Development costs

The development of the two services has gone hand in hand often leap frogging in a complementary sort of way. In considering development costs, I will ignore the costs associated with the development of the Foundation itself, though I make the point as, in the context of the role and purpose of the Foundation, they are cognitive factors. It will be appropriate enough to consider only those development costs which have some direct bearing on these two services. These are best examined by listing chronologically significant development milestones (Tellis, 1979). These are:

1. 1972: AMF Australia-wide information services survey to ascertain the needs of industry, assess the extent of information involved and the degree of participaton that could be expected from all sources—federal, state, academic and private industry (Dixon and Tellis, 1972).
2. 1973: ESRISAT commenced as a manually produced monthly current awareness bulletin, providing in addition experience and an experimental system for the Thesaurus and AESIS project to follow.
3. 1974: Development of an indexing vocabulary (Thesaurus) for the geosciences in Australia for potential Australia-wide use. The project was supported by the BMR, CSIRO and NLA and cooperatively undertaken with these organisations, the State Geological Surveys and Departments of Mines, academic and government agencies and many companies.
4. 1975: A first geoscience information seminar held at AMF which gave a general mandate for the creation of an Australian earth sciences bibliographic database.
5. 1976: Production of a first working edition of the *Australian Thesaurus of Earth Sciences and Related Terms.*
6. 1976: Pilot study and development of AESIS with some sample products on CSIRONET, CSIRO's computing network.

Table 5.1 Development costs: AESIS and ESRISAT.

	$	$
i. Survey		6 000
ii. Thesaurus		
a. Development	50 000	
b. Production (1979) edition	5 000	55 000
iii. Systems development		
a. Computing programs and routines	65 000	
b. Non-computing elements	12 000	
c. Computer terminal equipment, installation, connect fee etc.	5 000	82 000
Total		143 000

7. 1977–78: Stabilisation of AESIS products and production routines for multiple products: *AESIS Quarterly*, *AESIS Cumulation* on microfiche, *AESIS Special Lists*, retrospective search output formats.
8. 1979: Computer typesetting and production of the second edition of the Thesaurus in hard copy.
9. 1980: Transfer of ESRISAT from manual production to computer typesetting in the same format as *AESIS Quarterly*, with a new *ESRISAT Six-monthly Cumulation* on microfiche for international material in ESRISAT.
10. 1980: Mounting of AESIS on AUSINET for interactive public use Australia-wide.

For costing purposes the above can be grouped as shown in Table 5.1.

Initial computer programs for the Thesaurus were written at WRE in 1973/74 and subsequently developed by AMDEL's computing section. About 32% of the amount shown in Table 5.1 at ii.a is the estimated equivalent value for software contributed by these two organisations by way of technical assistance. The National Library of Australia contributed some funds towards the computing costs for successive iterations during the main development phase of the project. SADME participated in the technical development of the Thesaurus along with 15 other organisations, and also assisted with punching corrections and alterations. The Department had an active interest in the development of the Thesaurus for use in its own indexing program.

The computing programs and routines for AESIS were produced by CSIRO, CILES, using their GFMS and numerous subroutines specially developed for the AESIS project. The cost shown in Table 5.1 at iii.a is a generalised estimate of what it would have cost AMF if recourse to a commercial bureau and/or external software packages had been considered. It would be only right to add here that had the latter option been the only course available it would have radically changed time scales for the AESIS project.

Table 5.2 Processing costs: AESIS and ESRISAT.

	Qty	$
i. Scanning (ESRISAT)	2 800	
ii. Indexing (AMF)	2 700	
iii. Indexing and collation (Others)	1 050	18 000*
iv. Data preparation, data entry, correction, editing, updating		26 000
v. Computing	Total	44 000

*Generalised estimate of equivalent value of indexing done by the Geological Surveys etc., and AMF.

The cooperation of all these agencies and the participation of CSIRO, CILES in such a major way must be acknowledged as a significant contribution to the creation and maintenance of this valuable national resource.

4.1.2 Processing costs

Processing costs are considered under the following main elements: scanning and indexing; and data preparation, data entry, correction and editing, updating. These costs are obviously a function of the volume processed. It will be best therefore to examine them through current annual volumes and concommitant costs. While AESIS aims at comprehensive coverage of all Australian material that can be garnered, ESRISAT is a selective service with a much wider ambit requiring a large 'scanning' element in the processing routine. Scanning, though, also enables sighting material on Australia by non-Australian sources or Australian work in non-Australian publications. Besides books, reports and other monographic material, conference papers and proceedings, reprints and so on, about 430 journals and serials are systematically scanned for these two services.

In 1980 scanning and indexing covered an estimated 6500 papers, articles, books, reports and so on, with a resulting 3700 (3756 actual) items being indexed and processed into the two systems. Costs for these are shown in Table 5.2.

4.1.3 Cost of products

The following are currently produced:

i. ESRISAT: 12 issues a year.
ii. ESRISAT Six-monthly Cumulation: produced on microfiche in January and July each year.
iii. *AESIS Quarterly*: four issues a year.
iv. *AESIS Cumulation*: progressive cumulation on microfiche produced annually each December, in convenient segments.

Table 5.3 ESRISAT/AESIS products annual production costs, 1980.

Product	Quantity (annually)	Computing component	Total cost
		$	$
ESRISAT	400 × 12	(940)	6 000
ESRISAT Six-monthly Cumulation (microfiche)	50 × 2	(100)	
AESIS Quarterly	500 × 4	(1 130)	8 000
AESIS Cumulation (microfiche)	500 (+3 quarterly limited productions)	(7))	1 000
State lists (computer print-out)	8 × 4	(200)	
* *AESIS Special List* (9 lists in 1979–80)	9 × 50	(1 240)	4 000
Total			19 000

*Not produced annually; calculation based on those produced in 12-month period 1979–80.

Table 5.4 Management and support services costs, 1980.

	$
i. Management, administrative and support staff: Salaries and related costs (superannuation, payroll tax, holiday pay, workers compensation)	26 000
ii. Administrative overheads (as a percentage of non-salary administrative costs)	5 000
iii. Library books and serials*	32 000
iv. Computer terminal maintenance and routine line fees	1 000
v. Nominal supervisory, computing development, and temporary storage†	2 000
Total	66 000

*AMF and SADME equivalent current annual value as part of earth sciences resource sharing concept being developed at the Glenside Campus, Adelaide, South Australia.
†CILES technical assistance value.

Table 5.5 AESIS/ESRISAT unit costs (1980).

Cost element	Cost	Unit cost
	$	$
1. Direct costs: processing costs only	44 000	11.9
2. Direct costs (processing costs *plus* cost of products)	63 000	17.0
3. Direct costs *plus* management and support service costs	129 000	34.8
4. Direct costs *plus* modified management and support services costs*	97 000	26.2
5. Direct *plus* all indirect costs†	158 000	42.7
6. Processing costs *plus* modified management and support service costs	76 000	20.5

Note *Annual library books and serials costs removed.
†Development cost at one fifth—'amortised' over life of project.

v. State lists: lists of citations pertaining to the respective States of Australia, produced quarterly for the State Geological Surveys.
vi. *AESIS Special Lists*: produced on special topics as demand discerned.
vii. Retrospective searches.
viii. Control products:
  a. Master file: on microfiche, per quarterly update.
  b. Statistical reports: produced per update and as required.

Individual costs for these products, which include computer typesetting/micrographics, are given in Table 5.3.

4.1.4 Management and support services

Costs shown in Table 5.4 are calculated as percentages of time allocated in 1980 for staff associated with the two services, other than those committed full-time to actual processing (scanning, indexing, data entry and so on). Annual (1980) direct resource commitments are as shown.

4.1.5 Unit costs

To obtain some perspective on the many cost figures presented it is necessary to reduce them to unit costs, the unit in this case being a single citation—which is the basic end product of bibliographic systems.

The annual number of unique citations output by the two services as shown in Section 4.1.2 is 3700.

Which costs should be considered for computation of the unit cost depends on the purpose for which such costings are required. Undoubtedly some form of conventional cost accounting procedures could be applied but, as Lancaster (1979) says, 'realistic costing procedures for information products and services are generally lacking'.

To obtain a meaningful look at costs it is perhaps preferable to examine a series of unit costs using the desired variations in the cost elements to obtain an insight into cost distributions. Table 5.5 shows unit costs using different cost elements.

Having established this range of costs, can we make some observations on their relationship to the effectiveness of the system or benefits therefrom?

5. COST EFFECTIVENESS AND BENEFIT

Cost effectiveness is the 'relationship between level of performance and the cost involved in achieving it' (Lancaster, 1979). It is a good way of assessing alternatives. *Cost benefit* is the 'relationship between the benefits of a particular product or service and the costs of providing it' (Lancaster, 1979). Neither of these measures can be used without the basis for analyses recommended through the foregoing discussions.

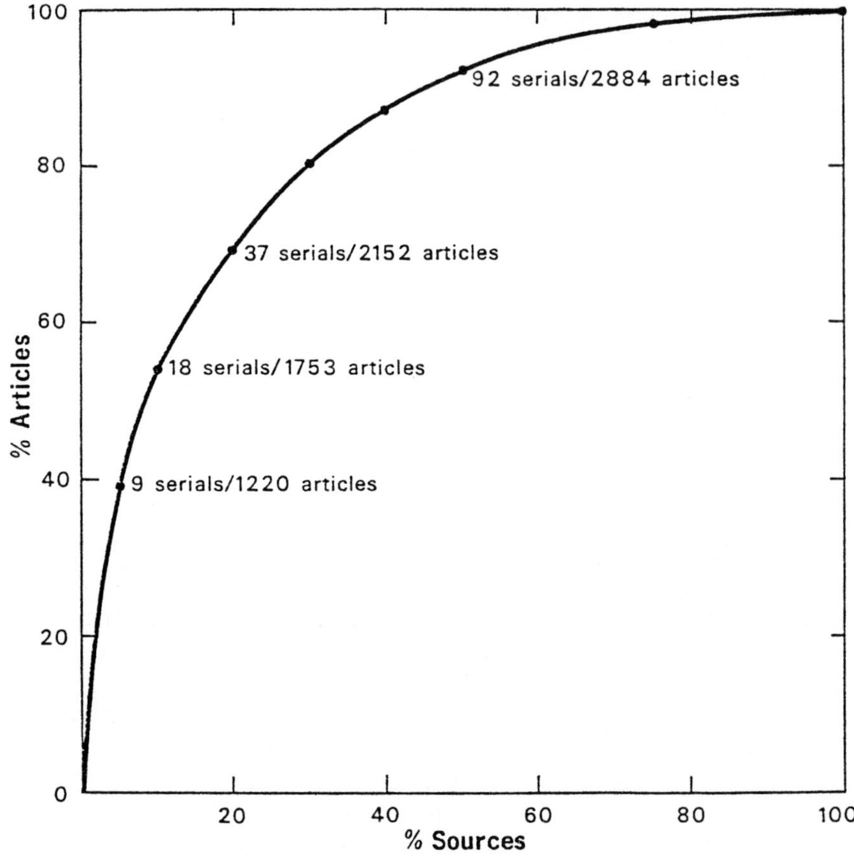

Fig. 5.7 Distribution of 3114 articles from 184 journals/serials in AESIS (1976–79).

Cost effectiveness analyses are an essential ingredient in any evaluation process when a choice of approaches, methods and systems is involved.

Indexing policy or the degree of coverage of the literature required in a database illustrate this factor. Both represent major costs and have what may be termed trade-off points at which increases in system performance can only be achieved through disproportionate increases in cost.

With *indexing policy* there is the question of 'free language' terms versus a controlled vocabulary or a combination of both. There is then the question of depth or exhaustivity of indexing. In every case there are different costs involved. A critical examination of the uses the system will be put to is required before indexing questions can be evaluated. The constraint of funding would then be the eventual moderating factor.

In AESIS we use a controlled vocabulary (AMFE, 1979). It is estimated that the development of the Thesaurus through to the second edition over the period 1974 to 1979 cost $55 000 (Tellis, 1981). Were an appropriate thesaurus already available such an expense would not have been incurred. However, some attention to uniformity and rationalisation in every indexing process is inevitable and the maintenance of uniform practice in indexing—format of names, corporate names, singular and plural usage, and so on—always has a direct cost element, or indirect costs in performance levels of the system. These latter costs may not be borne by the database system but rather by the users of the system in the problems they often create. Unless our analysis is detailed, and projections as thorough as possible such 'costs' are never considered. Should they be considered? For in-house systems surely they must be. For others, the viability of the database cannot be immune to such factors and therefore these costs must be consciously examined for decisions one way or the other.

In the normal indexing process it is probably true to say that, with a string of indexing terms, one half of the terms possibly takes twice as long to allocate as the other half. This obviously affects the cost of depth of indexing. Take another aspect: when using a controlled vocabulary, experience shows that over a period of time indexers could tend to use only those terms they readily remember. Is a reviewing editor/indexer then necessary? Again costs are involved. Identification of types of users, output products, and so on would help very much in discerning the course to take.

What about the *degree of coverage* of the literature. For earth sciences literature in Australia, Fig. 5.7 shows the distribution of articles and papers in AESIS over the period 1976 to 1979. In the usual Bradford distribution effect we see that 70% of papers are covered through 37 journals and serials. To cover the remaining 30% of papers in the presently identified literature a further 147 journals and serial titles would have to be acquired. The costs against effectiveness are radically changed. The objectives of the service would therefore have to be analysed very thoroughly.

Cost benefit is a less tangible area to assess as benefits of the system are not that easily measurable.

Lancaster (1979) suggests the following possible criteria for establishing a cost benefit ratio for information services:

i. Cost savings through the use of the service as compared with the costs of obtaining needed information or documents from other sources.
ii. Avoidance of loss of productivity—for example, of students, faculty, research workers—that would result if information sources were not readily available.
iii. Improved decision making or reduction in the level of personnel required to make decisions.

iv. Avoidance of duplication or waste of research and development effort on projects which either have been done before or have been proved infeasible by earlier investigators.
v. Stimulation of invention or productivity by making available the literature on current developments in a particular field.

He goes on to say:

> . . . most attempts at assessing benefits are content with asking a sample of users their opinions about the benefits of the service provided . . . 'user satisfaction' is a major concern . . . and it may be the only feasible approach to the evaluation of benefits in many circumstances.

At the AMF 'user satisfaction' is of paramount concern and if any success can be credited to the operations of the Foundation, and we have reason to believe this is so, it is due very much to our services being created against and moderated by user demand.

To help examine effectiveness and benefit analyses, some data from my paper (Tellis, 1981) giving cost and usage statistics for AESIS and our library and information services are given in Section 5.1 along with examples and discussion.

Overall, notwithstanding the successful creation and use of many database systems in Australia and overseas, almost without exception the evidence is that the development of and input to databases has to be subsidised. In Australia with our levels of user population, the case for subsidy in some form is even stronger.

5.1 Cost effectiveness and benefit: AESIS and ESRISAT

As mentioned earlier, cost effectiveness analysis is obviously best used for assessing alternatives. There are unfortunately very few details available for comparable systems in Australia for us to assess relative cost effectiveness. Discussions with colleagues indicate that we are working well within expected unit costs. Trade-offs within the system—35–40% distributed indexing, indexing depth, online input from documents themselves, majority use through membership, distributed partial subsidy—make us feel we are close enough to the most attractive options.

However, the indications are that cost benefit assessment could be the more worthwhile exercise as it is concerned more with whether the system is at least delivering the goods and is therefore taking the measure of 'effectiveness' through the user, rather than just examining the cost of one output or process against another. Effectiveness, benefits and costs are of course all inextricably linked and whilst one must not confuse one measure with the other, in the information world it is the 'benefits' that are more likely to permit existence before 'effectiveness' has the opportunity to hone the options.

Cawkell (1972) and Magson (1973) amongst others have suggested ways of evaluating effectiveness and benefits. These are either methods for making meaningful comparisons of alternative systems or making assessments against predetermined parameters. Cawkell does this through recording 'action hits'—if a notification provided by an information service causes the user to obtain an article, read it, and take some beneficial action, then this is defined as an action hit—and he accepts that 'obviously there are degrees of action'. Magson in a way uses a variation of Cawkell's action hit concept by establishing a relationship between items of information relevant to a predetermined 'target readership' established by prior questionnaires, and then formulates a method for arriving at the cost for an alternative service, thereby inferring the benefit of the present system.

I had hoped that Magson's and Cawkell's methods were examined in Flowerdew and Whitehead's (1974) extensive review published as an OSTI report on cost benefit and cost effectiveness analysis of information systems. Magson's concept appears very attractive and Cawkell's method, like most of his writings, is practical and direct. The other method that interested me is that suggested by Nightingale (1973), who is mentioned in the OSTI report and whose service parallels ours, in an appropriate industry too—petroleum.

To apply, even subjectively, some of these measures to AESIS and ESRISAT let us first look at some direct usage statistics for these two services, summarised in Tables 5.6 and 5.7.

The number of requests processed in 1980 is shown in Table 5.6 as 3876. However, this is the *least figure* as:

a. Only such requests as are related by the user to the two services in question are recorded as such in our statistics of usage of the two services.
b. 35–40% of the material in AESIS is not obtainable from AMF and therefore requests are directed to respective sources.
c. Unquestionably some percentage of requirement must be satisfied locally through access to company, institution or personal libraries and collections and local interlibrary loans and therefore not referred to us at AMF.

We estimate that all this must account for between 20% and 50% additional requests making for more representative usage figures of between 4650 and 5800.

Progressive usage statistics of requests to AMF as available are shown

Table 5.6 AESIS/ESRISAT usage statistics (1980).

Service	Number of recipients	Number of items disseminated	Possible number for request*	Number of items requested
1. *AESIS Quarterly* (4 issues a yr)	452	2 684	1 638	1 139
2. *ESRISAT* (12 issues a yr)	399	1 503	1 503	2 737†
				3 876

**AESIS Quarterly* has an average 35–40% citations covering theses, open-file exploration and Departmental unpublished reports which are available only from their respective sources and to whom requests are therefore directed. No statistics are available with us for the number of requests for this material. Also backup service for non-member subscriptions is not usually provided and so statistics for these are not known.

†More than one request for the same item.

Table 5.7 ESRISAT/AESIS progressive statistics 1974 to 1980.

Service	Number of items requested 1974–77	1978	1979	1980
1. *AESIS Quarterly* (June 1976 onwards)	52	306	501	1 139
2. *ESRISAT*	4 776	1 828	2 162	2 737
Total	4 828	2 134	2 663	3 876*

*Note: In 1981 this figure grew to 5 118, but has since settled back to about the 1980 figures.

in Table 5.7. Again these statistics reflect only those requests identified by the user as originating from these two services. The library has a separate 5100 requests recorded over the period 1974–80 not associated with these two services. Borrowings at the front desk are also not recorded in either of these statistics.

5.1.1 Cost benefit

Now applying Cawkell's measure, since each request is made after examining an annotation or keyword string, or both, I believe these requests must represent some degree of action hits and therefore show appreciable benefit to the user from the two services: AESIS and ESRISAT.

In the method reported by Nightingale (1973), of BP, London, the number of additional journals that users would have to scan if the current awareness bulletin were withdrawn, was assessed by questionnaire—taking the mean and not the average value—and then the cost that this would represent was calculated. The calculation was based on a time of 10 minutes per issue multiplied by the number of persons receiving the bulletin, at an

Table 5.8 Top 20 serials having the greatest number of citations on Australian geoscience in AESIS 1976–79.

Title	Citations	Issues per year
1. Australia. Bureau of Mineral Resources, Geology and Geophysics. Record	357	100*
2. Geological Society of Australia. Journal‡	293	4
3. Queensland Government Mining Journal	214	12
4. BMR. Journal of Australian Geology and Geophysics	173	4
5. Australian Mining	155	12
6 APEA Journal‡	155	2
7. Australian Society of Exploration‡ Geophysicists. Bulletin	147	4
8. Australasian Institute of Mining and Metallurgy. Proceedings‡	117	4
9. Search	102	12
10. Journal of Geochemical Exploration	102	6†
11. Alcheringa	93	4
12. Western Australia. Geological Survey. Annual Report	93	1
13. Tectonophysics	83	17†
14. Economic Geology	74	8
15. Contributions to Mineralogy and Petrology	69	6†
16. Australia. CSIRO. Division of Applied Geomechanics. Technical Report	61	23*
17. Mine and Quarry Mechanisation	56	10
18. Nature	55	52
19. Australian Coal Industry Research Laboratories. Published Report	54	14*
20. Australia. BMR, Geology and Geophysics. Bulletin	50	14†

*Number halved for calculating scanning time.
†Average for one year.
‡Professional society journal.

estimated hourly cost to the company. The cost of producing the current awareness bulletin was then subtracted from this cost to obtain the 'benefit' value.

Using the same principles and restricting ourselves to Australian material, that is AESIS, we see from Fig. 5.7 that, as is normal for these distributions (Bradford phenomenon), from a sample of about 3000 articles over the period 1976–79, about 10% of the journals and serials covered by AESIS account for about 55% of the articles and 20% for about 70%, respectively.

Table 5.8 shows the top 20 titles that have contributed this 55% in AESIS in the last four to five years. Assuming that managements would be happy for their professional staff to keep up with at least half the current Australian geoscience literature, we will accept this as the sample to be scanned, but, because of the subject spread, reduce it to half the number

Table 5.9 Alternative costs for benefit from AESIS Quarterly.

Annual Salary	Cost per hour	Scanning time	Number of persons	Total cost	'Benefit' ($)	
$	$	hr		$	A*	B*
15 000†	19.20	20	1 200 (400 × 3)	461 000	398 000	385 000
			800 (400 × 2)	307 000	244 000	231 000
20 000†	25.60	20	1 200 (400 × 3)	614 000	551 000	538 000
			800 (400 × 2)	410 000	347 000	334 000

*Benefit ($) A = Total cost minus (3 700 × $17.00); Cost element 2, Table 5.
*Benefit ($) B = Total cost minus (3 700 × $20.50); Cost element 6, Table 5.
†In 1983 there was at least a 30% upward movement in these figures. The relative resultant 'benefit' figures would be appreciably larger.

after removing the professional society journals which are taken as scanned anyway. Some weight must be applied to monographs in series as they are not scanned in the same way as journals. The resultant number of issues for scanning is taken as 122 per year.

Costs to the company of a professional person's time is taken at 233% of salary as in the BP case. The number of users would be 400 × 3 (see Table 5.6) as we believe at least three people use every copy of *AESIS Quarterly* (or ESRISAT). Let us also examine a more conservative user figure of 400 × 2.

Scanning time estimated in the BP study was 10 minutes per issue. The resultant equivalent costs are shown in Table 5.9.

Clearly some considerable level of benefits to the collective users of these services are apparent from these examples. How good the margins actually are I leave to local interpretation.

Notwithstanding such benefits and/or earnings from products and cooperative input by many organisations, such services cannot be self-sufficient unless there are unprecedented increases in levels of earnings. Some level of subsidy is therefore inevitable and justified to ensure continuance. This we believe is the experience of most database suppliers worldwide (Zwillenberg, 1980).

6. CONCLUSION

The development, management and control of database systems can only be accomplished through adequate analysis and appreciation of all the factors that affect systems, both external and internal. Sound objectives, strong user orientation, and assessment of up to date options coupled with cost-conscious design are inescapable for viable systems.

ACKNOWLEDGEMENTS

I am grateful to my colleagues at AMF for discussions and/or for statistics provided, principally: the Director Dean Crowe, Librarian Claire Conroy, Data Processing Librarian Julie Matthews, Ann Ninham, and Gloria Scheer and Sue Buckley (Library student)—both of whom are now with Delhi Petroleum Pty Ltd—Maureen Hodges for patiently putting it all together through successive word processor iterations, and Barry Frost of SADME for most of the diagrams. Permission by the LAA to use a substantial part of my paper presented at the LAA-NZLA Conference at Christchurch (Tellis, 1981) is also gratefully acknowledged.

REFERENCES

AMF (Australian Mineral Foundation). 1979. *Australian thesaurus of earth sciences and related terms*, 2nd edition. AMF, Adelaide.

AWRC (Australian Water Resources Council). 1982. 'Water information needs in Australia'. *Occasional Papers Series* No. 2.

Barwise, T. P. 1980. 'Possible means of stimulating investment in and improving the climate for the information industry: strategies for EEC intervention in the European information industry and market 1981–85'. *Aslib Proceedings* 32 (Supplement): 41–55.

Burch, J. G. and Strater, R. F. 1974. *Information systems: theory and practice.* Hamilton Pub. Co., Santa Barbara, California.

Cawkell, A. E. 1972. 'Cost-effectiveness and benefits of SDI systems'. *Information Scientist* 6:143–148.

CSIRO. 1980. *CRRERIS Manual of procedures.* CSIRO, Melbourne.

Dixon, P. and Tellis, D. A. 1972. *AMF information services survey.* Australian Mineral Development Laboratories (AMDEL) Report No. 911.

Flowerdew, A. D. J. and Whitehead, C. M. E. 1974. *Cost-effectiveness and cost benefit analysis in information science.* London, London School of Economics and Political Science. OSTI Report No. 5206.

Harrison, E. F. 1975. *The managerial decision-making process.* Houghton-Mifflin, Boston.

Lancaster, F. W. 1979. *Information retrieval systems: characteristics, testing and evaluation*, 2nd edition. John Wiley, New York.

Magson, M. S. 1973. 'Techniques for the measurement of cost benefit in information centres'. *Aslib Proceedings* 25:164–185.

Marron, J. 1969. 'On costing information services'. *American Society for Information Science. Proceedings* 6:515–520.

Nightingale, R. A. 1973. 'A cost-benefit study of a manually-produced current awareness bulletin'. *Aslib Proceedings* 25:153–157.

Park, M. K. 1981. 'Decision-making processes for information managers'. *Special Libraries 72*(4): 307–318.

Tellis, D. A. 1979. 'Managing the creation and implementation of a bibliographic data base'. Seminar on Australia Data Bases—Creation and Management held by LAA Information Science Section, New South Wales Group, Sydney 24th October, 1979. (Published in microform).

Tellis, D. A. 1981. *Australia-wide information services for the mineral and petroleum industries: cost aspects.* LAA-NZLA Conference, Christchurch, New Zealand, 19–23 January 1981. Proceedings. LAA, Sydney.

Townley, H. M. 1978. *System analysis for information retrieval.* Andre Deutsch, London.

Zwillenberg, H. J. 1980. 'Funding of modern information services'. *Australian Academic & Research Libraries* 11:167–171.

6. Staffing and other management questions

Peter Judge

1. Introduction
2. Staffing questions
   2.1 Identification of tasks
   2.2 Staff requirements for generation of a database
   2.3 Staff requirements for operation of a database
3. Marketing and other output considerations
4. Copyright
5. Legal responsibilities
6. Conclusion
Further reading

1. INTRODUCTION

If you are concerned with a home database, clearly you can skip this chapter. However, if building a database is part of your business activities, it may be important. Databases, however small, need to be integrated into the other activities of the business. You will have to justify what you are doing in terms of the resources you will need in both personnel and money. Some of what follows may provide you with the answers to your own queries, or the ammunition you need when under fire from your management.

2. STAFFING QUESTIONS

Asking how many staff will be needed to run a database, at the beginning of the planning exercise, is a little like asking 'How long is a piece of string?' Nevertheless, after 'What will it cost?', the second question managers ask when a new activity like a small database is suggested, is 'How many people

SMALL SCALE DATABASES
ISBN 0 12 391970 3

is it going to take?' They may also want to know what kinds of people, at what levels, and whether they will have to be new people or can be found among existing staff members. It is no good giving the truthful answer, that you don't know. So, where do you find the answers to questions like these?

A search on LISA, using terms like DATABASE, INFORMATION and MANAGEMENT, is likely to produce a list of material on DBMS but very little that can convince your boss about numbers and costs of staff required to run your new database. If you contact a few of your friends who are operating databases elsewhere, you will be impressed not only at how easy they make it all seem, but also at the different answers each gives.

There is a very good reason for these differences; not only is every in-house database unique, but so is the 'house'. Nearly every new database is set up in an environment which already has certain staff, skills, equipment and so on. If you are very lucky, and if it really is a very small database, the answer to how many new people will be needed may very well be none. If you are not so lucky, the answer will be, um, well . . . some 'guesstimate' which is likely to be politically acceptable.

Note that our ideal managers have asked 'How many people will you *need*?' Others take a less generous approach, they ask 'How many people can you *save* by starting up this database?' This question can be a tricky one and it is wise to think about possible answers to it *before* you propose the database. It is not unreasonable for your boss to suppose that the database is designed to do something more efficiently than the old manual ways, therefore that it should need fewer staff, not more.

In the simplest case, the answer may be that the database *will* save staff, once it is fully operational. You may even be able to predict how many staff it should save. Equally, you may expect that there will be *no* staff savings. The database may be intended to give better control of some operations (to which the riposte from that doubting Thomas, your manager, is 'How have we managed so far, then?'); to do something entirely new (and useful); or to enable an in-house system to interact with another (perhaps also recently computerised) service in the organisation or outside. But if there are going to be *no* clear gains, and if it is not obvious why this is so, beware! You may be barking up the wrong tree, and pursuing a private hobby down a blind alley. . .

A Punch cartoon from the early days of computers, shows a giant machine with tape-drives and switches and flashing lights and about 30 (expensive!) systems experts and technicians clambering over it. The caption is 'Yes—we've managed to save about 30 clerks'. This kind of saving is best left to the joke books.

However, the initial question remains: 'How many staff will be needed?' and because it is a real question of management importance, a workable answer must be found. As a means of sharing experience, a small survey was made of database staffing and costs in Australia in early 1982, through a questionnaire (Fig. 6.1) addressed to all operators of publicly accessible databases. This was not a large sample—only 40, and only about half responded—but it did enable us to get some feeling for the size and range of the staff and costs involved.

The questionnaire shows the variety of tasks which have been identified and was the product of some discussion and trial runs. While it was originally intended for Australian use, it is probable that the resource elements identified are generally applicable. Obviously, staff and other cost elements will differ from country to country.

The answers to the questionnaire showed a wide variation which tended to reflect the complexity rather than the size of the databases. However, about half the replies clustered around certain values and those most frequent—the 'modal'—values have been shown in Fig. 6.1 where applicable. These figures should be interpreted with great caution. However, they do give some guide to the relative levels of resources said to be needed by one group of database operators in one country. Since I know of no similar surveys elsewhere, I have no way of knowing whether these figures are likely to be typical of practice in other countries. But they do offer a guide, which may be of some help when answering questions about resource needs.

2.1 Identification of tasks

My approach in this section will be to look at the tasks identified in the questionnaire to see where specialised staff are needed; the use of a bureau or other outside personnel can save costs; and where effort is needed to ensure that the database is used.

Some databases are virtually one-person operations; others, even 'small' databases, are the product of a team of half a dozen or more individuals, each contributing skill and some part of their time. As I suggested earlier, the environment in which a database is to be established is an important determinant of resource requirements.

The first and most important finding from the survey was that it is not the smallness or otherwise of the database which determines how many people will be needed, but the nature and complexity of the records in the database. At one level, large files of simple records, like herbarium labels, may be set up with little more effort than the typing of labels would have taken anyway. Indeed, either the labels or the database could be considered as a byproduct of the effort put into the other, however the database provides a powerful analytical tool as a bonus. At the other extreme, records of factual information, such as research in progress, may require visits by

AUSTRALIAN DATABASES
Staff and costs

(Please give "best guestimates" where no hard data are available)

A. IDENTIFICATION

1.1 *Name of Data Base* "MODAL"	
1.2 *Person responsible*	
1.3 *Address:*	
1.4 *Telephone:*	1.5 *Telex:*

B. NATURE AND SIZE

2.1.1	*Nature* of data base:	Bibliographic	✓	Tick for yes
2.1.2		Factual		"
2.1.3		Other (please specify)		
2.2.1	*Size of data base* at end of 1981			Records
2.2.2	Average *monthly growth rate*		250	Records/month
2.3.1	Records are	bibliographic data	✓	tick for yes
2.3.2		plus "expanded" titles		"
2.3.3		plus index terms	✓	"
2.3.4		plus abstracts	✓	"
2.3.5		plus full text		"

C. INITIAL DESIGN AND ESTABLISHMENT

3. *Early planning*

3.1	Working party or committee?	✓	Tick for yes
3.2	If so, how many people?	5	
3.3	How many meetings?		
3.4	Over how long a period?	12	months
3.5	Staff involvement?	6	man months

4. *Software*

Either 4.1.1 Standard package(s)? Which? .... Yes ....

4.1.2	Initial cost of software?	$	1000	
4.1.3	Implementation costs (software modifications etc.) By bureau?	$		
4.1.4	or by own programmers?	$		
or 4.2.1	Developed in-house?			Tick for yes
4.2.2	Design cost?		6	man months
4.2.3	Development cost?		6	man months

(Give pro rata cost or incremental cost as appropriate, if the software is used for more than one application).

	Thesaurus? Own production?			
4.3.1.1	Staff time to establish		18	man months
4.3.1.2	Staff time to update (monthly)			man months
or 4.3.2.1	Use a "standard" thesaurus? Which			
4.3.2.2	Update or mods per month		0.1	man months
	Other setting-up costs in			
4.4.1	staff		6	man months
4.4.2	hardware purchase	$	4000	
4.4.3	hire	$		
4.4.4.	computer charges	$		
4.4.5	etc. (please specify)	$		or man months

5. *Data*

	Selecting and obtaining *initial* material			
5.1.1	Staff time			man months
5.2.2	Purchase of *initial* material (including retrospective material)	$		

D. OPERATING (Give *monthly* figures—e.g. "man months *per month*")

6. *Input*

6.1.1	Obtaining material	$		
6.1.2	Selecting material		0.3	man months
6.2	Indexing		0.5	man months
6.3	Data entry		0.5	man months
6.4	Checking and post-editing		0.2	man months
6.5	Other? (which?)			

7. *Systems maintenance* (per month)

	Software support			
7.1.1	In-house staff			man months
or 7.1.2	Bureau charges	$		
	Processing (computer costs)			
7.2.1	Data entry	$	500	
7.2.2	Data base maintenance, utility processing	$		
7.2.3	Output processing, (lists, COM, photocomposition)	$	300	
7.2.4	Storage . . on-line	$		
	. . . off-line	$		

8. *Searching*

	Searching data base for self or clients			
8.1	Staff		0.1	man months
8.2	Computer costs	$	150	
or 8.3	Bureau costs in lieu	$	100	
8.4	Are these costs recovered from			
	. . . in-house users			Tick for yes
	. . . external users			"
	indicate approximate *percentage* of cost recovery.		100	%

9. *Printed or microform output*				
9.1	Editing, page make-up, etc.		0.2	man months
9.2	Reproduction, distribution	$		
	User aids			
	Writing search manuals, brochures, advertising, etc.			
9.3.1	Writers		0.2	man months
		$	500	
9.3.3	Postage	$		
10. *Overheads*				
10.1	Costs	$		
10.2	What do these include			....
	....			....
11. *Training*				
11.1	How much time to train your staff? (Ave. per month)		0.05	man months
11.2	your users? (Ave. per month)		0.05	man months of *your* staff
12. *Any other costs?*				
12.1	Staff			man months
12.2	Hardware costs?	$		
12.3	Bureau charges?	$		
12.4	Other (please specify)?	$		

How does your answer satisfy you? Does it give a reasonable picture of numbers *and levels* of staff involved?
If not, please specify and/or comment further.

Fig. 6.1 Survey questionnaire on staff and costs of Australian databases.

professional staff to establish accurate data. Each record may be the product of an interview or an enquiry, and in Australia such a visit may cost $100 or more. If each record is to carry such a price tag, it raises serious questions about the database objectives, its future use and cost effectiveness.

Whether you believe the modal numbers or not, I urge you to look closely at the questionnaire. Most of the questions relate to tasks which your database will entail, or to costs incurred to offset the employment of staff to perform certain tasks. The questionnaire can also help serve as a check list to estimate resource requirements. But do not be intimidated by it; a survey by the City University in London showed that 65% of the organisations contacted had used *only* their existing data processing staff to implement new databases.

Problems, where they arise, may be more 'political' than technical. Political questions may include such issues as 'who is to be responsible'? There may be competition in your organisation *to set up* a particular database, or to *avoid* responsibility for it. If there is to be cooperative input, agreement will need to be reached with potential contributors. This may not be an easy task. For example, an attempt to establish a cooperative database, intended to catalogue research projects, foundered on the issue of whether the database was to be structured around the research workers or around the research projects. Some potential contributors to the database already had systems operating based on projects, and others on workers. Because no compromise could be found, even after many months of discussion and pilot experiments, the project was eventually dropped.

Agreement also needs to be reached with potential users of the database, and they should be included on any planning committee. Later in this chapter I shall discuss the problems of marketing a database and getting it used effectively. Many of these problems could be ironed out during the planning stage if users were brought in earlier. Too many databases, and the information services based on them, are designed more for the operators' convenience than the users'. Even a small in-house database could be thought of in terms of its future users ('market') and planned accordingly.

There are other kinds of problems which may also arise at this early stage. For example, a professional society planned to develop a database of its publications to provide a better service to its members. Many of these members complained most vociferously; they could not see the benefit of such a database but did see a risk of their membership dues rising in order to pay for the database. Paradoxically, and just as much a problem at this stage, there may be a lack of opposition for proposals for a new database. There is so much talk of computers and the information society, that people accept any computer-related proposal as normal and necessary. This uncritical acceptance is potentially as harmful as irrational opposition. Objectives, costs and benefits need to be determined as precisely as possible and widely discussed among those who will pay for the database to be generated and those will will pay to use it. (Use is never free! The user may not pay money to the database provider but will have to pay for the time spent using the database which will hopefully be less than the time required to obtain the information in some other way. If not—why?) An early concensus on such matters can prevent a great deal of trouble later.

2.2 Staff requirements for generation of a database

These days few databases are developed in a back room by individuals. Usually there are endless committee meetings to debate *whether* to do it, and if so *how*. In the Australian survey, respondents said that such a decision phase may last three to 24 months or more, depending on the support (technical, financial, political) the idea attracts. Indeed, the effort put into this early planning stage is more likely to depend on the amount of argument the proposal generates than its future size or cost. (Remember Parkinson's Law of Triviality: the time spent on any item of the agenda will be in inverse proportion to the sum involved.) The modal staff time involved in this phase may be up to six man months, not only to service the committee but also to liaise with the technical experts and perhaps to act as 'product champion' to maintain the interest and momentum of the project. If it is to be an important and widely used database, it is worth putting such resources into the early planning phase to ensure that the project starts on a sound basis. But these resources need to be kept in proportion.

Once there is agreement in principle to go ahead, decisions will also have to be taken on data selection, software and hardware. These have been discussed in earlier chapters of this book, and all will influence staff requirements. It is important from the outset to distinguish between the contribution which *you* have to make from your own staff because you have the expertise, and the contribution that you can obtain more cheaply from outside.

In Australia, the government research organisation, CSIRO, has advised on the establishment of more than 50 databases, and has also used outside consultants in setting up others. Such sources of know-how, whether available from the public sector, private consultants or commercial bureaux, cannot be overestimated. At different stages of setting up a database, different skills are needed, sometimes quite briefly. Unless these skills already exist in your organisation, it may be quite uneconomic to buy, acquire, or learn them yourself. This is where know-how and experience count. Objective advice, from a colleague engaged in a similar operational database, or from a professional consultant who is not tied to particular hardware or software, can save much time, cost, heart searching and later recriminations.

Obviously, you (and probably also your planning committee, including some future users) will define what the database is to do, and hence what data elements should go into the database. Defining the objectives and content of the database is part of your skill, and if you are confident that you are right, you should not allow yourself to be talked into doing something entirely different in order to fit in with somebody else's preconceptions and prejudices. This being said, if small compromises can enable you to make use of an existing system at a fraction of the cost of developing an entirely new system to do things exactly the way you had imagined them, clearly those compromises are worthwhile. Commonsense only asks: 'will it still satisfy the *essential* objectives?'.

Standard software packages for most information retrieval applications are now available from the major hardware firms and specialised software houses. Many of these standard packages will need some modifications in specific applications. An example quoted of bureau costs for a modification in a fairly complicated situation was \$3000—equivalent to about three weeks salary and overheads for a programmer on your own staff. However, another respondent to the survey developed a program from scratch at a cost of 12 man months. Clearly, you would need to be sure that the difference in efficiency would be significant in order to justify the greater programming cost. There is another aspect to this decision. If it is intended that the database will develop into a service accessible to the public, future users will want familiar file structures and search procedures so that their experience on other systems helps them to interrogate the database. Hence choosing a standard program package helps the user as well as the budget.

Even after agreement has been reached with your collaborators and potential users on the objectives and general structure of the database, and the software and hardware have been chosen, there may be other details of establishing the database which absorb staff and management time. Respondents to the survey suggested from two to six months may be absorbed in miscellaneous activities at this stage. The moral is to allow plenty of contingency resources, they are likely to be needed.

One highly significant 'detail' is vocabulary control. A thesaurus, the list of preferred terms you intend to use for indexing the records in your database, can easily develop into a bottomless bucket into which you are pouring staff time and money. Once again, commonsense should be the guide. It is ridiculous to have a controlled list of tens of thousands of terms for a database which will run into only a few thousand records. In my own organisation, we discontinued the thesaurus which had been developed for the master list of our publications, because it proved too expensive to maintain. A thesaurus is in constant evolution and somebody has to spend time on update and maintenance.

Those respondents to the survey who developed their own thesauri thought that it took between one and three days each month to update and maintain it. In an analysis made of the costs of AESIS, the cost of thesaurus development was estimated at $50 000 initially, plus a further $5000 to issue an updated edition. Will such a development be necessary in your case? In general, this will depend on the complexity of the subject, the size of the database, and the number of indexers required for input. If most of the indexing is being done by one or two people working closely together, the likelihood is that they will soon develop a feeling for the terms to be used, so a simple list of preferred subject headings may be sufficient as a guide to consistency of indexing.

One special kind of database, (although this may not be a 'small' database) is the computerised library catalogue. Librarians are well aware of the needs for an effective Authority File. This is an essential part of the structure of a catalogue, but can also run away with staff time and costs. In my own organisation, which has nearly 50 research libraries and a book and serial vote approaching $3 million, the Authority File takes 1.5–2 people to maintain it, and is likely to continue at this rate for some years to come. However, no library is an island. The likelihood is that your library is linked with others in its field, or in its region, and that usable Authority Files already exist for the catalogues with which you will need to interact. In this case, it is evident that you should be using the same terms as your collaborators, and this is an instance where you may be able to take an existing Authority File, with only minor additions to suit your special needs, or to develop formal collaboration to reduce the load on your own time.

2.3 Staff requirements for operation of a database

Once the database is established, and the system is running, there is a steady input requirement which will depend on the nature of the database and the way it operates. Experience shows that it should be possible for an indexer to prepare 50 to 100 straightforward records for input in the course of a working week. These will then have to be keyed into the computer by the data entry operator. In some very small systems, this may be one and the same person, or an experienced data entry operator may be able to work straight from the original text for at least part of the record, for example the bibliographic elements, leaving the indexer to prepare the rest of the record for input.

You may of course be able to use keyboard staff who are already in your organisation. There are obviously economies of scale possible. A couple of data entry staff may be able to cope with the input to half a dozen different databases and such economies of scale can significantly reduce individual costs. Moreover it is becoming increasingly common for organisations to have word processing systems linked to a computer; in this case the skills of the word processing operator may be available for data entry to your system.

Indeed, small word processing systems are now becoming so common, that many secretarial staff are familiar with terminals and VDUs and will be able to deal with this kind of input as a normal part of their duties. Clearly, there are limits to the additional load that can be placed on willing individuals, but there may be opportunities for rationalisation in a small department to make time available for this purpose. If not, it may be worth considering whether the database work can be linked to some new development in office automation, so using the new equipment more efficiently and making gains in efficiency which can include the typing tasks as a by-product of the database operation.

As you can see, the database may benefit from the skills of many individuals already employed in various parts of the organisation and who can contribute a little time to provide know-how and advice, or even a significant proportion of their time to gather information, index, or key in data. Sharing staff in this way has obvious advantages, provided it is done under control and management realises what is happening.

Staff sharing is very common, and is one of the reasons why it is difficult to get good figures for the costs of databases. Some figures always seem to be swept under the carpet, either by accident or design, for a variety of motives. There are times when we want to minimise the apparent costs, just as there are times when we want to emphasise how much effort we are putting into an activity. This lack of precision may prevent management having an accurate feeling for cost benefit, which could help in making the database more effective. Equally, it may prevent an appreciation of true costs, which if known should result in the database being reassessed before these costs become outrageous.

There is another disadvantage to sharing staff, whether formally or informally. Because you have no real responsibility for their activities, you may have little real say in when they do your work or in the control of the quality of that work. These implications should be brought into the open during the early planning phase, and agreement reached with the management responsible for these staff about the likely nature, quantity and quality of their collaboration.

The *nature* of the system will also influence staff requirements. For example, if a system offers online input and output through a shared network, this will reduce the demands on staff for input but increase the demands for training others who are sharing in the online input. It will also increase the demands for the control of this input to maintain a satisfactory and consistent standard. Do not underestimate the training component of a shared system. Our computerised library catalogue required us to run training seminars at widely separated locations; these took about three man months of effort and heavy travel expenses. It was also necessary to write a detailed manual to ensure a common practice throughout the system. This work was spread over 5 years as the system developed and absorbed about two man months of effort. However, this catalogue could not be considered a 'small' database, and training activities and a manual of procedures for a small system could obviously be more modest. This does, however, highlight another advantage of a shared system; once the system is set up and running, each contributor supplies only a small part of the input, but benefits from the total database. Another clear instance of economies of scale.

The object of putting records into a database is not only to store or list them, but to process and selectively retrieve information so providing a service to oneself or to others. At least, this is true in most cases. In a few instances, respondents to our survey were using the database primarily for archival purposes, and no regular use was being made of the stored material. In other cases, there was no general access to the database, but the material was distributed as a publication, and the database was being used to sort and index the material for typesetting. There is nothing wrong with these approaches: the sale of printed indexes is how many large national and international databases recover their costs. But, if you intend to operate in this way, this needs to be clearly identified and agreed to during the early planning stage. It may also need different staff skills; a good editor may not be a good online searcher and vice versa.

If there is to be an online or batch output from the system in response to user interrogation, this requires staff in a number of capacities: user advice, database interrogation and document delivery. Within one's own organisation there is relatively little problem. Those who are putting in the data have a detailed knowledge of the file structure, search procedures and command language, and can be relied upon to make the best possible use of the system. For many years the US Department of the Interior would allow only its own staff to search the Selected Water Research Abstracts file on behalf of American users, because it felt that only they knew the system well enough to do it justice.

Practice makes perfect, one reason why an estimated 97% of online searches on bibliographic databases are performed for their enquirers by information staff is that the common and search procedures for different files are soon forgotten, and time spent online looking up the Manual soon becomes expensive and frustrating. Moreover, if users are to search the database online directly, they will need a search manual to explain how to do it. For a small database, the manual need not be complicated, and users who will do such work for themselves are already likely to have some familiarity with computers. However, the preparation of such a manual is another element which must appear in the forecast of expenses and is likely to require at least some continuing work to maintain it.

Users will also need some general help with formulating the kinds of question which the database can answer. If the question, once it has been clearly identified, is unsuited to the database, advice will be needed on where your frustrated user should turn next; this general attitude of helpfulness is part of turning the database activity into a *service*. It is seldom good enough to say 'Sorry, not my field'!

Above all, the user has come to you for information; in most cases he does not want simply 'to use the database'—the database is a tool and a means to an end, and if that end could be better attained in some other way he would happily use that instead. Moreover, if it is a bibliographic database, the service does not end with the print-out; in most cases the *document* is needed as well, and in some in-house services an analysis or synthesis of the documents will also be required. All of this implies greater versatility on the part of your database operators, where subject skills and an out-going personality may be as vital as dexterity on the keyboard.

3. MARKETING AND OTHER OUTPUT CONSIDERATIONS

For the operator of a new database there may be a requirement not only to develop the database but to set up a service by which it can be *used.* If the output is in the form of a printed publication, this will involve distribution and perhaps sale of the publication just like any other. If the output is in the form of an online service, perhaps in addition to a printed publication, manuals and training courses will have to be provided for users. In both cases, the system has to be made known; within the parent organisation by means of the normal channels of communication, and in the case of a publicly accessible service, through advertisements or technical papers and popular articles in appropriate journals, trade magazines and other media. But which are the 'appropriate' journals?

This introduces concepts of marketing. The first and most important of these is to identify the particular market sector at which your service is aimed. This needs to be defined with some care as it will affect the design of your database in two ways.

Firstly, identifying the market sector will enable you to estimate the potential user population. With a very specialised database, this user population may be so small that the cost benefit equation becomes alarming. However this may not be a reason for not undertaking the database, the importance of its content may be the overriding factor in taking a decision to go ahead. It may imply however, that your organisation will have to provide a continuing and growing subsidy with little apparent return, and this factor should be clearly presented during the early decision stages.

Secondly, the particular market sector at which you are aiming may be either technically rather sophisticated, or quite the opposite. This may affect both the way in which your database record is structured, and the form of output. Be realistic in your assessment of the rate at which potential users will adopt your system. Old habits die hard, and even after 3000 years of books, it is still difficult to persuade busy people to read, let alone acquire new skills which they believe will result in overloading them with even more information.

Somehow, potential users have to be made aware of the value of your system, and its ability to select from the mass of material in their field and provide them with *less* but more *relevant information.* Who is to prepare this publicity material? For many database staff writing about their systems and services is a labour of love, although obviously some do it better than others. It is, however, a continuing labour. Every year your user population changes, people leave, new people join. Samuel Johnson said 'If a man does not make new acquaintances as he advances through life, he will soon find himself alone. A man, Sir, should keep his friendship *in constant repair*'.

What is true for your friends, is true for your users, and this repair process requires an important part of your marketing effort. It must be admitted that the results of such publicity can be disappointing; many of our potential users seem unwilling to read, listen to or in any way respond to the claims we make for new services. If only they would just *try* them, we feel, they would be convinced! So it may be difficult, perhaps for many years, to justify a new database solely on its level of use, or by the revenue it returns.

However, each new database benefits from the efforts of its predecessors. People are becoming more conscious of the 'information society', and the explosion of personal computer usage is producing a new generation predisposed to accept databases as part of a normal way of life, like books, journals, or office memoranda.

The situation varies from country to country. A few years ago, the Asian Institute of Technology sent out some 3000 brochures about its databases to technical institutions in the countries in its region; these resulted in only a dozen or so enquiries. The 5 million online searches performed annually in the USA represent only a little more than two searches per 'technical professional' after a growth period of over ten years; how many technical professionals do you have in your target market sector?

In summary, no matter how good your database, it will be worthless unless it is used. The marketing effort is just as much the responsibility of you and your staff as are the input or the processing, and must be budgeted for in the same way, as other essential activities. This may seem very obvious and straightforward, but experience in the past has shown that database operators as a class are not very good at marketing their wares. A better mousetrap will *not* automatically make the world beat a path to your door, the world first has to know your address and second be convinced that it suffers from mice. The key element in all of this, from initial design to point of use, is *communication*, this is what a database is about and this is the key role of its staff.

What is more, the communication must be two-way. The criticisms of users—and non-users!—may be vital in getting your service 'right', to the point where it becomes viable. If for some reason there will be a delay in responding to a particular enquiry, let the user know immediately what that delay is likely to be, the reasons for it and make sure that the information will still be needed. It may turn out that the information required can be provided more quickly in some other way. A good service requires some degree of personal attention to users, as well as the prompt but impersonal provision of the information or data requested. Such courtesies and thoughtfulness are not an extraneous afterthought or some kind of a frill on the service, they are an integral and necessary part of it, and one of the ways by which you ensure that your user is satisfied and will return to use the database again.

All of the above is valid whether the database is being offered commercially or not. Even for an in-house information service, for which no charge is made to users, or for any other kind of database which is intended to be given away gratis, the concepts of marketing are vital to ensure that the product is correctly matched to the target audience and that the target audience is aware of the possibilities offered by the product. However, if a real charge is to be made, and money collected, questions of what costs are to be recovered and how prices are to be set immediately arise.

This book has dealt mainly with bibliographic databases, and has not made much mention of numerical and factual databases which form an increasingly large proportion of commercial databases, particularly those offered to the business sector. Such business databases are frequently highly profitable, as is testified by their proliferation. However, bibliographic databases, with rare exceptions, do not recover their full costs. That is to say, offered commercially, they are only viable if they are integrated into a mix of related products, in which case their costs will probably be carried by revenue from the hard copy printed version. For example, a few years ago the tape services of the CAB contributed only 5% to total revenue, 90% coming from the printed publications and the remainder from other services.

If the database is being offered to the public through one of the commercial hosts in Europe or North America, the organisation generating the database may recover only a quarter or less of the money paid by the user, the remainder goes to the commercial hosts and to the network operators providing the communications facilities. These harsh economic facts should be appreciated before you undertake to recover any particular proportion of the costs of generating the database. Practical experience shows that at best, by setting prices roughly equivalent to those current for other similar databases in your country, you may be able to recover the marginal direct costs of offering the service on the database—a very different and much smaller return than the true total costs of producing and operating it.

When charges are introduced for using a database, they are generally computed in three parts: a communications cost of reaching the computer on which the database is stored; a connect-time cost which is based on the total time the user spends online; and a 'per hit' cost, where the user pays for each usable piece of information retrieved and printed. Clearly, these elements are capable of variation. Recently, the CAB reduced its connect-time charges but increased its per hit price. This was intended to encourage the potential user to choose the CAB databases for his search, and to spend more time online in the expectation that he would be able to search more successfully and so be willing to pay for a greater number of hits.

Other databases have lower rates for subscribers to their printed version. Others will only sell subscriptions to their tapes after which the subscriber can use the tape for his own purposes in any way he chooses; this use may be limited to a particular individual or organisation, or it may provide full commercial rights. Others may negotiate lease or exchange of tapes. Exchanging databases is, as we saw earlier with cooperative production of databases, an efficient way for many to gain access to a large body of information of which each has provided a small part.

It is in the nature of information that almost all cooperative arrangements are good but be sure that you can honour your commitments before you sign. An undertaking to provide abstracts where formerly you only added a few indexing terms may require another member of staff. Watch also that you do not become totally dependent on such a cooperative arrangement. If the other partner crashes for some reason, you may be drawn down with him, or suddenly have to find additional resources to avoid this.

4. COPYRIGHT

The law of copyright differs so much in different countries that it is difficult to provide general advice in a book of this kind. A bibliographic database raises copyright questions at two stages: input, and document delivery.

A bibliographic database is making use of titles, author names and possibly also author abstracts contained in copyright publications. In most cases the publishers concerned will be delighted that you are drawing attention to their publications and will raise no difficulties in your using material in this way. However, this may not be universal, even in countries with liberal copyright laws. If there is any doubt, it is always best to write to the publishers of the publications concerned to ask their permission. Moreover, some publications are specifically exempted by their publishers from inclusion in databases, possibly because the publishers concerned have databases themselves and wish to retain the monopoly on their contents. Once again, in all such cases, formal permission should be sought. In many cases, particularly when material is to be used only in an in-house database, permission once sought will be freely given.

Document delivery, so far as a bibliographic database is concerned, usually means making photocopies of articles, scientific papers or parts of books, either for individuals or for transmission to a library on behalf of an individual reader who has requested the publication concerned. Once again, legal requirements differ greatly from country to country and should always be complied with. For in-house users there are unlikely to be any difficulties but, regardless of copyright considerations, the publisher is justified in taking action to protect his sales.

5. LEGAL RESPONSIBILITIES

If your database is being used to provide answers to questions, you have a legal responsibility to do your best to ensure that those answers are correct. To some extent, the nature of that responsibility depends on who is the questioner. If it is a colleague within your organisation, the situation may be defined by the rules relating to such matters in that organisation. However, in providing information or advice to people outside your organisation, in most cases the law of your country will be quite explicit as to what is expected of you. The situation may be complicated slightly by whether giving information is a normal part of your duties, or whether it is only incidental to your main activity in the organisation.

Australian law, for example, requires the *employer* 'to exercise reasonable skill and diligence' to ensure that:

- Information and advice provided by staff and upon which the recipients are likely to rely for serious purpose, are accurate.
- Staff are sensitive to the use an enquirer may make of information or advice sought.
- When there are doubts about the reliability of information, or the authority of the provider of that information these are made known to the enquirer.
- Where information or advice is being given on a matter that has not yet been finalised, the interim nature of such advice is also made clear.
- Where advice is sought from a *technical* information service on *policy* or *legal* matters, such questions should normally be passed to those more appropriately placed to answer them.

In general, legal liability for giving incorrect information rests on proof of negligence, and it is not possible to spell out what this means in every circumstance.

The principle of law involved is perhaps best summarised in a case in Australia in 1968 (the Shaddock Case):

> ... wherever a person gives information or advice to another person upon a serious matter in circumstances where the speaker realises, or ought to realise,

> that he is being trusted to give the best of his information or advice as a basis for action on the part of the other party and it is reasonable in the circumstances for the other party to act on that information or advice, the speaker comes under a duty to exercise reasonable care in the provision of the information or advice he chooses to give.

The computer has neither added to nor reduced the requirement to be thoroughly conscientious; it has merely made it easier and quicker to get *an* answer, right or wrong, for which you are responsible, not the computer.

6. CONCLUSION

Most of these management questions seem straightforward commonsense. This may be why they are so often overlooked. Every database is developed *for* somebody: perhaps just for the originator of the database, but more often for a wider use. Make sure that the effort expended on the database is justified by the value of the use expected from it, and that what the database offers is really what is wanted. Consultation with the users (the 'market survey'!) can contribute positively to the design of your database, and alert those users to the fact that something good is on the way.

Finally, advice from William of Occam, which is still good after 650 years. 'Occam's razor' says, in effect: 'Keep it simple. The simplest way is probably best'. Computers can do such fascinating things that there is sometimes an overwhelming temptation to sophisticate a database just because it's possible. Fight that temptation! Know your users, and give them exactly what they need. They will thank you for it.

FURTHER READING

Cronin, B. (Ed.) 1981. *The marketing of library and information services* (Vol. 4, Aslib reader series). London, Aslib.

Roberts, S. A. (Ed.) 1984. *Costing and economics of library and information services.* (Vol. 5, Aslib reader series). London, Aslib.

Many other references will be found in recent issues of the *Annual Review of Information Science and Technology.*

7. Management with a DBMS

Ian S. McCallum

1. Introduction
2. Information retrieval
   2.1 Autonomous information retrieval
3. A 4GL DBMS
   3.1 Focus
4. Building the database
   4.1 The growing eucalypt
   4.2 Entering data
5. Searching the database
6. Conclusion
Acknowledgement
References

1. INTRODUCTION

This chapter describes how a database management system may be used for creating, searching and maintaining a file of records containing both alphabetic and numeric data. A prototype system was developed using FOCUS running under TSO on an IBM 3081 computer. The performance of the software, illustrated with a database of 154 records related to eucalypts suitable for growing in south-eastern Australia, was tested against five of six contemporary user requirements for computer based information retrieval. In the areas of user convenience, data maintenance and data manipulation, the system was found to be superior in performance to conventional inverted file information retrieval systems. Suitability for microcomputers was assumed, but not tested.

SMALL SCALE DATABASES
ISBN 0 12 391970 3

2. INFORMATION RETRIEVAL

In Australia, information retrieval—the process of creating, storing and accessing information in electronic form—is moving into its third development phase. From the early 1970s offline or batch systems were used to match search terms against database contents. Processing usually took place overnight while searchers waited to determine the effectiveness of their queries. By the mid 1970s batch systems had given way to online systems in which the matching process took place interactively—both online and in real time. Breakfast no longer came between search request and search results. The results were available in seconds rather than hours. This speed of response led to major improvements in search effectiveness since the first set of search results could immediately be used as input to the second set of queries, and the second set of results could be used to refine the third set of queries, and so on until the information seeker was satisfied that the search was complete. This allowed the searcher to match information requirements against the database with speed and precision not previously possible with batch systems. Success in retrieving information led to a high incident of repeat use and to general appreciation of the role of computers in information retrieval. Online text retrieval systems are now in general use. Their characteristics are taught in all library courses, and their virtues are extolled by most librarians and information workers.

But the first and second phases of information retrieval were limited in their appeal by requiring trained searchers to conduct searches on behalf of information seekers. The searcher became an intermediary for the requester by translating the subject of the search into the vocabulary, grammar and syntax of the command language which was understood by the software controlling retrieval. Unfortunately this was a less than ideal position for the information seeker, blissfully ignorant or perhaps frustrated by the idiosyncracies of AUSINET or MEDLINE or ORBIT. The end user had no guarantee that the request as specified to the software corresponded exactly with the information requirement which prompted the request in the first place. Interrogation of the file was delegated, and with it the ability to control the amendment, addition and deletion of records. Until the inverted file systems become easier to use, their potential for managing information will not be realised. Thankfully, a healthy trend in this direction is emerging. The searchers are closing in on the store.

The third phase of information retrieval in Australia began when the system operators realised that the people who consume information generate most of it themselves. Whilst it is possible to dip into the public pool of stored data, people's perceptions of the value of information are largely determined by the uses to which they put the results of their own searching and synthesising processes. Since the application of retrieved information to problem solution is a highly individualised activity, most of the information applied tends to come from personal sources. And since there is so much information available the need is to find computer solutions to information problems which permit the computer to do what it does best—to extend medium and long-term memory, and at the same time displace the intermediary by simplifying the rules for storing and searching. This enables the end user to have direct access to a store of items already screened for relevance at the input stage. The intermediary is then freed of the responsibility, and the hazards, of attempting to interpret someone else's information requirements. He or she may then turn to more productive tasks, such as increasing the quantity or improving the organisation of information which may be readily shared. The end user is able to significantly reduce the time and the cost of identifying, storing and retrieving relevant material. And most importantly, the end user is at last in direct control of the route to his or her information destination. The benefits of such control, faster access and improved throughput, should lead to more informed decision making.

2.1 Autonomous information retrieval

What then are the requirements of a personalised information retrieval system? What major characteristics must it possess in order to facilitate immediate interaction between intellect and information?

i. The system should be easy to learn and simple to use. This is the most important requirement. If it is not met there is little progress beyond systems requiring intermediaries. Commands should be few in number and as close to English as possible. System prompts for data entry and for retrieval should be maximised. Ideally, the user should be able to select tasks from menus, never be in doubt about what the system is doing, and be able to sign off from the system at any point in the dialogue.

ii. The system should be capable of storing and manipulating quantitative data as well as textual data. 'Information' is not confined to words. The system should be capable of at least simple calculations where numbers are stored with text. In this context, even a rudimentary capability for generating graphs is useful.

iii. The system should support online retrieval, and also online addition, deletion and amendment of records. For the database to reflect current information interests, it is essential that data maintenance be performed as soon as the need for it becomes evident. Record maintenance should be just another aspect of online interrogation. To complement retrieval the system should permit printing of results on either low speed local or high speed remote printers.

iv. The system should possess both local processing capability plus the ability to connect to host computers. The end user needs to be able to search for information stored in databases on many different host systems. Once relevant items are found, the user should be able to download or transfer them from the host to the personal system. Conversely, the end user also needs to be able to upload, to send items from the personal to the host system. The implication is clear. The most versatile, flexible type of terminal is a microcomputer. Local intelligence, and with it the ability to run software unrelated to information retrieval, can be a key factor in justifying equipment acquisition.

v. All functions of the system should be available either through dedicated telecommunications lines or by dial-up part-time connection. High volume users will need the capacity and response times of permanent connection between terminal and host. Low volume users need the convenience and portability of establishing temporary telephone links when the need arises. The full range of functions should be available through either access method.

vi. The system should provide a service with a value or payback in excess of its purchase and operational costs. This is the cost effectiveness requirement. If the user considers that the costs of system use are greater than the benefits of the results obtained, then there is a fundamental flaw in the application design or in the method of operation.

3. A 4GL DBMS

An online search of the library and information science databases will attest to the recent growth of literature on the use of DBMS for information retrieval. However, the impetus for the development of DBMS has come not from librarianship, but from commercial data processing hardware and software vendors.

To quote Martin (1981), an influential DBMS evangelist:

> The data within a corporation (or any other organisation) will increasingly be regarded as a basic resource needed to run the corporation. As with other basic resources, professional management and organisation of the data are needed. The importance of efficient use of data for production control, marketing, accounting, planning and other functions will become so great in a computerised corporation that it will have a major effect on the growth and survival of corporations in a competitive marketplace.

According to Martin (1981), DBMS provides the key that unlocks the data:

> The intention of a database is to allow the same collection of data to be shared and serve as many applications as is useful. Hence, a database is often conceived of as the repository of information needed for running certain functions in a body such as a corporation, factory, university or government department.

The DBMS provides a conceptual structure for managing the information repository, and in most cases also contains a subsystem to access the organised records.

Libraries and other information centres are really no different from Martin's 'corporation'. Their stock in trade is the management and provision of information; indeed their funding can depend upon their success in providing service from stored data. Many libraries, be they special, public, university, state or national, either have or have access to DBMS now. The DBMS might have been acquired to run a personnel, shares, ratepayers or financial system, but the fact remains that their implementation is spreading. Most public and private organisations with data processing capability and with responsibility for the provision of information services either have, or soon will have, DBMS. They are as fashionable in computing as the light blue colour IBM paints its hardware.

But a DBMS by itself is not sufficient for our notional system. There are many DBMS' available for a variety of computers: ADABAS, DB2, FOCUS, IDMS, IMS, INQUIRE, RAMIS II, SYSTEM 2000, TOTAL and others for mainframe computers, down to DBASE II and LOTUS 1-2-3 and others for microcomputers. However it is not the case that every DBMS has a high level 4GL programming language and our system calls for a simple, English-like command language which permits operation by people not trained in programming. We need a 4GL with a DBMS. That is, we need to be able to issue simple commands which can be translated by the computer into more precise instructions, and we need to issue these commands to a system which organises information in a manner which reflects the use we wish to make of the database contents. Our user will be making a productivity trade-off between machine resource usage and rapid system development.

3.1 FOCUS

FOCUS is such a high level, user oriented, understandable, English language information management system. It is a 4GL with a DBMS and can perform a range of online tasks from simple inquiries to complex 'What if?' analyses.

FOCUS has done much to establish the concept of 'programmerless programming', and it assists the development of quite intricate systems without insisting that the users possess a high level of programming ability.

Information Builders Incorporated (1983), the US company which developed FOCUS, describes its product as a 'comprehensive information control system':

> It contains facilities for describing files, both simple ones and complex interconnected ones; for entering, changing and deleting records in the files; and for preparing reports from the information in the files.

FOCUS is available for both mainframe and microcomputers at around $100 000 for the former, and $4500 for the latter. For the technically minded, the FOCUS configuration for our system is running on an IBM 3081 with MVS/SP as the operating system, TSO as the teleprocessing monitor, and requires up to one megabyte of virtual memory. The microcomputer version has all the functions of the mainframe version, is designed for the IBM Personal Computer Model XT with DOS, 256K of main memory (an additional 512K comes with the FOCUS board), and also needs a 5 megabyte fixed disk.

Since ACI Computer Services offers FOCUS as part of its time-shared bureau services, and the project was satisfactorily justified to management, computer facilities were made available. Mainframe rather than micro FOCUS was chosen because of the sophisticated performance analysers already implemented on the larger machine.

4. BUILDING THE DATABASE

With a 4GL/DBMS, a computer and a terminal, all that remained was to build a database. Since this chapter began life in 1982 as a seminar paper, and since 1982 was the Year of the Tree, what better subject than eucalypts, uniquely Australian trees?

4.1 The growing eucalypt

The first task was to determine a structure for the information and to design the file. But before that could take place, the uses of the database needed to be clarified and an appropriate source of information identified. Fortunately there is an excellent reference work on Australian trees (Simpfendorfer, 1975) which lists the main eucalypt species and provides sufficient details to answer such queries as:

i. Which eucalypts have red flowers?

ii. Here is a dark green gum leaf. It is 20 cm long and 2 cm wide. It came from a tree with smooth bark, peeling in ribbons. To which species does it belong?
iii. Which eucalypts are suitable for planting in high rainfall, saline soil areas of Victoria?
iv. What is the average rainfall requirement of eucalypts suitable for both commercial timber production and bee-keeping?
v. Can I plant stringy bark and yellow box on a steep slope with very rocky soil?

and so on.

By considering first how the file might be used and then determining what information might be stored to satisfy file enquiries, we proceed to the design of the database. And now we notice a major difference between DBMS and an inverted file text retrieval system such as STAIRS. All data in FOCUS is stored in fields of fixed length. While this characteristic permits online updating, it does impose constraints upon the entry of text material which may be of unknown length. FOCUS cannot perform the word in context searches of the text retrieval systems. Its searching capabilities are restricted to scanning strings of characters to match search terms with file contents. How significant will this limitation prove to be?

The layout of Simpfendorfer's book, *An introduction to trees for south-eastern Australia*, with standard descriptions for species, makes it easy for us to design the file. Taking his data, it is straightforward to extract the elements considered most likely to answer our questions. The structure of our database, called 'EUC' for short, is shown in Fig. 7.1.

In Fig. 7.1 'FIELDNAME' is the label for the section of the record in which data is stored—the name of the field. 'ALIAS' is an abbreviation for convenient reference to the name of the field. 'FORMAT' species the type of field (A = mixed alphabetic and numeric data, I = integer or unmixed numeric data), and the number of characters available for storing data.

For example, the field 'BOTNAME' will contain the botanical name of the species. We can refer to it using the shortened form 'BN', and the field will contain mixed alphabetic and numeric data to a maximum length of 20 characters. Similarly, 'RAINFALL' will contain the tree's rainfall requirement in millimetres. 'RA' is the abbreviated name, and there are four character positions for storing numeric data.

Our records may have up to 29 fields. Nine fields will contain numeric data, and 20 fields may contain a mixture of both text and numeric data. Note that the locality, growth and shape fields contain coded data. In the locality field each Australian State is indicated by a number: 1 = NSW (New South Wales); 2 = NT (Northern Territory); 3 = QLD (Queensland); 4 = SA (South Australia); 5 = TAS (Tasmania); 6 = VIC (Victoria); and 7 =

Fieldname	Alias	Format Length
BOTNAME	BN	A20
COMNAME	CN	A25
LOCALITY	LO	A7
LC2		A1
LC2		A1
LC3		A1
LC4		A1
LC5		A1
LC6		A1
LC7		A1
MAXHGTM	HH	I2
MINHGTM	LH	I2
RAINFALL	RA	I4
GROWTH	GR	I1
SHAPE	SH	I1
SOILS	SO	A35
USES	US	A50
MAXLEAFL	HL	I2
MINLEAFL	LL	I2
MAXLEAFW	HLW	I2
MINLEAFW	LLW	I2
BUDS	BU	A40
FRUIT	FR	A40
BARK	BA	A40
FLOWERS	FL	A25
DESCRIPTION1	ID1	A60
DESCRIPTION2	ID2	A60
DESCRIPTION3	ID3	A60
DESCRIPTION4	ID4	A60

Fig. 7.1 Structure of the Eucalypt database.

WA (Western Australia). 'A1' redefines the locality field in seven single character fields which are separately searchable. At the time of retrieval, FOCUS will convert from the number which is stored to the name of the State.

In the shape field, tree shapes at early maturity have been grouped into nine basic forms, Fig. 7.2. In the rate of growth field, 1 = slow (below 0.5 m p.a.), 2 = moderate (about 0.5 m p.a.), 3 = fast (more than 0.5 m p.a.) and 4 = very fast (more than 1 m p.a.).

Note also that the last four fields (DESCRIPTION 1–4) provide for four fields each of 60 characters, giving us 240 character positions for the entry of textual data. It is here that text searching will be conducted. A complete record is shown in Fig. 7.3.

4.2 Entering data

FOCUS has been given a set of instructions called a procedure to prompt

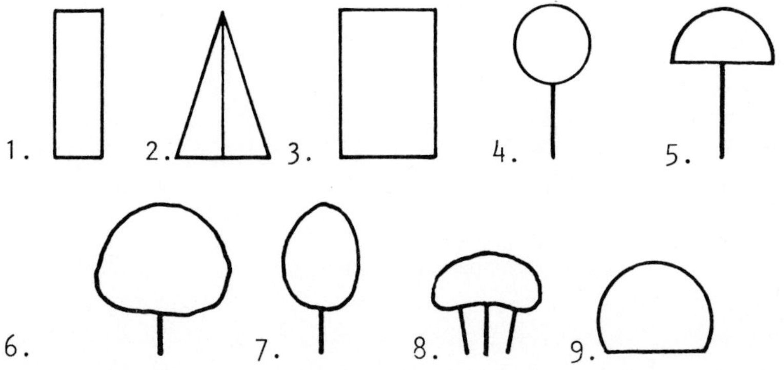

Fig. 7.2 Coded data for tree shapes. From Simpfendorfer, 1975.

for field names one at a time until full details of new records have been added to the file. We invoke this procedure by typing its name: 'LOADEUC'. FOCUS then asks whether we wish to add, change or delete records. To begin, we answer 'ADD'. The data entry procedure than asks us to enter each field in succession.

The first prompt is: BOTNAME = and we answer with the botanical name: GLOBULUS then FOCUS prompts for the common name: COMNAME = and we answer: TASMANIAN BLUE GUM; and so on until the last field has been entered. See Fig. 7.4.

Note that in the 'USES' field a single quote has been omitted from the end of the line. Opening and closing single quotes are used to indicate that the field may contain punctuation and other special characters, so FOCUS finds the omission and tells us we have forgotten the closing quote. Then it prompts again for the same field. This rudimentary validation process is performed for each field in the record.

The next time we remember the quote, but type a line which is longer than the 50 characters we have allowed for in the file design. FOCUS tells us we have exceeded the specified line length and prompts again for the field's contents.

When all fields have been entered correctly, FOCUS prints a message telling us that the species named has been added to the file, and prompts for the botanical name of the next record. At this point we notice that the value in the rainfall field should have been 750 mm rather than the 789 mm we entered, that the maximum and minimum leaf lengths should have been 40 and 30 cm, not 409 and 20, and that we have misspelled 'resists' in the second line of the description. We therefore type 'END' to end the updating procedure, and select 'CHA' to change the fields in error. See bottom of Fig. 7.4.

Fieldname	Data	
BOTNAME	*camaldulensis*	
COMNAME	river red gum	
LOCALITY	1234567	
MAXHGTM		30
MINHGTM		20
RAINFALL		500
GROWTH		3
SHAPE		6
SOILS	best on deep moist silty soils	
USES	windbreaks shade parks farm forests honey	
MAXLEAFL		20
MINLEAFL		12
MAXLEAFW		4
MINLEAFW		3
BUDS	5–10 conical, 8–10 mm long, conical cap	
FRUIT	globular, 5–7 mm, protruding valves	
BARK	smooth ashy grey	
FLOWERS	creamy to white	
DESCRIPTION1	the only eucalypt to occur naturally in all mainland states	
DESCRIPTION2	narrow when young, spreads with age if space permits	
DESCRIPTION3	drought and frost resistant, tolerates moderate saline	
DESCRIPTION4	closely related to *E. blakeyi,* and *E. tereticornis*	

Fig. 7.3 Sample record from the Eucalypt database.

```
  LOADEUC
ADD CHANGE OR DELETE EUC INFORMATION ?>ADD
>
 BOTNAME      =>GLOBULUS
 COMNAME      =>TASMANIAN BLUE GUM
 LOCALITY     =>'    56 '
 MAXHGTM      =>40
 MINHGTM      =>25
 RAINFALL     =>789
 GROWTH       =>4
 SHAPE        =>4
 SOILS        =>DEEP WELL DRAINED LOAMS
 USES         =>'FARM FORESTS TALL WINDBREAKS SHADE PARKS AVENUES HONEY
(FOC300) MISPLACED QUOTE IN DATA REPLY,DISREGARD:
'FARM FORESTS TALL WINDBREAKS SHADE PARKS AVENUES HONEY
 USES         =>'FARM FORESTS TALL WINDBREAKS SHADE PARKS AVENUES HONEY'
(FOC209) DATA VALUE EXCEEDS ITS LENGTH SPECIFICATION:
FARM FORESTS TALL WINDBREAKS SHADE PARKS AVENUES HONEY
 USES         =>'FARM FORESTS WINDBREAKS SHADE PARKS AVENUES HONEY'
 MAXLEAFL     =>409
 MINLEAFL     =>20
 MAXLEAFW     =>6
 MINLEAFW     =>5
 BUDS         =>'SINGLE BLUISH ROUGH 15-20MM DIAM'
 FRUIT        =>'LARGE 2CM DIAM ROUGH'
 BARK         =>SMOOTH DECIDUOUS IN RIBBONS
 FLOWERS      =>CREAMY
 DESCRIPTION1=>'TALL STRAIGHT TREE CLEAN TRUNK. FLORAL EMBLEM OF TASMANIA'
 DESCRIPTION2=>'PRODUCES STRONG CONSTRUCTION TIMBER, RESTS FROST'
 DESCRIPTION3=>'DENSE CROWN HEAVY BRANCHING, SUBJECT INSECTS IN DRY AREAS'
 DESCRIPTION4=>'WIND FIRM, MATURE LEAVES DARK GREEN'

 GLOBULUS HAS BEEN ADDED TO THE FILE

 BOTNAME      =>END
>ADD CHANGE OR DELETE EUC INFORMATION ?>CHA
```

Fig. 7.4 Example 1.

```
>
BOTNAME      =>GLOBULUS
CONNAME      =>.
LOCALITY     =>.
MAXHGTM      =>.
MINHGTM      =>.
RAINFALL     =>750
GROWTH       =>.
SHAPE        =>.
SOILS        =>.
USES         =>.
MAXLEAFL     =>40
MINLEAFL     =>30
MAXLEAFW     =>.
MINLEAFW     =>.
BUDS         =>.
FRUIT        =>.
BARK         =>.
FLOWERS      =>.
DESCRIPTION1=>.
DESCRIPTION2=>'PRODUCES STRONG CONSTRUCTION TIMBER. RESISTS FROST'
DESCRIPTION3=>.
DESCRIPTION4=>.

GLOBULUS INFORMATION HAS BEEN UPDATED

BOTNAME      =>END
>ADD CHANGE OR DELETE EUC INFORMATION ?>END
>>
```

Fig. 7.5 Example 2.

```
  TEXTFIND
WOULD YOU LIKE TO SEARCH 1, 2 OR 3 TEXT STRINGS ?>3
PLEASE ENTER THE FIRST TEXT STRING>FLORAL EMBLEM OF TASMANIA
PLEASE ENTER THE SECOND TEXT STRING>DENSE CROWN
PLEASE ENTER THE THIRD TEXT STRING>MATURE LEAVES DARK GREEN
PLEASE SELECT 'AND' LOGIC, OR 'OR' LOGIC>AND
>


NUMBER OF RECORDS RETRIEVED IS        1


 BOTANICAL NAME  GLOBULUS
 COMMON NAME     TASMANIAN BLUE GUM
 DESCRIPTION     TALL STRAIGHT TREE CLEAN TRUNK. FLORAL EMBLEM OF TASMANIA
                 PRODUCES STRONG CONSTRUCTION TIMBER. RESISTS FROST
                 DENSE CROWN HEAVY BRANCHING, SUBJECT INSECTS IN DRY AREAS
                 WIND FIRM, MATURE LEAVES DARK GREEN


WOULD YOU LIKE TO SEE THE RECORD DETAILS ?>Y
```

Fig. 7.6 Example 3.

FOCUS asks us to enter the botanical name to help find the record, then prompts field by field as it did for the 'ADD' command, see Fig. 7.5. If we do not wish to change the data in a particular field we type a full stop and the procedure moves on to the next field. When we come to a field we wish to change, we enter the correct information which replaces the current field contents, and move on to the next field. At the end of the record FOCUS performs the update and announces that it has done so.

```
BOTANICAL NAME  GLOBULUS
COMMON NAME     TASMANIAN BLUE GUM
LOCALITY                         TAS VIC
MAX HEIGHT (M)  40
MIN HEIGHT (M)  25
RAINFALL         750
GROWTH          4
GROWTH DESC     VERY FAST
SHAPE           4
SOILS           DEEP WELL DRAINED LOAMS
USES            FARM FORESTS WINDBREAKS SHADE PARKS AVENUES HONEY
MAX LEAF LENGTH 40
MIN LEAF LENGTH 30
MAX LEAF WIDTH   6
MIN LEAF WIDTH   5
BUDS            SINGLE BLUISH ROUGH 15-20MM DIAM
FRUIT           LARGE 2CM DIAM ROUGH
BARK            SMOOTH DECIDUOUS IN RIBBONS
FLOWERS         CREAMY
DESCRIPTION     TALL STRAIGHT TREE CLEAN TRUNK. FLORAL EMBLEM OF TASMANIA
                PRODUCES STRONG CONSTRUCTION TIMBER. RESISTS FROST
                DENSE CROWN HEAVY BRANCHING, SUBJECT INSECTS IN DRY AREAS
                WIND FIRM, MATURE LEAVES DARK GREEN


WOULD YOU LIKE TO CONTINUE FOCUS TEXT SEARCH ?>N
>>
```

Fig. 7.7 Example 4.

```
 TABLE FILE EUC
>COUNT BN
>END
 NUMBER OF RECORDS IN TABLE=    154  LINES=    1

 PAGE     1


 BOTNAME
 COUNT
 -------
     154

>>
```

Fig. 7.8 Search 1. Count the number of species entered in the database. "TABLE FILE EUC" means prepare a tabular report from the eucalypt file. "COUNT BN" uses the abbreviated name and specifies that all botanical names should be counted.

5. SEARCHING THE DATABASE

There are two main ways to search for information:

i. By using the report request language with its basic verbs: list; print; count; sum and write. English sentences are used to direct which records are to be retrieved, what calculations are to be performed, how the results should be sorted, and how the report should be presented.

```
 TEXTFIND
WOULD YOU LIKE TO SEARCH 1, 2 OR 3 TEXT STRINGS ?>1
PLEASE ENTER TEXT>SNOW
>


NUMBER OF RECORDS RETRIEVED IS        23


 BOTANICAL NAME  ACACIAEFORMIS
 COMMON NAME     WATTLE LEAF PEPPERMINT
 DESCRIPTION     ATTRACTIVE DENSELY CROWNED SPREADING DARK GREEN TREE
                 HARDY. WITHSTANDS LIGHT SNOW, SUIT COOLER DISTRICTS


 BOTANICAL NAME  AGGREGATA
 COMMON NAME     BLACK GUM
 DESCRIPTION     UPRIGHT TREE, DENSE SPREADING CROWN
                 BRANCHES TO WITHIN 1-3 M OF THE GROUND
                 SUITABLE NON SALINE WET SITES, PART. AT HIGHER ELEVATIONS
                 RESISTS FROST, WITHSTANDS COLD AND LIGHT SNOW

 BOTANICAL NAME  ARCHERI
 COMMON NAME     ARCHER ALPINE GUM
 DESCRIPTION     VARIABLE SMALL TREE OFTEN WITH TWISTED TRUNK
                 WITHSTANDS SNOW AND EXPOSURE IN ALPINE AREAS
                 TOLERATES SOME WETNESS


 BOTANICAL NAME  CHAPMANIANA
 COMMON NAME     BOGONG GUM
 DESCRIPTION     SPREADING SHORT BOLED MANY BRANCHES. NEW INTRODUCTION
                 FROST RESISTANT, WITHSTANDS PROLONGED SNOW
                 LEAVES ARE SLIGHTLY BLUISH
```

Fig. 7.9 Search 2. Search for any species suitable for planting above the snow line, then display four brief records.

ii. By invoking a procedure, specially written for this application, which permits simple Boolean searching of the contents of the four description fields.

For example, let us assume that we wish to know which eucalypt is the floral emblem of Tasmania, and that we already know that it has dark green foliage and a dense crown. We ask FOCUS to begin the search by typing 'TEXFIND', Fig. 7.6. FOCUS then asks how many text or character strings we wish to search, and gives us a choice of up to three. Then it prompts in succession for each string, and asks whether we wish to use 'AND' or 'OR' logic to control retrieval. We select 'AND' logic since we want only those records containing all three strings. FOCUS finds a matching record and prints its botanical and common names plus the description. We next have the option of printing the full record—which is the same as the one we earlier entered and amended, Fig. 7.7.

There are many other searches we could perform. Figs 7.8–21 show details of searches which are broadly representative of FOCUS' capabilities.

```
 TABLE FILE EUC
PRINT COMNAME USES
>>IF USES CONTAINS WINDBREAKS
>IF LOCALITY CONTAINS 6
>END
 NUMBER OF RECORDS IN TABLE=     35  LINES=   35

 PAGE     1


 COMNAME                   USES
 -------                   ----
 BLACK GUM                 WINDBREAKS SHADE ROADSIDES
 GRAMPIANS GUM             LOW WINDBREAKS PARKS ROADSIDES
 BROWN STRINGYBARK         FARM FORESTS WINDBREAKS
 GIPPSLAND GREY BOX        FARM FORESTS WINDBREAKS SHADE PARKS HONEY
 GOOSEBERRY MALLEE         LOW WINDBREAKS PARKS ROADSIDES
 RIVER RED GUM             WINDBREAKS SHADE PARKS FARM FORESTS HONEY
 BOGONG GUM                WINDBREAKS SHADE PARKS
 CANDLEBARK GUM            FARM FORESTS WINDBREAKS HONEY PARKS ORNAMENTAL
 WOOLLYBUTT                WINDBREAKS FARM FORESTS HONEY
 RIVER WHITE GUM           FARM FORESTS WINDBREAKS PARKS AVENUES ORNAMENTAL
 SLENDER LEAF MALLEE       LOW WINDBREAKS SHELTER ORNAMENTAL HONEY
 YORRELL                   WINDBREAKS SHADE ROADSIDES HONEY
 BLOODWOOD                 FARM FORESTS SHADE HONEY WINDBREAKS PARKS
 CIDER GUM                 WINDBREAKS SHADE FARM FORESTS
 BOG GUM                   WINDBREAKS ROADSIDES ORNAMENTAL
 YELLOW GUM                HONEY BIRDS FARM FORESTS WINDBREAKS PARKS SHADE
 RED STRINGYBARK           FARM FORESTS WINDBREAKS SHADE PARKS HONEY
 SPOTTED GUM               FARM FORESTS HONEY WINDBREAKS SHADE PARKS ROADS
 YELLOW BOX                FARM FORESTS WINDBREAKS SHADE HONEY PARKS
 YELLOW STRINGYBARK        FARM FORESTS WINDBREAKS SHADE HONEY
 MESSMATE                  FARM FORESTS TALL WINDBREAKS SHADE HONEY
 RED BOX                   FARM FORESTS WINDBREAKS SHADE PARKS HONEY
 RED IRONBARK              FARM FORESTS HONEY BIRDS WINDBREAKS SHADE PARKS
 MANNA GUM                 FARM FORESTS WINDBREAKS HONEY PARKS AVENUES
 BLACK BOX                 FARM FORESTS WINDBREAKS HONEY
 GREY BOX                  FARM FORESTS WINDBREAKS SHADE HONEY
 WEEPING SALLEE            WINDBREAKS LOW SHELTER PARKS ORNAMENTAL
 SWAMP GUM                 WINDBREAKS HONEY
 WHITE SALLEE              WINDBREAKS SHADE
 SNOW GUM                  WINDBREAKS PARKS ORNAMENTAL HONEY
 NARROW LEAF PEPPERMINT    FARM FORESTS WINDBREAKS SHADE
 SILVERTOP                 FARM FORESTS WINDBREAKS SHADE HONEY
 BLUE GUM                  WINDBREAKS SHADE FARM FORESTS HONEY
 GREEN MALLEE              EUCALYPTUS OIL HONEY LOW WINDBREAKS PARKS
 TASMANIAN BLUE GUM        FARM FORESTS WINDBREAKS SHADE PARKS AVENUES HONEY


>>
```

Fig. 7.10 Search 3. Print the common name and uses for all trees suitable as windbreaks and native to Victoria.

```
 TABLE FILE EUC
>PRINT COMNAME USES
>IF LOCALITY CONTAINS 6
>IF RA GE 450
>IF SH EQ 5 OR 6 OR 7
>END
 NUMBER OF RECORDS IN TABLE=     14  LINES=   14

 PAGE     1


 COMNAME                   USES
 -------                   ----
 SOUTHERN MAHOGANY         SHADE AVENUES PARKS STREAM BANKS
 RIVER RED GUM             WINDBREAKS SHADE PARKS FARM FORESTS HONEY
 BOGONG GUM                WINDBREAKS SHADE PARKS
 TINGIRINGI GUM            LOW SHELTER PARKS ORNAMENTAL
 BLOODWOOD                 FARM FORESTS SHADE HONEY WINDBREAKS PARKS
 BOG GUM                   WINDBREAKS ROADSIDES ORNAMENTAL
 SPOTTED GUM               FARM FORESTS HONEY WINDBREAKS SHADE PARKS ROADS
 YELLOW BOX                FARM FORESTS WINDBREAKS SHADE HONEY PARKS
 YELLOW STRINGYBARK        FARM FORESTS WINDBREAKS SHADE HONEY
 RED BOX                   FARM FORESTS WINDBREAKS SHADE PARKS HONEY
 OMEO GUM                  LOW SHELTER ROADSIDES PARKS
 WEEPING SALLEE            WINDBREAKS LOW SHELTER PARKS ORNAMENTAL
 SPINNER GUM               LOW SHELTER ORNAMENTAL
 BLACK SALLEE              LOW SHELTER SHADE ORNAMENTAL HONEY


>>
```

Fig. 7.11 Search 4. Print the common name and uses for all trees native to Victoria with an annual rainfall requirement of at least 450 mm in shape classes 5, 6 or 7. (Some abbreviated field names are used.)

```
 TABLE FILE EUC
>PRINT COMNAME BARK MAXLEAFL MINLEAFL
>IF MAXLEAFL FROM 18 TO 22
>END
 NUMBER OF RECORDS IN TABLE=     17  LINES=   17

 PAGE      1

 COMNAME                BARK                                     MAXLEAFL  MINLEAFL
 -------                ----                                     --------  --------
 CABBAGE GUM            SMOOTH                                       20        10
 GIPPSLAND GREY BOX     ROUGH, SMOOTH ON BRANCHES                    18         8
 RIVER RED GUM          SMOOTH ASHY GREY                             20        12
 LEMON SCENT GUM        CHALKY WHITE TO GROUND LEVEL                 18        10
 CUP GUM                SMOOTH, SHED IN FLAKES                       20        12
 CANDLEBARK GUM         SMOOTH WHITE DECIDUOUS                       20        12
 RIVER WHITE GUM        SMOOTH GREYISH WHITE DECIDUOUS               20        10
 TUART                  LIGHT GREY FIBROUS AND PERSISTENT            18        12
 BLOODWOOD              ROUGH WITH TILE LIKE FLAKES                  18        10
 SPOTTED GUM            SMOOTH MOTTLED GREYISH PATCHES               20        10
 MESSMATE               FIBROUS, PERSISTENT SMALLER BRANCHES         18        10
 MANNA GUM              SMOOTH DECIDUOUS RIBBONY                     20        10
 SYDNEY BLUE GUM        SMOOTH AND BLUISH                            20        10
 WALLANGARRA GUM        SMOOTH AND WHITE                             20        10
 SILVERTOP              FURROWED AND HARD                            18        10
 GOLDFIELDS GUM         ROUGH BUTT SMOOTH HIGHER UP                  20        12
 FOUR WING MALLEE                                                    20        15

>>
 TABLE FILE HOLD
>PRINT BOTNAME COMNAME BARK
>IF BARK CONTAINS 'ASHY GREY'
>END
 NUMBER OF RECORDS IN TABLE=      1  LINES=    1

 PAGE      1

 BOTNAME             COMNAME              BARK
 -------             -------              ----
 CAMALDULENSIS       RIVER RED GUM        SMOOTH ASHY GREY
```

Fig. 7.12 Search 5. Print the common name, bark type and maximum and minimum leaf lengths for all trees with a maximum leaf length between 18 and 22 cm. Then save or hold the answer set and perform a further search on the retrieved items, selecting only species with ashy grey bark.

6. CONCLUSION

The project began to test a 4GL/DBMS for its suitability for information retrieval. After working through the examples we are in a position to comment on performance in relation to the characteristics of our autonomous system.

i. The system is not difficult to use. Some familiarity with a command language is required, but the language itself is sufficiently English-like for the educated layman to master.
ii. The system can certainly store and manipulate text and numeric data, and it can produce simple graphs.
iii. The system supports online retrieval as well as online addition, deletion and amendment of records.
iv. We did not test the system using a microcomputer as a terminal, but this capability is present. Downloading and uploading are provided for.
v. The system is available through either dial-up or leased lines and performed satisfactorily in both communication modes.
vi. Determining value in relation to cost is difficult. Costs, although situation dependent, are relatively straightforward to calculate. But the

```
  TEXTFIND
WOULD YOU LIKE TO SEARCH 1, 2 OR 3 TEXT STRINGS ?>3
PLEASE ENTER THE FIRST TEXT STRING>RESIST
PLEASE ENTER THE SECOND TEXT STRING>FROST
PLEASE ENTER THE THIRD TEXT STRING>DROUGHT
PLEASE SELECT 'AND' LOGIC, OR 'OR' LOGIC>AND
>



NUMBER OF RECORDS RETRIEVED IS       41



 BOTANICAL NAME  ACCEDENS
 COMMON NAME     POWDER BARK
 DESCRIPTION     SMALL TREE PINKISH TRUNK PRODUCES DENSE HEAVY TIMBER
                 SUITABLE FOR WARMER DISTRICTS
                 HARDY, FROST AND DROUGHT RESISTANT


 BOTANICAL NAME  ANNULATA
 COMMON NAME     OPEN FRUIT MALLEE
 DESCRIPTION     TYPICAL MALLEE. COMPACT, SPREADING, WELL SHAPED.
                 DROUGHT AND FROST RESISTANT
                 LEAVES NARROW AND DARK SHINING GREEN


 BOTANICAL NAME  BROCKWAYII
 COMMON NAME     DUNDAS MAHOGANY
 DESCRIPTION     SPREADING DENSELY CROWNED, BRANCHES ASCEND SHARP ANGLE
                 RELATIVELY NEW INTRODUCTION, PRODUCING GOOD FARM TIMBER
                 USUALLY SINGLE STEMMED BUT MULTI STEMMED NOT UNCOMMON
                 VIGOROUS PREFERS LOAMY SOILS RESISTS DROUGHT FROST SALT

  TABLE FILE HOLD
>PRINT COMNAME OVER LOCNAME OVER MAXHGTM
>IF MAXHGTM GE 20
>IF LOCNAME CONTAINS NSW OR VIC
>END
 NUMBER OF RECORDS IN TABLE=      1  LINES=     1

 PAGE     1


 COMNAME  RIVER RED GUM
 LOCNAME  NSW NT  QLD SA  TAS VIC WA
 MAXHGTM                                    30

>>
```

Fig. 7.13 Search 6. Carry out a text search for species which resist both drought and frost, print a few records, then hold the result and print the common name, locality and maximum height for trees taller than 20 m and native to NSW or Victoria.

value of the system—its worth to the end user, is not easy to quantify. And in the case of a personal information retrieval system, it seems likely that only the person can judge.

ACKNOWLEDGEMENT

Writing this paper and building its database would have been much less interesting for me, and I suspect for you as well, had it not been for the generous permission of K. J. Simpfendorfer and his publisher to reproduce records already painstakingly compiled in a definitive work. I am most grateful to have been granted the opportunity to bring the magnificent eucalypt to your notice.

```
 TABLE FILE EUC
>PRINT CN BY HIGHEST HH
>IF LO CONTAINS 4 OR 5 OR 7
>IF US CONTAINS WINDBREAK
>IF US CONTAINS FOREST
>END
 NUMBER OF RECORDS IN TABLE=     28  LINES=   28

 PAGE      1


 MAXHGTM  COMNAME
 -------  -------
      40  WOOLLYBUTT
          JOHNSTON GUM
          TASMANIAN BLUE GUM
      35  BROWN STRINGYBARK
          MANNA GUM
          BLUE GUM
      30  RIVER RED GUM
          CANDLEBARK GUM
          YELLOW STRINGYBARK
          SILVERTOP
      25  SUGAR GUM
          YELLOW GUM
          RED STRINGYBARK
          MESSMATE
          RED MORRELL
      20  DUNDAS MAHOGANY
          TUART
          CIDER GUM
          SALMON GUM
          WANDOO
      18  BROWN MALLET
      15  BLACK BOX
          SWAMP YATE
          TALL SILVER PEPPERMINT
      12  DUNDAS BLACKBUTT
          MERRIT
          BLUE MALLET
          ROCK GUM


>>
```

Fig. 7.14 Search 7. Print common names in descending sequence by tree height for South Australian, Tasmanian and Western Australian trees useful as windbreaks or for farm forests.

```
 TABLE FILE EUC
>SUM AVE.RA PRINT CN RA
>IF LO CONTAINS 6
>IF US CONTAINS SHADE
>END
 NUMBER OF RECORDS IN TABLE=     26  LINES=   26

 PAGE      1


 AVE
 RAINFALL  COMNAME                     RAINFALL
 --------  -------                     --------
      591  BLACK GUM                        700
           GIPPSLAND GREY BOX               650
           SOUTHERN MAHOGANY                550
           RIVER RED GUM                    583
           BOGONG GUM                      1000
           ARGYLE APPLE                     600
           PINK GUM                         450
           YORRELL                          250
           BLOODWOOD                        650
           CIDER GUM                        750
           YELLOW GUM                       400
           RED STRINGYBARK                  550
           SPOTTED GUM                      450
           YELLOW BOX                       500
           YELLOW STRINGYBARK               600
           MESSMATE                         650
           RED BOX                          500
           RED IRONBARK                     500
           GREY BOX                         450
           ACORN OR OIL MALLEE              300
           WHITE SALLEE                     550
           NARROW LEAF PEPPERMINT           700
           SILVERTOP                        650
           BLACK SALLEE                     750
           BLUE GUM                         900
           TASMANIAN BLUE GUM               750


>>
```

Fig. 7.15 Search 8. Add the rainfall requirements of Victorian species providing good shade; determine and print the average with common names and rainfall requirements.

```
  TABLE FILE EUC
>HEADING CENTER
>"DISTRIBUTION OF EUCALYPTS NATIVE TO NSW"
>COUNT BN BY LO IF LO CONTAINS 1
>END
 NUMBER OF RECORDS IN TABLE=     57  LINES=   12

 PAGE     1

 DISTRIBUTION OF EUCALYPTS NATIVE TO NSW
          BOTNAME
 LOCALITY  COUNT
 --------  -------
 1               8
 1    6         10
 1   56          6
 1  4            1
 1  4 6          7
 1  4 67         3
 1  456          4
 1 3             8
 1 3  6          5
 1 34 6          3
 1 3456          1
 1234567         1


>>
```

Fig. 7.16 Search 9. How many species of eucalypt are native to NSW, and how many NSW species have been found in the other States? Include a heading in the report.

```
  TABLE FILE EUC
>HEADING CENTER
>"SPECIES FOR APIARISTS IN WET AREAS"
>PRINT CN RA OVER USES
>IF USES CONTAINS HONEY
>IF RA GT 600
>IF RA LT 850
>END
 NUMBER OF RECORDS IN TABLE=     13  LINES=   13

 PAGE     1

             SPECIES FOR APIARISTS IN WET AREAS
 COMNAME  GIPPSLAND GREY BOX          RAINFALL   650
 USES  FARM FORESTS WINDBREAKS SHADE PARKS HONEY
 COMNAME  SWAMP MAHOGANY              RAINFALL   650
 USES  WINDBREAKS ROADSIDES PARKS HONEY
 COMNAME  VARIETY TAS BLUE GUM        RAINFALL   750
 USES  ORNAMENTAL SHADE PARKS HONEY
 COMNAME  CANDLEBARK GUM              RAINFALL   650
 USES  FARM FORESTS WINDBREAKS HONEY PARKS ORNAMENTAL
 COMNAME  BLOODWOOD                   RAINFALL   650
 USES  FARM FORESTS SHADE HONEY WINDBREAKS PARKS
 COMNAME  MESSMATE                    RAINFALL   650
 USES  FARM FORESTS TALL WINDBREAKS SHADE HONEY
 COMNAME  MANNA GUM                   RAINFALL   700
 USES  FARM FORESTS WINDBREAKS HONEY PARKS AVENUES
 COMNAME  LITTLE SALLEE               RAINFALL   650
 USES  LOW SHELTER PARKS HONEY
 COMNAME  SWAMP GUM                   RAINFALL   650
 USES  WINDBREAKS HONEY
 COMNAME  SNOW GUM                    RAINFALL   800
 USES  WINDBREAKS PARKS ORNAMENTAL HONEY
 COMNAME  SILVERTOP                   RAINFALL   650
 USES  FARM FORESTS WINDBREAKS SHADE HONEY
 COMNAME  BLACK SALLEE                RAINFALL   750
 USES  LOW SHELTER SHADE ORNAMENTAL HONEY
 COMNAME  TASMANIAN BLUE GUM          RAINFALL   750
 USES  FARM FORESTS WINDBREAKS SHADE PARKS AVENUES HONEY


>>
```

Fig. 7.17 Search 10. What eucalypts are useful for apiarists in rainfall areas of between 600 and 850 mm p.a.? Print the common name and the rainfall arranged above the uses.

```
 TABLE FILE EUC
>HEADING CENTER
>"NSW SPECIES - TALL TRUNKS, ROUNDED FOLIAGE - GROUPED BY RAINFALL"
>PRINT CN BN BY RA IN-GROUPS-OF 50
>BY LO BY SH
>IF LO CONTAINS 1
>IF SH CONTAINS 4
>IF RA GT 400
>IF RA LT 800
>END
 NUMBER OF RECORDS IN TABLE=     18  LINES=   18

 PAGE     1

      NSW SPECIES - TALL TRUNKS, ROUNDED FOLIAGE - GROUPED BY RAINFAL
 RAINFALL  LOCALITY  SHAPE  COMNAME                      BOTNAME
 --------  --------  -----  -------                      -------
      450  1 3  6        4  GREY BOX                     MICROCARPA
      500  1             4  GREY IRONBARK                PANICULATA
           1 3           4  NARROW LEAF IRONBARK         CREBRA
           1 3  6        4  RED IRONBARK                 SIDEROXYLON
      550  1             4  SLATY BOX                    DAWSONII
           1  4 6        4  RED STRINGYBARK              MACRORHYNCHA
      600  1    6        2  ARGYLE APPLE                 CINEREA
           1  4 6        4  BROWN STRINGYBARK            BAXTERI
      650  1    6        4  GIPPSLAND GREY BOX           BOSISTOANA
                            BRITTLE GUM                  MANNIFERA
           1   56        4  SILVERTOP                    SIEBERI
           1  456        4  MESSMATE                     OBLIQUA
                            SWAMP GUM                    OVATA
           1 3           4  WILLOW LEAF PEPPERMINT       NICHOLII
           1 3456        4  CANDLEBARK GUM               RUBIDA
      700  1   56        4  BLACK GUM                    AGGREGATA
           1  456        4  MANNA GUM                    VIMINALIS
      750  1    6        4  RIVER WHITE GUM              ELATA
```

Fig. 7.18 Search 11. What species occur in NSW, have tall slender trunks with rounded foliage at the top, and require from 400–800 mm of rain? Group them by rainfall in ascending increments of 50.

```
 TABLE FILE EUC
>"RAINFALL REQUIREMENT BY REGION"
>SUM AVE.RA BY LO
>END
 NUMBER OF RECORDS IN TABLE=    154  LINES=   24

 PAGE     1

 RAINFALL REQUIREMENT BY REGION
           AVE
 LOCALITY  RAINFALL
 --------  --------
                500
       7        370
      6         666
     5          750
     56         833
    4           400
    4  7        300
    4 6         425
    4 67        300
   3            500
  2 4 67        300
  23   7        500
 1              656
 1    6         700
 1   56         783
 1  4           250
 1  4 6         364
 1  4 67        266
 1  456         637
 1 3            731
 1 3  6         510
 1 34 6         466
 1 3456         650
 1234567        583

>>
```

Fig. 7.19 Search 12. What are the average annual rainfall requirements of species grouped by region?

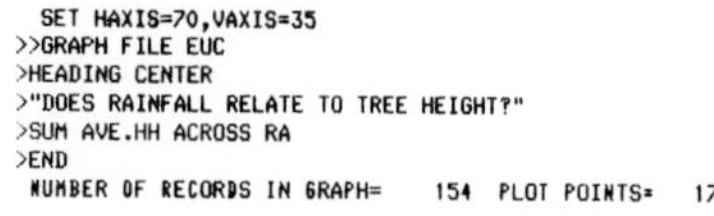

```
 SET HAXIS=70,VAXIS=35
>>GRAPH FILE EUC
>HEADING CENTER
>"DOES RAINFALL RELATE TO TREE HEIGHT?"
>SUM AVE.HH ACROSS RA
>END
 NUMBER OF RECORDS IN GRAPH=    154  PLOT POINTS=   17
```

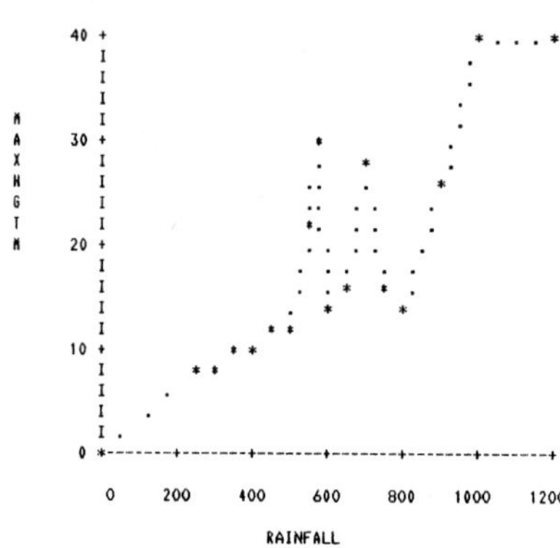

>>

Fig. 7.20 Search 13. Plot the relationship between average heights of mature trees against rainfall requirements.

```
 SET HAXIS=75
>>SET VAXIS=35
>>SET GRID=ON
>>GRAPH FILE EUC
>HEADING CENTER
>"TREE HEIGHT RELATED TO RAINFALL"
>SUM AVE.RA ACROSS HH
>END
 NUMBER OF RECORDS IN GRAPH=    154  PLOT POINTS=   17
```

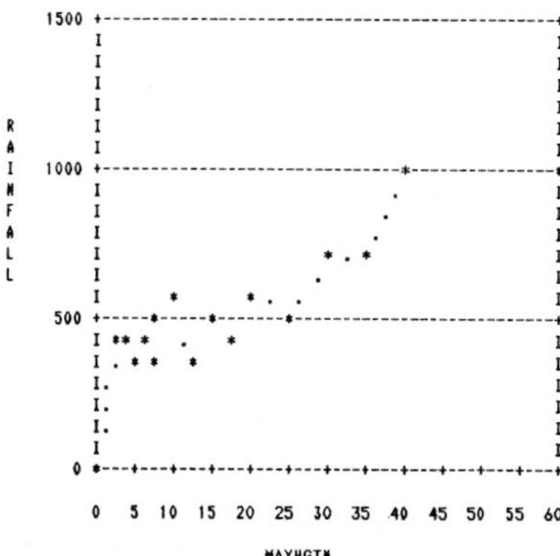

Fig. 7.21 Search 14. Now show in a grid, average rainfall against mature tree height. Who said eucalypts don't like water?

REFERENCES

Information Builders, Inc. 1983. *FOCUS users manual, 1983.* New York, Information Builders.

Martin, James. 1981. An end user's guide to database. *Computerworld* May 4: 3.

Simpfendorfer, K. J. 1975. *An introduction to trees for south-eastern Australia.* Melbourne, Inkata Press.

8. Input processing and editorial responsibilities

George Levick

1. Introduction
   1.1 Terminology
2. Primary document handling
3. Maintenance of data standards
   3.1 Control data
   3.2 Variable data
   3.3 Computerised checking
Further reading

1. INTRODUCTION

In this chapter I will discuss input processing and editorial responsibilities from the point of view of personal experience as managing editor of an established system. This system is a bibliographic database established according to normal bibliographic conventions and is independent of any other purpose (such as maintenance of a library catalogue or management of a library collection).

The primary tasks of a managing editor are to arrange a smooth flow of documents and data and supervise the everyday quality standards of the data that is entered. My general approach to the managing editor's job is a practical one. While we naturally wish to meet the highest requirements possible, the resources available to us are limited in relation to the extent of our responsibilities. Thus we must aim at economy as well as efficacy.

1.1 Terminology

The terminology used is based on a system in which 'indexers' describe

SMALL SCALE DATABASES
ISBN 0 12 391970 3

'documents' in a process that results in completed input forms. These forms, and the corresponding computer impressions, I call collectively 'data', while a unit of data that is sufficient to describe an individual document is an 'entry'. Within an entry, identifiable subunits are 'elements', and the spaces (literal or metaphorical) occupied by elements are 'fields'. Thus an author's name might be an element, and would then properly occupy an 'author name field'.

2. PRIMARY DOCUMENT HANDLING

Document handling prior to data input may range from totally 'distributed' input, with no central document handling, to total in-house handling, storage and provision of documents. Our database falls between these two extremes and we borrow needed documents from a library or equivalent store for the period necessary to discharge our particular responsibilities.

Unless the flow of documents involved is small in relation to the resources that can be devoted to it there will always be a discernible time lag between the arrival of a document and the appearance of the corresponding database entry in accessible form. This time is needed for documents to be distributed to indexers; input forms to be collated and edited; and data to be entered, processed, and added to the searchable file. Even if circumstances allow this time to be reduced, for example documents could be analysed individually and the data entered online, it might not be economical to operate in this way. Batch processing is generally cheaper in computing terms than online entry. I would suggest, too, that indexing and editing are also more efficiently performed on batches of documents and data, respectively, than on individual items. (The basis for this suggestion is that there are 'overhead costs' of time in preparing for a session of such activities—assembling reference materials, reacquainting oneself with conventions, and so on—which for efficiency and economy should be distributed over a number of unit entries). If batch operations are adopted, then inevitably some documents are delayed while the number of documents needed for a batch is accumulated.

After the indexing process is completed there should be few occasions where an entry is so defective as to require a second reference to the original. Such occasions, however few, are disproportionately costly. The extent of the disproportion will vary with circumstances—notably the ease with which we gain access to the documents after they have left our control. In principle, the effect of having to relocate and reobtain a document is to double the cost of handling it. Thus it is prudent to retain documents at least until the corresponding data has passed the stages of editing and validation for acceptance into the main file.

If this period is considerable—that is, too long for personal memory of individual documents to be reliable—then responsible handling requires that some records of the physical movements of documents are kept; at least of their acquisition and disposal. These records make up what I call an 'interim file'. There is an element of duplication of the database itself in doing this and for the overall efficiency of the operation it is necessary to keep the interim file to a minimum level of complexity and cost. It is also desirable that it should be a 'desk top' facility—immediately and easily accessible at any time. If a computerised system—not necessarily that used for the database—can be used in this fashion there are obvious advantages, otherwise some form of 'card' index is ideal.

In scientific (and many technological) subject fields, where the dominant form of publication is an article in an issue that can in some way be identified as a member of a series, it is practical to maintain an index to names of the series. The records that need to be kept are then entered by referring to the position of the individual document within the series (for example its serial number). Even for monographs within series, as opposed to typical journals, this is still a convenient and effective device, involving a minimum of duplication of effort. It also has the incidental but important advantage of providing an authority file of the series names.

For documents that have no serial characteristics, the practical compromise depends on the particular circumstances in which the documents are acquired. Essentially, what is needed is a systematic arrangement whereby either: (a) the interim file contains a minimal bibliographic reference in order to identify and locate each document; or (b) the reference is directly transferable to the data input for the database.

In the case of (a), suppose that we obtain all our documents from a particular library whose acquisition interests are similar to those of our databases. Then it should be possible, in consultation with the library, to devise an abbreviated form of reference (even, perhaps, a simple numerical sequence) that can be expanded by coordination with the library's own records when necessary. In such a situation one major use of the interim file will be to protect the interests of the library, and this sort of arrangement will be beneficial to both parties.

In the case of (b), minimum bibliographic details of a new document are entered on an input form. The form is then duplicated; one copy forms the basis of the interim record, while the other is completed by the indexer to meet the requirements of the database.

In any case, interim records of non-serial items should be discarded as soon as the documents are disposed of and the corresponding entries made accessible in the database.

3. MAINTENANCE OF DATA STANDARDS

In the maintenance of data standards editorial responsibilities centre upon ensuring adequate and responsible service at a reasonable cost. The first consideration is the extent of intellectual checking and proofreading and the second is the extent to which the computer can edit the data.

It goes without saying that the highest standards of editorial attention are the most costly in terms of time and effort. These involve a careful character by character check of input sheets as received from indexers, with absolute insistence on the most rigid requirements of adherence to convention and general correctness of all data elements. If there is a time in the routine input operation at which data is 'keyboarded' from the input sheets, but not yet submitted to the computer for validation, a similar proofreading of the keyboard output would be required. In what respect, and to what extent, can we relax these standards—in effect, place our trust in those applied by indexer and data entry operator respectively—without serious detriment to the performance of the database?

This question emphasises the need to train and encourage indexers and data entry operators to recognise and follow conventions. Although it may seem easier and more economical to simply correct errors when we notice them, time spent in discussion with their originators is an investment not a loss, even if it only imparts our concern for correctness.

The extent to which the computer can relieve us of our responsibility for maintaining data standards is related to the type of data being processed. The data with which we deal is of two types: control data, and data which varies from entry to entry, that is the actual descriptions of individual documents.

3.1 Control data

'Control' data is exemplified by the tags that identify fields within each entry, and the symbols that delimit them (mark their beginnings and ends). There can be no compromise with this type of data; it must be present and correct for the database to work effectively. Fortunately, since by its nature it is directed to the functioning of computer programs, it is well-suited to mechanised checking. However, as I will show later in this chapter, there are clear limits to the extent to which such checking relieves us of our editorial function, and vigilance when input is being prepared is always justified.

3.2 Variable data

However the bulk of the data with which we deal is information relating specifically to particular documents, that is variable data. In dealing with this data we should firstly aim at reducing the actual size of entries. Every character that is proposed for entry will need to be written, checked, keyboarded, processed, stored, and made available for retrieval; every character thus has a cost which must be justified by its value to the user. Secondly, we must ask how rigidly we need to apply high standards of adherence to convention and general correctness to individual elements.

As I have implied above, the yardstick is the extent of success in serving the users of the database. Users, we assume, approach a database with some general expectations of its coverage, but with little or no privileged foreknowledge of the details of its contents. As entries are presented to them in response to suitably formulated queries, users judge entries by the extent to which the corresponding documents are likely to meet their needs. Of those entries that satisfy this criterion, they make copies in some form, which are presented to a library, in the expectation that the corresponding documents will be found and delivered within an acceptable time.

From our particular point of view, the characteristics of each of these stages are:

a. At the *search* stage, users have no choice but to put their trust in the database and its attendant systems. Since most retrieval systems still depend at some stage on literal mechanical matching of strings of characters, even small, forgiveable, and easily overlooked typographical errors can result in failure to retrieve references that would otherwise satisfy the terms of a request. These failures are also potentially irrevocable, in that users are unaware that relevant information exists in the field. Thus, elements that are intended primarily as search terms (such as subject descriptors and classification symbols) must be the subject of careful, detailed checking and editing; and moreover should not contain abbreviations or compressions, unless they are rigidly controlled in a way that is accessible to users.

b. At the stage of *relevance judgement* by contrast, users have the opportunity, and the materials, for intelligent coordination and interpretation, both between entries and between elements within entries. Since they are reading data in context, they can allow for obvious typographical errors and expand meaningful abbreviations and compressions. Editing of elements intended mainly for this purpose can legitimately be more relaxed, with emphasis on brevity (that is, economy) rather than on correctness rigidly applied.

   The difficulty here is in determining which elements are designed simply for this purpose. Any suggestions I make will be controversial as a general statement, for it is a characteristic advantage of a bibliographic database that any element is a candidate for searching; moreover, databases differ in respect of the cues that might be useful for document identification.

However, the type of data I have in mind is descriptive data such as abstracts; author affiliations; non-bibliographic details, for example of conferences; and general explanatory notes relating to the form and origin of documents. In my judgement, this type of data should be treated as optional for inclusion (whole classes of documents can be defined for which abstracts are redundant, for instance); and if included should be edited with a view to brevity and to avoiding duplication of information given by any other element.

c. At the *document location* stage, a situation roughly intermediate between the first two stages confronts us. As in the relevance judgement stage, the participants have before them the entire context of the entry; but as in the search stage, the detailed content of any particular reference will usually be unpredicted (that is, the library will not know in advance that retrievals from a particular database will refer to a particular book or journal issue).

If we take citations as the paradigm of this kind of data, clearly any numerical matter—volume and issue numbers, for example—must be carefully checked. Policies as regards the treatment of textual data—monograph or series titles, for example—are less well agreed upon. Notwithstanding the existence of proposed standard lists of abbreviations, either of whole titles or of words that occur within them, my own experience supports a recommendation that document and series titles should be presented to the user in full. Again, however, since they are intended to be read in context, it is not necessary to guard too conscientiously against an occasional typographical error. (These recommendations, incidentally, are not in conflict; the more context that is provided, the less important a minor typographical slip is likely to be).

If most entries relate to items from serial issues, one can attempt to have the best of both worlds by representing series-titles by unique mnemonic codes (analagous, say, to CODENs). The computer can then be programmed to expand the codes into full titles from a stored authority list. The effect is to economise on input and storage costs while still presenting users (and their librarians) with unequivocal references at the output stage. A system such as this, however, requires careful editorial attention, since it is always possible for a typographical error to result in a valid but erroneous code being entered, making the resultant references quite incomprehensible.

3.3 Computerised checking

It is common to include in the database production system a sequence in which data presented to the computer is automatically compared with stored specifications before being accepted as part of the database file. Such a sequence is virtually mandatory for what I have referred to earlier as 'control' data, simply because errors of this kind have the capacity to degrade the operation of the database as a whole. However, with some limitations, it can also be applied to the informative data in each entry.

With control data, typically each entry is examined to ensure that at least a minimum of designated mandatory fields is present, and that each is occupied and suitably delimited. This can be elaborated, just to give one example, so that different standards are applied to entries referring to monographs and serial items respectively.

Similarly, automated checking of the content of fields can vary from simply checking that they meet some simple condition (for example that all characters are alphabetic), through comparing them to entries in a glossary of acceptable terms (for example an authority file of classification codes), to demanding quite complex structures involving text, spacings and punctuation (for example that the contents of an author field must be in the general form 'Author, A. J.').

There is quite clearly much more to be said on this topic, but all I wish to do here is to point out that while this form of checking is a most useful aid, it does not take the place of careful initial editing.

The reason is that the detection of an error at these stages can result in no more than a 'report' setting out the error detected and the entry in which it occurs. In other words, the entries involved are simply returned for further editing (which is why it is inaccurate to call these subsystems 'editing' or 'validation' programs—they are simply error detection systems). Depending on the nature of the errors detected, what is required of the editor may range from correcting a simple typographical slip to finding and consulting the original document to supply missing data.

Wherever in this range a particular case may fall, there is always some degree of double handling of the entry; and therefore of potentially avoidable effort and cost. In this, as in much else, it is best to 'get it right first time'.

FURTHER READING

Dierickx, H. and Hopkinson, A. (Eds.) 1981. *Reference manual for machine-readable bibliographic descriptions.* (Unisist International Centre for Bibliographic Descriptions). Second rev. edition. Paris, UNESCO.

[various authors]. 1966-1969. Articles entitled 'Content analysis, specification and control'. *Annual Review of Information Science and Technology,* 1-4.

[various authors]. 1970-1974. Articles entitled 'Document description and representation'. *Annual Review of Information Science and Technology,* 5-9

9. Subject control

Brenda Gerrie

1. Introduction
2. Terminology
3. Current issues in subject control
4. The power of online retrieval
5. The role of a controlled vocabulary
6. Vocabulary control in a total system
7. Recall devices
   7.1 Synonym control
   7.2 Control of wordforms
   7.3 Hierarchical term linkage
   7.4 Summation of document sets
   7.5 Other devices
8. Precision devices
   8.1 Logic devices
   8.2 Syntactic devices
   8.3 Weighting devices
9. Design of a total system
10. Conclusion
References

1. INTRODUCTION

It is a reasonable assumption that a viable database will identify a significant body of information, that some attempt will be made to analyse the information sources to display content, and that information retrieval from the file will be possible by means of online, interactive software (for example STAIRS, DIALOG, ORBIT). The fundamental objective in the design of any database is to store the *maximum* amount of information in the *minimum* of storage. The difficulties which persist in information retrieval are associated with information indexing and the meaning of terms—an

SMALL SCALE DATABASES
ISBN 0 12 391970 3

ongoing issue, rekindled more than two decades ago by Maron and Kuhns (1960), that centres upon how best to identify and reveal the contents of documents. Indexing decisions are no less important in a small scale database environment because small databases may eventually grow to be large databases and poorly conceived design decisions may be magnified many times over by the sheer number of records involved.

Indexing decisions relate closely to the way in which a conventional information retrieval system operates. In such a system descriptions of sources of information are analysed and indexed during the process of creating a record to represent (and describe) that source of information in a database file. Later a client expresses a need which in its turn is analysed, and a strategy for retrieving the required information prepared. The retrieved records either represent the information required or point to the source of potentially useful information. These activities are depicted in Fig. 9.1 and are representative of a range of retrieval systems and databases. Whether the database describes documents, institutions that offer particular services or the characteristics of eucalypt trees, the choice of vocabulary used in the description and indexing of each record is central to the retrieval process because it determines what information is retrieved. The vocabulary may be derived originally from the text of the information sources, may influence clients to express a need in what they perceive to be 'the language of the system', and may influence the construction of a search strategy and affect the search and retrieval process in many subtle ways.

Bibliographic databases are by far the most common databases currently in wide use. In Australia AUSINET (operated by ACI Computer Services) makes available close to half a million records of Australian origin in 24 files that provide a range of information from research into ant populations to statistics on national income and expenditure in Australia (ACI Computer Services, 1984). I would estimate, based on Williams (1980), that there are upwards of 500 publically available machine readable databases with in excess of 140 million bibliographic records available online through various services in North America, Europe and Australia. These databases can be interrogated interactively online and are often used to produce printed products (indexes and catalogues). For this reason the following discussion on subject control and subject access to databases draws upon bibliographic type examples but the principles apply equally to other kinds of textual information files.

2. TERMINOLOGY

The terminology associated with computer-based retrieval systems is new and is still changing. The choice of *indexing system* is a key decision in the

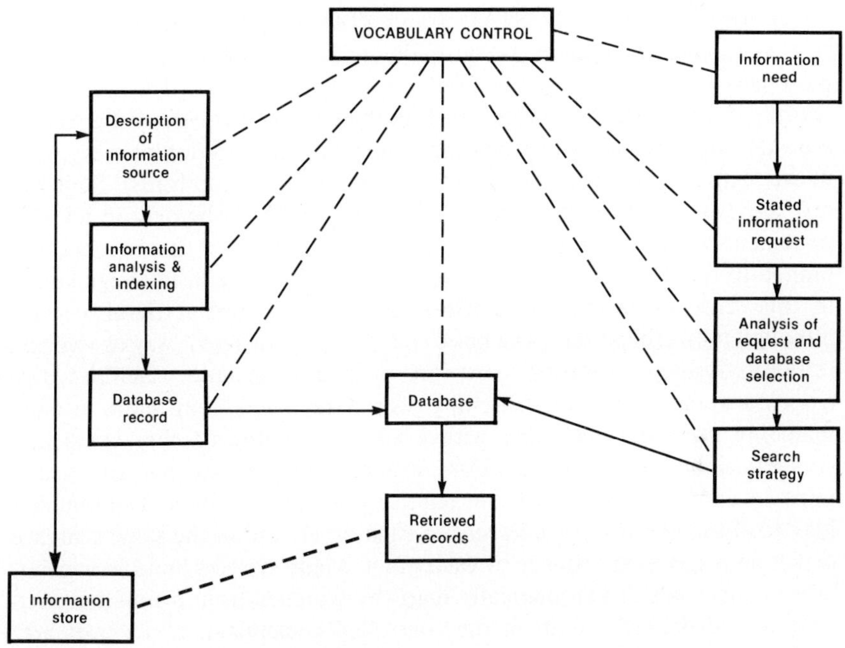

Fig. 9.1 An information retrieval system.

database design process. The indexing processes form a part of indexing systems, and these encompass the process of document analysis (deciding what a document is about), and concept manipulation and indexing (deciding how best to express the document's subjects). The indexing system may utilize an indexing model (that indicates the syntax or grammar and the amount of coordination of concepts and an accompanying *vocabulary or index language* that indicates semantic relations established as broader, narrower, and related terms). *Index terms* are derived from this model according to certain rules pertaining to the use of that vocabulary and in concert with an indexing policy (that relates to the extent of document analysis). In the broadest sense the index language from which the index terms are derived may be the natural or free text of the document itself, a prescribed list of subject headings, a thesaurus, or even a coded language or classification scheme. The index terms can be *descriptors* (that is terms actually assigned to a document); *identifiers* (that is free form terms, usually proper names, geographic names, acronyms and so on); *subject headings* (usually terms assigned to books in a manual system); and *classification or category numbers* (coded terms which group like subject together for shelf arrangement or some other collocating retrieval purpose).

Retrieval software like STAIRS and STATUS, are often referred to as *free text retrieval systems* because the initial design of these software packages was based upon the need for retrieval of text. The significant feature, in general terms, is that words in the searchable fields of the records are automatically indexed so that the occurrence and position of every word in the text is recorded (possibly with the exclusion of stopwords). So a free text retrieval software may enable *full text searching* when entire texts of documents are stored in a database file. The main point is that access is not limited to the database fields to which index terms have been assigned and in this sense DIALOG and ORBIT are also free text retrieval systems although they achieve the same basic end in quite a different way to free text retrieval systems. Retrieval software normally includes facilities like *truncation* (a device for searching word fragments, but more usually matching all terms beginning with a specified string of characters) and *contextual* or *proximity* operators which enable a searcher to specify retrieval conditions based on the relative position of words. The searcher may wish the words to be adjacent to each other, within the same sentence or within a specified distance of each other. Many systems build in vocabulary linkages which automatically map the searcher from a non-preferred term to the preferred term in the controlled vocabulary, or an '*explode*' facility which enables a group of related search terms to be searched automatically, provided their relationship is expressed in the controlled vocabulary through the narrower term relationship.

3. CURRENT ISSUES IN SUBJECT CONTROL

The longstanding methods of subject control of information in a library context have been to arrange the physical documents sytematically by subject classification number. This broad arrangement of documents by subject facilitates browsing but probably lacks pinpointing capabilities for specific subjects and scatters topics covered from different points of view through the collection. Access to specific subjects is usually provided through an alphabetical, specific subject catalogue, the prescribed headings chosen by indexers from a subject heading list or thesaurus. Specific access is limited to the major topics in each document and, apart from economic considerations, the primary concerns are how specific should a subject heading be and what linkages are necessary between and among headings to house and maintain an organised store of information? In an environment like this, the inventory purpose is paramount and rules for specific entry, word order and subject subdivision are geared to the collection of related material.

But the anomolies in authorities such as the LCSH attest to the impossibility of keeping subjects together, systematically over time. Allen (1981) is one of many practitioners who have devised methods of indexing that espouse the importance of content analysis and information access. Allen's five basic principles are: use of natural language as far as an order of terms is concerned; use of multiple entry; use of precoordinate terms only when the size of the file warrants it; use of single concepts on the whole; and limited use of subdivision of subjects. The stimulus to provide more information access has largely come from the development of online, interactive information retrieval. Just as these systems have provided new approaches to subject searching, there is a growing feeling that new approaches to indexing are also required (Atherton, 1978; Allen 1981; Schabas, 1982). Specificity of subject headings and linkages between headings are still important in computer-based retrieval systems because the ability to pinpoint specific information is as important as the ability to relate or associate information that may be relevant to the same request. But the approach to indexing can be quite different. Firstly, automated systems are more hospitable to more exhaustive indexing since the addition of further index terms to a record makes only a marginal difference to storage and manipulation costs (this is Allen's principle of multiple entry). Secondly, the collocation purpose can be de-emphasised in favour of more natural language indexing that is expressive and useful for interactive retrieval. Thirdly, software facilities like truncation, proximity or contextual operators, mapping and explosion facilities for linkages can be used effectively by a searcher to define search requirements, make linkages between subjects and compensate generally for a lack of prior control over the vocabulary.

In designing a database, and in particular in choosing an indexing system (encompassing the indexing model, the language and the policy) one must not only look ahead to the retrieval requirements and the information need but also take into account the retrieval capabilities of the software. In fact Svenonius (1981) asks the question—why develop indexing techniques at all—would it not be better to develop search strategies to be used at the time of retrieval?

4. THE POWER OF ONLINE RETRIEVAL

By means of retrieval software facilities a searcher can orchestrate a search and in a sense control the vocabulary of a database in ways that are not possible manually. The power of retrieval software must be considered during the database design phase, and further, database indexers must have knowledge of information retrieval systems to index effectively.

The power of online retrieval can be demonstrated by considering, a straight forward example of a search protocol, SEARCH CHILD$3, which may mean retrieve all records in the database in which the word root 'child' and up to three following characters occurs. In a free text environment in which words have been indexed discretely by the machine this protocol may retrieve records containing free text segments in which the root 'child' forms a part, as well as records containing index terms assigned from a controlled vocabulary and of which the root 'child' forms a part. Retrieval of records would result where there is a match on: text words (usually from titles and abstracts) like '. . . the individual child's basic rights. . .'; index terms which contain the *word* CHILD like CHILD ABUSE, CHILD REARING; index terms which contain the *root* child and no more than three characters following that root, for example CHILDREN but not CHILDHOOD; and all the more specific phrases to which either of the above conditions pertain like ADOPTED CHILDREN, MIGRANT CHILDREN, ABUSED CHILDREN.

In this kind of environment it may be less critical for a searcher to know the circumstances under which an indexer may assign a heading CHILD ABUSE in preference to ABUSED CHILDREN (because the illustrated protocol would match on both). It is important for the searcher to know the form of headings, for example that CHILDCARE is entered in the database as one word in preference to two words (because the illustrated search protocol would not match on CHILDCARE). Clearly a searcher can, through the retrieval system, exercise powerful post-control over the vocabulary of the system.

5. THE ROLE OF A CONTROLLED VOCABULARY

What then is the role of a controlled vocabulary in a computer-based environment? Lancaster (1972; 1979) has written excellent texts on the subject and justifies the need for some kind of controlled vocabulary on the basis that it facilitates communication between searcher and system. By using a controlled vocabulary indexers and searchers are able to represent subject matter consistently because the vocabulary, through its content, structure and organisation, is a retrieval tool in its own right from which index terms and search terms can be selected.

A vocabulary attempts to avoid dispersing like subjects and collocation of unlike subjects through normalisation, synonym and near synonym control and homograph control. In principle, and in order to achieve these kinds of controls a single term is preferred and 'see' or 'use' references made from the non-preferred terms to assist with a manual search through a print-on-paper product. Online, the retrieval software may automatically map a searcher from a non-preferred term to the preferred.

Whether the mode of access to the database is online interactive search or manual search through a printed product the decision as to which term to prefer can be a difficult one. The decision not only relates to the principles of vocabulary control in relation to terms warranted by the literature and the user but also to the mode of access. Filing and collocation are primary considerations in planning a printed product and formulation of a search statement is a basic consideration in an online search. In reality one author's choice may not be another's choice. Standardised terminology in existing vocabularies may go against conventional preferences because indexers are often forced to make decisions about a developing literature before the terminology settles down, and there may be good reason why the term prevailing in the literature is not the best index term.

For example, which of the terms STRIKES and INDUSTRIAL DISPUTES might be preferred with regard to synonym/homograph control? STRIKES may appear to be the prevailing term in the literature and therefore a user's choice but it is a homograph (military strikes, baseball strikes, industrial strikes). On the other hand, choosing the term INDUSTRIAL DISPUTES has a far-reaching policy decision in that it is an umbrella term for specific subjects like STRIKES, LOCKOUTS, SIT-INS, to which specific access may well be lost. Far better to qualify the specific term by choosing to use either INDUSTRIAL STRIKES or STRIKES (INDUSTRIAL). In an online information retrieval environment the difference between the terms would be reflected in the way the search statement is formulated and would favour natural language. Of course in a printed product the position of entries allocated the chosen heading, relative to other entries, is affected and the issue of filing and collocation must be considered. Collocation on the word STRIKES would serve no useful purpose.

A controlled vocabulary through its structure links semantically related terms in order to facilitate the conduct of comprehensive searchers and spares searchers having to draw all the related terms from their own heads. Broader/narrower term relations like the relationship between PARASITES and LIVER FLUKE are straight forward. But it is a considerable and demanding task to identify and record the variety of other relationships in a systematic way. For example the relationships between TEACHER and EDUCATION, COPPER and PIPES, EARS and HEARING, FACTOR ANALYSIS and CORRELATION, and DEATH and PROBATE may not be readily identified as instrumentality, material, utilisation, explanation, and cause and effect respectively. In any case what does it matter? Are not these relationships best identified during query analysis as a part of the problem solving activity?

A controlled vocabulary, by its very existence can create problems.

When it lacks specificity a searcher limited to using the vocabulary cannot separate a specific subject from its broader subject (differentiating between INDUSTRIAL DISPUTES, STRIKES and LOCKOUTS). An indexer may also be at a loss as to how to index a specific subject not represented in the controlled vocabulary. When the vocabulary lacks adequate structure and linkages between related terms, indexers and searchers may both overlook suitable terms particularly if they become 'switched off' to the need to consider candidate terms not listed in a controlled vocabulary. At the other end of the spectrum there may be no controlled vocabulary in an information retrieval system and the natural language of a title and/or abstract identify and reveal subject content. Without a controlled vocabulary to indicate preferred terms and wordforms there may be subject scattering and inconsistency in the way subjects are identified. As a consequence, searchers must think of all possible synonymous words and expressions if they wish to locate all possible information on a topic.

In summary the arguments for a controlled vocabulary are:

a. The cost of information input may be high because of the intellectual effort expended on indexing, but storage costs may be minimised because of the high concentration of information through the vocabulary.
b. A controlled vocabulary means that like subjects are brought together and separated from unlike subjects for the purposes of retrieval of sets of information from the database file.
c. Comprehensive searches are facilitated when a controlled vocabulary properly identifies broader/narrower/related term relationships.

Using a controlled vocabulary for indexing and searching, by definition means that the language is restricted and is not fully specific.

On the other hand an 'indexing free' natural language representation means:

a. The language is completely specific to the content of the database record.
b. Input costs may well be less than would be the case if assigned, intellectual indexing using a controlled vocabulary is performed.
c. Storage costs may be high because of the need to store significant portions of text for retrieval purposes.
d. The burden of information analysis shifts to the searcher who must consider all the natural language possibilities of expression to begin to get comprehensive retrieval.
e. A search strategy based on natural language terms is more readily transferred to another database of a similar ilk.
f. In a natural language environment a *subject specialist* requesting the minimum of information to solve a problem may feel more comfortable.

g. The *information specialist* wishing to exploit the database to produce printed products tailored to suit particular purposes has to face problems of arrangement and determination of suitable sort keys for each record, and in effect 'index' the database.

But of course in a computer-based environment we need not have an either/or situation and in a well designed retrieval system in which the database structure and content marries well with the retrieval software the free text and controlled vocabulary components of a logical record complement each other for retrieval purposes.

One way to test a good design that integrates database and software is to note the extent to which the *maximum information* occupies the *minimum storage space* for each logical record of a database designed for free text retrieval of information. For example a text entitled *Snakes and Lizards of Australia* could be assigned the subject headings SNAKES–AUSTRALIA–IDENTIFICATION and LIZARDS–AUSTRALIA–IDENTIFICATION following the LCSH model. This being so, then the fundamental axiom to store maximum information in the minimum of storage has not been followed. The sway of the argument that such headings are necessary to systematically arrange a printed product or to define a search (by limiting retrieval to subject heading fields) is closely tied to the number of records in the database on that subject.

6. VOCABULARY CONTROL IN A TOTAL SYSTEM

A significant body of information not readily accessible, and a clearly defined clientele wishing to make use of this information are the basic prerequisites for a viable database. But it is unlikely that a single 'best' method of indexing could serve the variety of retrieval purposes and information services required from that database. The mode of information access—either search and retrieve online interactively or manually by scanning a print-on-paper product—require different approaches to indexing and vocabulary control considerations.

Firstly, for online interactive retrieval accessible information must be machine indexed otherwise real time responses cannot be achieved and the interactive capability is lost. Currently operating retrieval software relies on automatically indexing the contents of database records (in their entirety or in part, into a single file or series of files).

In this regard, there is a requirement for a natural language component of each record which is expressive of the document's content and useful for retrieval. The title should be expressive of the overall document's content and if the title is lacking it can be enriched by the addition of free form identifiers assigned to the record from the document text. If storage costs permit, informative abstracts should be included, so that a basic principle of including the maximum information in the minimum of storage space is followed.

The retrieval software that offers online interactive capabilities will undoubtedly offer truncation, mapping, explosion, back-referencing and other facilities. Such facilities can be routinely used by an experienced searcher to exercise vocabulary control at the point of the search, thus providing the flexibility to tailor a search to a particular information need.

Finally, for all practical purposes, it may still be necessary to consider using a controlled vocabulary to index the major concepts in each document so that the information is logically grouped into a variety of subject sets to provide:

i. A capability for retrieval of significant portions of the database and comprehensive search.
ii. A capability to produce systematically arranged print-on-paper products as alternative forms of information dissemination.

The development of a set of subject categorisation and indexing guidelines are essential particularly when the activities associated with the preparation of database input records and subject analysis are decentralised. The input manuals prepared by the National Library of Medicine (1983) for the Medlars database, and the Food and Agriculture Organisation of the United Nations (1979) for ASFIS are examples of sets of guidelines for the preparation of database input that take account of an online interactive retrieval environment. These guidelines relate most closely to the exhaustivity of indexing—the nature and number of index terms intellectually assigned to each item in the database. The major concerns are the depth to which the content of an information source is revealed (related to what terms are chosen and the number of index terms assigned to each record) and the manner in which a record is integrated into a collection of other records (related to what terms are chosen and the number of records associated with each term). There are no definitive answers to the questions—what is the optimum number of index terms to be assigned to each record? and what is the optimum number of records to be assigned to each index term?

The growth of online information retrieval over the past decade has been substantial as evidenced by the growth in literature about the subject and reviewed by Hall and Dewe (1980) and Hawkins (1981). Collier (1978) and Kent (1978) are but two authors who discuss the diminishing importance of derived database products. There is a range of information sources rich in examples of search strategies published in the journal literature, particulary *Online* and *Online Review.* Texts like *Online Searching* (Henry *et al.*, 1980) and *Online searching: a primer* (Fenichel and Hogan, 1981) are but two examples that cover the protocols and mechanisms of online searching. The designer of a database ought to be familiar with this literature and the implications of online retrieval discussed by Gerrie (1983) in order to properly relate the choice of an indexing (and searching) vocabulary and the method of indexing to the anticipated retrieval requirements.

The environment in which information retrieval online interactively is performed is determined to a large extent by the retrieval software. Basically, when developing search tactics a searcher is either attempting to retrieve wanted information—possibly more information—by expanding a search or attempting to exclude unwanted information by refining a search. Retrieval software has various recall and precision devices for achieving these ends.

7. RECALL DEVICES

Recall devices are used to increase the number of relevant documents in the retrieval set and there are many different devices that may be available through the retrieval software to improve recall, and each device can be implemented in several different ways. The four recall devices most common to conventional retrieval systems are synonym control, control of wordforms, hierarchical term linkage, and the summation of document sets.

7.1 Synonym control

When synonyms are controlled at the point of indexing the searcher may have to identify the preferred term for use in a search by consulting the controlled vocabulary. When some kind of mapping facility is available through the retrieval software a searcher may successfully use a non-preferred term for which the software automatically substitutes the preferred term during retrieval. In either case the controlled vocabulary may restrict the searcher when terms which are not truly synonymous are treated as such (for example a thesaurus may direct an indexer to use INFORMATION STORAGE instead of the term FILING SYSTEMS) leading to a possible loss of discrimination between like terms. An alternative is to input terms as authors have used them and define equivalence relationships to suit a particular user group. Software packages usually have some facility for this: STATUS (Croall, 1977) has a macrologic; STAIRS (ACI Computer Services, 1980) has the SYN operator; other software may have a SAVE SEARCH (DIALOG for example) facility. This throws responsibility for considering synonyms onto the searcher but at least equivalence relationship can be defined to suit a particular group of users.

7.2 Control of wordforms

Normalisation of words (choosing to use the term IMPEDANCE not IMPEDING or IMPEDE) on input can be determined by the controlled vocabulary or automatically by means of a computer algorithm which reduces various words to a single morphological form (for example MORPHOLOGICAL and MORPHOLOGY can be reduced to the root MORPHOLOG). This is known as conflation of wordforms. If these kinds of normalisation are performed on input there may be a loss in meaning and the searcher has no flexibility to distinguish between words such as LEGISLATION and LEGISLATORS. Confounding wordforms by means of suffix truncation at the point of the search is more usual in conventional systems and provides the flexibility to distinguish different meanings in different wordforms. String searching which can be thought of as a truncation device to match strings of characters is a feature of ORBIT and ELHILL and operates in a different way. Truncation involves locating index terms in the inverted file which match a stem whereas string searching enables a search of a sequential printfile for a specified character string in a subset of a file. String search initiates a sequential search of a small subset of a large database file that is selected according to some earlier search strategy and is normally used as a precision device because of this subsearch quality.

7.3 Hierarchical term linkage

Normally a document's specific subjects are identified in indexing. A searcher wishing to generically survey a database for information may find facilities for linking hierarchically related terms useful. ELHILL provides the facility to automatically match generically related search items taken from the controlled vocabulary using an explosion facility. A searcher need not know the exact relationships that have been established in the controlled vocabulary nor know what the narrower terms are. The convenience of this facility can be offset by the automatic inclusion of undesirable terms in a search strategy. Deficiencies in the structure of a controlled vocabulary are carried through to the search stage and selective explosion is generally impossible.

7.4 Summation of document sets

The facilities discussed so far involve some form of linkage of terms which, for retrieval purposes, can be considered equivalent or substitutable in a search. The explicit summation of document sets using Boolean 'OR' logic is the most common recall device in conventional systems. There is another useful logic facility, 'OR NOT' described by Martinez and Zarember (1975). OR NOT is explained in terms of Venn diagrams in Fig. 9.2. Under certain circumstances the logical expression A AND B may be too constraining in that not all wanted documents explicitly contain B. Recall can be improved by identifying alternatives to B, for example A AND (B OR D OR E). Another option is to identify some undesirable concept C. The search strategy A AND NOT C may eliminate unwanted documents as well as some wanted documents which contain both A AND B. The compromise is (A AND B) OR (A AND NOT C) which takes account of those documents containing A and explicitly mentioning B whilst rejecting documents explicitly mentioning C. This composite expression is equivalent to (A AND B) OR NOT C and represents a broader search strategy than A AND B and a narrower strategy than a simple search for A.

7.5 Other devices

Other recall devices such as weighted retrieval and quorum logic (Gerrie, 1983) are being studied but are not as yet in evidence in conventional retrieval systems. They do hold promise for qualitative retrieval (weighting in order to rank output in an order of preference) and for brevity of expression of a retrieval condition (quorum logic makes use of the logical construct 'x out of n' instead of having to express all the possible permutations of logic).

8. PRECISION DEVICES

Precision devices are used to limit the number of retrievals and involves coordination and linkage of information at various stages of the document indexing, search and retrieval process. The distinction normally made between postcoordinate and precoordinate indexing becomes blurred, particularly in an online environment which provides capabilities for a variety of linkage, and precoordinate index languages may be broken down for postcoordinate retrieval. Possibly a better approach is to view precision devices as either logic devices, syntactic devices, or weighting devices. A fourth approach is bibliographic coupling which takes advantage of similarities between document bibliographies in the retrieval process.

8.1 Logic devices

Logic devices include Boolean operators like AND, and AND NOT. Contextual logic is a simple extension of Boolean logic and takes account of positional information in the retrieval process in order to increase the

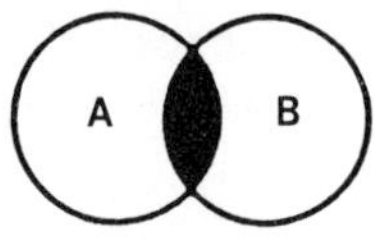

(i) A AND B

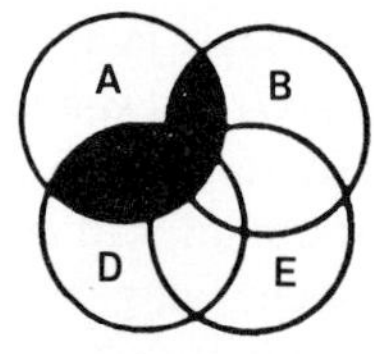

(ii) A AND (B OR D OR E)

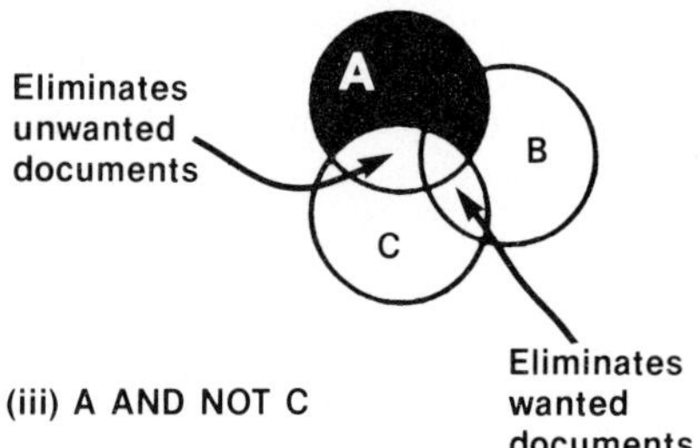

(iii) A AND NOT C

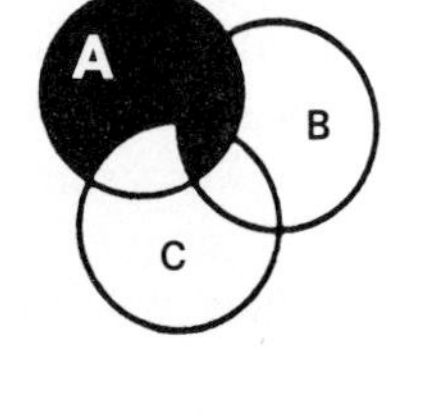

(iv) (A AND B) or (A AND NOT C)
≡ (A AND B) OR NOT C

Fig. 9.2 An illustration of 'OR NOT' logic as a recall device.

strength of association between terms and hence the precision of a search. Quorum logic is not normally a feature of conventional IR systems, but experimentally the method holds promise in the ease with which a search strategy can be reformulated simply by adjusting the values of 'x of n', to further refine a search.

8.2 Syntactic devices

Both links and roles are applied at the point of indexing in indexing systems like PRECIS (Austin, 1974) but are not normally exploited online interactively. This could be because interest in links and roles as precison devices which eliminate false coordination has waned over the years as other means of avoiding the problem existed. Systems which use precombined index terms or headings/subheading combinations are more attractive than uniterm systems when these index terms are used to systematically arrange entries in printed products. The advantages of uniterm systems are achieved if the text is processed into a single concordance or inverted file. The earlier example which used the construct CHILD$3 illustrated the power of online retrieval. But the advantages of both precoordinate and postcoordinate systems are combined in conventional online systems like DIALOG by means of double postings in the inverted index, so the phrases can be matched as phrases and single word components of the phrase are also accessible.

8.3 Weighting devices

In conventional systems weighting is normally achieved at the point of indexing when an indexer separately identifies major and minor concepts in a document. Weighting at the point of a search is normally provided by qualifying a search term in various ways, for example:

- The construct SEARCH PENICILLIN may retrieve all documents in which the word occurs be it in a title, an abstract or in an index term.
- The construct SEARCH PENICILLIN/DE may retrieve the subset of documents in which the word PENICILLIN occurs as an index term or descriptor of *part* of an index term or descriptor.
- The construct SEARCH *PENCILLIN/DE may retrieve an even narrower subset of those documents in which PENICILLIN occurs as an index term or part of an index term but only in a major concept (flagged by an asterisk*) in a document.

This kind of weighting does not allow a searcher to express an interest in some term A over term B for reasons not connected with the use of the terms in the set of documents. SIRE (Noreault *et al.*, 1977) is one example of an experimental system that has been developed to provide this kind of flexibility in retrievals of continuous sets of documents according to an explicit rank order determined by the searcher (weighting at the point of retrieval).

System-orientated weighting as exemplified in EUREKA (Burket *et al.*, 1979) is also an experimental technique in which the weights rather than being oriented towards the relative importance of terms in a document or terms in a search, take account of the distribution of terms in a document collection (weighting at the point when the document enters the system).

9. DESIGN OF A TOTAL SYSTEM

The available range of recall and precision devices in an online, interactive retrieval environment shows how a searcher can compensate for a lack of prior control over a vocabulary. It also lends support to Svenonius' argument (1981) that it may be more fruitful to develop search strategies than to develop new indexing techniques.

There is one more point to consider in relation to vocabulary control in a computer-based information retrieval system. Every person who has searched online will have noticed spelling errors, the variant wordforms and the 'junky' index terms associated with many databases. The inverted indexes and word dictionaries used online give spelling errors a high visibility which they would not otherwise have. On the other hand, in a manual search the human eye compensates for and even overlooks error in a way that cannot, as yet, be emulated by machine. These variations which may matter little on the printed page can lead to blind failure in a conventional computer-based retrieval system. And so, quality control in the most basic sense is very important in a computer-based system.

How then does the designer of a database relate the choice of vocabulary and the indexing to the database's intended use? Unfortunately there is no recipe for success; database design is a complex activity in which the combined effects on retrieval of the form of presentation of input data, construction of searchable indexes and query language protocols must be examined. The following worked sample illustrates the combined effect of input, construction of searchable indexes and query language protocols on the design of a database.

For simplicity consider *one* protocol that is not supposed to be indicative of any particular system. The protocol uses a 'search' command, AND, OR, AND NOT Boolean logic, and NEXT indicates an adjacency relationship (contextual logic). Consider also two different approaches to the construction of searchable index.

In System A the index to the database comprises single words arranged in a single alphabetical index or concordance. A word is defined as a string of characters surrounded by punctuation marks or spaces, and stopwords are removed.

In System B there is a basic alphabetical index of terms which are double posted, so that a phrase AB is entered in the index three times as the phrase AB, and the word A and the word B. There are separate author indexes and title word indexes.

a. The input data ON-LINE can be handled in system A in one of two ways. Either the data is handled as one word and an exception is made of embedded hyphens when the searchable index is constructed. The retrieval protocol would be straightforward and identical in consequence to system B: SEARCH ON-LINE.

   But, if the word is broken down in system A (by virtue of the hyphen) the successful retrieval protocol no longer represents the input data: SEARCH ON LINE.

   Worse, suppose the word is not only broken down but stopwords are removed, then the retrieval protocol is ridiculous and there is a serious information loss because the concept 'off-line' cannot be distinguished from the concept 'on-line' because the only possible and successful search strategy would retrieve both concepts: SEARCH LINE.

b. The subject data TELEVISION AND VIOLENCE will be broken down in system A and the stopword 'AND' likely removed. This means that the retrieval protocol: SEARCH TELEVISION AND VIOLENCE which appears to match the subject heading in fact invokes the logical AND will retrieve documents in which both terms occur with a high probability that they will be unrelated. In system B the subject heading will remain intact and retrieval based on multiword index terms and is very straightforward, except that in this case the grammatical 'AND' would likely have to be distinguished from the logical 'AND' by, say, a single character mark. Thus: SEARCH TELEVISION A#D VIOLENCE.

c. The subject term that uses punctuation, for example CHILDREN, DELINQUENT is handled in system A by simply using connective logic: SEARCH CHILDREN NEXT DELINQUENT.

   Whereas in system B the heading remains intact, but the searcher must *exactly* match the input with regard to punctuation and spacing for successful retrieval: SEARCH CHILDREN, DELINQUENT.

10. CONCLUSION

One can concoct an endless variety of examples which demonstrate the vagaries of online information retrieval. All such examples relate more to the input form and conversion through the searchable indexes, and all problems raised are solveable. The critical point is that the information content of each record be identified and revealed for accurate information retrieval. The computer-based environment offers variety in the range of available information retrieval controls. A hybrid system possibly offers maximum flexibility if:

i. A controlled vocabulary is used to identify primary or major concepts to satisfy the needs of information specialists for comprehensive search facilities in support of serious research and the need for systematic arrangement of printed products.

ii. A controlled vocabulary is used to systematically arrange printed products derived from the database.

iii. A range of post-control facilities is available to operate effectively on natural language in order to satisfy the information requirements of subject specialists who may require a *minimum* of information to solve given problems of such variety that the problems cannot be anticipated at the point when a database is created.

REFERENCES

ACI Computer Services. 1980. *BRS/STAIRS manual.* 2nd ed. Melbourne, ACI Computer Services.

ACI Computer Services. 1984. *Information Retrieval Systems Newsletter* No. 30.

Allen, L. 1981. Alphabetical subject access: LCSH and a non-traditional approach. *Cataloguing Australia* 7 (4): 32–41.

Angione, P. V. 1975. 'On the equivalence of Boolean and weighted searching based on the convertibility of query forms'. *Journal of the American Society for Information Science* 26(2): 112–24.

Atherton, P. 1978. 'Improving subject access to books in on-line library catalogs'. In *1st International on-line Information Meeting, London, 1977.* Oxford, Learned Information, pp.131–8.

Austin, D. 1974. *PRECIS: a manual of concept analysis and subject indexing.* Council of the British National Bibliography.

Burket, T. G., Emrath, P., and Kuck, D. J. 1979. 'The use of vocabulary files for on-line information retrieval'. *Information Processing and Management* 15 (6): 281–9.

Collier, H. R. 1978. 'Online retrieval demands on new generation of data-bases, but they will be slow in coming'. In *2nd International Online Information Meeting, London, 5–7, December, 1978.* Oxford, Learned Information, pp.13–18.

Croall, I. F. 1977. *An introduction to the STATUS II information retrieval system.* Version 2. Harwell, AERE, Computer Science and Systems Division.

Fenichel, C. H. and Hogan, T. H. 1981. *Online searching: a primer.* Oxford, Learned Information.

Food and Agriculture Organization of the United Nations. 1979. *Aquatic sciences and fisheries information system: subject categories and scope descriptions with guidelines.* ASFIS Reference series No. 215.

Gerrie, B. 1983. *Online information systems: use and operating characteristics, limitations and design alternatives.* Arlington, Va, Information Resources Press.

Hall, J. L. and Dewe, A. 1980. Online information retrieval, 1976–1979. (ASLIB Bibliography 10) ASLIB.

Hawkins, D. T. 1981. 'Online information retrieval systems'. In *Annual Review of Information Science and Technology* 16: 171–206.

Henry, W. M. 1980. *Online searching: an introduction.* London, Butterworths.

Kent, A. K. 1978. 'Dial-up and die: can information systems survive on-line age?' *Information Scientist* 12(1): 3–7.

Lancaster, F. W. 1972. *Vocabulary for information retrieval.* Arlington, Va, Information Resources Press.

Lancaster, F. W. 1979. *Information retrieval system: characteristics, testing and evaluation.* 2nd ed. New York, Wiley.

Lockheed Information Retrieval System. 1980 (and updated) *Guide to DIALOG searching.* Lockheed Corporation.

Maron, M. E. and Kuhns, J. L. 1960. 'On relevance, probabilistic indexing and information retrieval'. *Journal of the ACM* 7(3): 216–44.

Martinez, C., and Zarember, I. 1975. 'OR NOT: the unused operator'. *Journal of the American Society for Information Science* 26(2): 112–124.

National Library of Medicine. *Medlars indexing manual parts I and II* (available NTIS PB254-270, PB 84-104280).

Noreault, T., Koll, M., and McGill, M. G. 1979. 'Automatic ranks output from Boolean searchers in SIRE'. *Journal of the American Society for Information Science* 28(6): 333–9.

Williams, M. E. 1980. 'Database and online statistics for 1979'. *ASIS Bulletin* 7(2): 27–9.

Schabas, A. H. 1982. 'Post coordinate retrieval: a comparison of two indexing languages'. *Journal of the American Society for Information Science* 33(1): 32–7.

Svenonius, E. 1981. Directions for research in indexing, classification, and cataloguing. *Library Resources and Technical Services* 25 (1): 88–103.

10. Document acquisition and selection criteria

Sherrey Quinn
Margaret A. Findlay

1. Introduction
2. Identification
3. Acquisition
   3.1 Legal deposit
   3.2 Coercion
   3.3 Gift
   3.4 Exchange
   3.5 Purchase
   3.6 Interlibrary loan
   3.7 Unobtainable documents
   3.8 Document 'surrogates'
   3.9 Problems
4. Selection
   4.1 Appropriateness of content/subject matter
   4.2 Types of document
   4.3 Quality of content
      4.3.1 Contribution to knowledge
      4.3.2 Relevance
      4.3.3 New application of knowledge
      4.3.4 Effectiveness of presentation
      4.3.5 Timeliness
      4.3.6 Authority of author, source, sponsor
      4.3.7 Audience
      4.3.8 Availability
5. Cooperative acquisition arrangements
6. Research in progress and directory information
7. Conclusion
References

SMALL SCALE DATABASES
ISBN 0 12 391970 3

1. INTRODUCTION

Databases vary in purpose and content. The aim may be to index documents in a defined subject area, imprints from a particular country or region, a particular form of publication or the contents of a particular collection; to document research in progress or produce a directory; or a combination of these objectives.

First principles of database creation and management require clearly defined and stated objectives. These will encompass the subject matter of the database, and the form, level and time-span of material to be included and/or excluded. Document coverage is the most important consideration of any database and results of searches will be affected by the source and scope of the documents selected. The value and strength of the file is in the continuous inclusion of documents which relate to, cover and reflect the objectives of the system. Criticisms of certain systems by users often reflect the lack of knowledge of the scope of documents intended to be captured for the file and it is the responsibility of the database producer to clearly define the document selection and acquisition criteria to the users.

The needs of the potential user groups or the market which the database is intended to serve should be considered and determined. Often the groups are varied and represent many different viewpoints. As examples, the groups can include:

- Policy-makers (legislators; institutional directors).
- Administrators (managers; principals; superintendents).
- Practitioners (engineers; chemists; teachers).
- Researchers.
- Librarians.
- Students (at all levels).

Within this framework potentially relevant documents or other material (for example directory information) must first be identified and acquired, then assessed according to the criteria for inclusion in the database. Well structured policies for these tasks are essential and should be clearly defined within the objectives of the system. The selection principles should serve as guidelines and relate the nature and scope of documents or information to the defined subject and users' needs and thus ensure stability and comprehensiveness in acquisition.

This chapter discusses the identification, acquisition and selection processes and these are illustrated in the flow chart in Fig. 10.1. The procedures for and problems encountered in identifying and acquiring research in progress or directory information are somewhat different from bibliographic documents and are therefore considered separately at the end of the chapter.

DATABASE OBJECTIVES

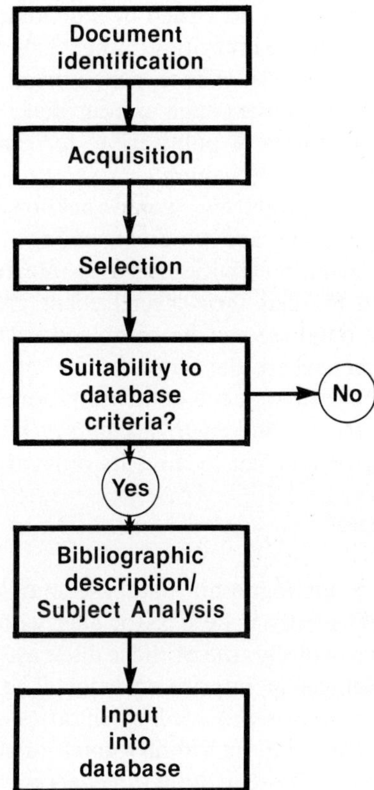

Fig. 10.1 Document acquisition and selection.

2. IDENTIFICATION

There are practical problems associated with identifying documents, and the methods used are those well-known to selection librarians. The amount of effort put into this activity will vary according to the type of database, but in general the task involves scanning journals, reviews, bibliographies, publishers' lists, press releases, conference programs, library accession bulletins, lists of reports issued by government and private enterprise bodies (sometimes available separately, sometimes incorporated in annual reports), and searching other databases in related or fringe subject areas. Indexers should also be alert to note relevant previously unknown items which are cited in material already selected.

Certain forms of publications are difficult to identify, particularly government reports which are issued by individual authorities or by consultants on behalf of those authorities, rather than through organised government publishing channels. Those government publishers who are well organised, or who document their output make the task of identification much easier. Other forms of publication, for example theses, may be easy to identify but difficult to acquire.

Most database producers would acknowledge that although the scanning task is tedious and time consuming it is most essential. Those whose database creation activities form an integral part of the information services provided to their own special client group are fortunate in that selection for the database can be combined with selection for the library collection. In cases where the scope of the database is broader than the subject scope of the library, the database producer must take care that his scanning is not merely limited to his library intake, or the database will become unbalanced and fail to meet its objectives.

3. ACQUISITION

A producer of a bibliographic database may compile and manage his database most efficiently if he is associated with a library or information service. This is particularly true of those database producers concerned with comprehensive subject or imprint coverage. The database producer needs access to all the services provided by libraries—procedures for ordering, accessioning and payment, interlibrary loans, directories and other reference materials, and so on. Those without direct access to this type of support will need to develop it, and will eventually build up library style services around themselves.

There are a number of means by which database producers may acquire documents: legal deposit, coercion, gift, exchange, purchase, and interlibrary loan.

3.1 Legal deposit

Database producers who enjoy legal deposit rights for published material are usually those charged with the responsibility of maintaining the national collection and compiling the national bibliography. Producers of specialist databases rarely obtain documents directly by legal deposit. However, the national bibliographies are useful to the small database producer as a means of checking his own coverage of published works; they are rarely current enough or specialised enough to be other than a backup selection tool. Most specialist database producers can identify and index relevant material in their special subject areas long before it appears in the national file.

3.2 'Coercion'

Coercion is perhaps the closest that a small scale database producer can get to legal deposit. It is most simply described as the administration insisting that reports or papers produced by the organisation (and its associates or member organisations) be deposited with the library or database production centre. A most important attribute of a database producing organisation is that it has its own publishing house in order. Coercion works best in small centralised organisations (Lay, 1979), and may be unsuccessful in larger, more decentralised organisations. The prudent database producer will monitor documents produced by his own organisation to ensure all are deposited.

3.3 Gift

Gift is an arrangement whereby the database producer is supplied with complimentary copies of publications, perhaps all publications or just those in certain subject areas. Ad hoc donations from interested individuals are also to be encouraged. Material from many organisations is free; the database producer should take the initative and request it. Database producers should not forget the 'old boy network' as a means of acquiring documents. They should take advantage not only of their own personal contacts but also of those of the staff in their own organisations if possible. This avenue can be quite successful in research organisations or academic institutions, especially if the research staff are aware of and sympathetic to the activities associated with creation of the database.

3.4 Exchange

Exchange arrangements require the database producer to supply its own (or other) publications in return for others. Both gift and exchange work most efficiently if they are formal arrangements subject to periodic review. Gift and exchange based on personal commitment or interest can be successful but is prone to disruption by staff departure, change of duties, and so on. Check lists should be kept to ensure the material is received.

3.5 Purchase

Purchase is the most common method of obtaining documents. If the database producer also runs a library the purchase may be assessed in terms of both relevance to the collection and relevance to the database. If the database producer provides a document backup service then purchase is necessary unless another equally accessible document source is available.

Purchase is the only option available in cases where the item cannot be obtained by other means. Tighter economic conditions and shrinking library budgets will in future make purchase a less attractive option, especially in the cases where the item is required only for potential indexing in the database but not for the database producer's library.

3.6 Interlibrary loan

Interlibrary loan is a very useful means of acquiring documents for indexing in the cases where the document is not required to be a permanent acquisition of the database producer. Usually the items sought on interlibrary loan have been identified in library accession lists and mostly but not always, the library will be one collecting in a similar or related subject area to the database producer.

Interlibrary loan of monographs presents no legal problem to the database producer at the document acquisition stage, although at the indexing stage there may be copyright questions he needs to consider (for example, the permissibility of including the document abstract in the database). However, when using interlibrary loan to obtain copies (for example photocopies of journal articles, or microforms of theses) for selection and indexing he must ensure he is complying with the provisions of the relevant copyright law.

3.7 Unobtainable documents

At times a database producer will identify a potentially relevant document but may not be able to obtain it by any acceptable means. In this case 'availability' becomes a prime selection criteria. If the document is not accessible to his client group he should, in general, exclude it from his database.

3.8 Document 'surrogates'

On occasions when the database producer may find a document difficult or impractical to obtain, a summary may be readily available. An experienced indexer with subject expertise may find that a summary or abstract and contents list provides sufficient detail for the item to be indexed adequately. This approach is taken by ACER when including theses in the AEI database. Theses are indexed for AEI from abstracts deposited with ACER by tertiary institutions.

3.9 Problems

There are two categories of documents which can be singled out as problems: unpublished material and conference papers. Unpublished material including report literature, is an important category of document in many special subject fields. Unpublished material may be difficult to identify and often is even more difficult to obtain. Only by constant vigilance can any measure of success be attained. Characteristics may include small print runs; lack of a coherent publication procedure in many organisations, particularly government departments; and poor bibliographic presentation.

Published conference proceedings present no particular problem; once they are identified, acquisition may be made by one of the variety of methods described earlier. Unpublished conference papers, however, often present a greater problem than unpublished reports. The conference organiser may not have required written papers from participants. Alternatively, the organiser may be a committee which disbands immediately after the conference and becomes impossible to locate. Preprints of papers may be available, but may be incomplete, inconsistent in naming the conference, or state 'may not be quoted'.

An associated problem is the conference organiser which assiduously issues comprehensive preprints of, for example, the Workshop on ABC, and then, perhaps years later publishes proceedings in which the conference is referred to by a different name, for example ABC Seminar. Whenever possible, the database producer should try to establish whether or not formal publication is planned before assessing preprints for inclusion in his database.

4. SELECTION

Selection is the decision making function for implementing the collection or acquisition goals. In most cases documents are acquired selectively and the decisions are made in the absence of the actual document. These decisions should be regarded as preliminary to the final selection process and it is at the stage of document acquisition that the final selection takes place. The following four factors will be considered as selection principles:

- Appropriateness of content/subject matter;
- Suitability of format, medium or document type;
- Quality of content;
- Availability of document.

PsychINFO subject areas		
Psychology	**Fringe areas**	**Nonrelevant**
Sexual behaviour	Sexual hormones	Fertility patterns
Smoking behaviour	Nicotine pharmacology	Lung cancer
Visual illusions	Nystagmus	Retinal cell structure
Verbal communication	Linguistics	Vocal cord physiology
Mon-machine systems	Technology and work	Computer programming

Fig. 10.2 PsychINFO subject areas.

Quality is the single most important selection criteria and although a document may satisfy other criteria, it should be rejected if the quality is not sufficient. Conversely, a high quality document may be considered although there are problems in availability.

4.1 Appropriateness of content/subject matter

As most small databases are subject orientated, it is important that the intent of subject coverage is well defined and an ongoing awareness of the important developments in the discipline is maintained. Consideration can be given to needs of users, however it is unlikely that a database can try to serve as a file for all knowledge or for any document that might by any stretch of the imagination be used by the potential users or in the context of the discipline. Most databases will have related areas in which specific consideration must be shown during selection. In general, database producers aim to cover the core subject areas comprehensively and review documents within the fringe areas on the relevance to the core subject. PsychINFO which strives to cover the world's literature in psychology and related disciplines deals with material in three areas; core psychology, fringe areas and nonrelevant; see Fig. 10.2.

4.2 Types of documents

Appropriate to the objectives of the database, a guide to the suitability of the different document types should be maintained. In a possible model, the many different document types are subdivided in three categories: most suitable, acceptable, and unsuitable.

In the first category, 'most suitable', documents are included as well as research and technical reports; descriptions of programs, projects, practices; evaluation and study reports; state-of-the-art papers and reviews; conference papers and proceedings; journal articles.

In the 'acceptable' category documents are selected when applicable from: annual reports; speeches and presentations; manuals; directories; material produced by local agencies; newsletters and bulletins.

Databases may also wish to include non-print material in the 'unsuitable' category, as well as ephemeral material which may be considered too transitory and without sufficient subject content; and news releases and interim progress reports which are generally preliminary in nature and are later superseded by final documents.

There are some considerations which apply to specific types of documents beyond the criteria pertaining to quality, availability and document types. These document types include short documents which can be evaluated on the uniqueness of content, utility to users or loss to the subject field if not included in the system. Opinion papers often fall into this category.

If candidates for a national database, documents containing material of local interest may have little value and should be selected only if they have some significance or utilisation beyond the narrower confines.

Journals are generally preselected and identified as indexed totally or selectively. In general, the application of qualitative criteria is not as relevant in selecting individual journal articles. Problems can arise with articles outside the subject or the country areas and those reprinted from other sources. In addition to the regular journals some databases elect to input good quality relevant articles which may be located in other journals not regularly covered. It should be remembered, however, that the user may have difficulty locating these titles and assistance by way of a note to the publisher's address should be cited in the document description.

The selection policy of *Sociological Abstracts* for journal articles is based on three criteria: '*inclusiveness*—to abstract the entire range of sociological journals and those in related disciplines irrespective of language of publication; *systematicity*—to abstract fully every core sociological journal and select from related journals those articles directly pertinent to sociology and those written by sociologists; and *continuity*—to abstract journals in chronological sequence of their publication whenever possible' (Chall and Wurzel, 1977, p.1.1).

4.3 Quality of content

As mentioned earlier, the quality of content, although elusive and subjective is the most important factor. The quality of a document can be ascertained through several specific characteristics.

4.3.1 Contribution to knowledge

Substantive contributions to knowledge will always have priority in selection, especially when based on well-designed research or an orderly presentation of data. Evidence which challenges or contradicts existing knowledge or common opinion can be as useful as that which confirms or merely extends what is already known. Papers prepared for learned societies or other special interest groups (for example professional organisations) often reflect the trends of new research and explorations not yet formally produced. Documents which add to or enhance the knowledge base of the field, or which provide an impetus for further research or action, should also be selected.

4.3.2 Relevance

Relevance in selection is defined as the extent to which the document deals with issues that are current, and of contemporary interest to the discipline.

4.3.3 New application of knowledge

There is always a need for documents which describe the application of tested or known methods to new areas and new problems.

4.3.4 Effectiveness of presentation

Though it may discuss a well-known subject, a document may add value because it presents the subject with exceptional clarity and vigor. It may present new insights, show the subject in a new context, or in language or form particularly suit the understanding of the intended audience. It is a disservice to users to select documents where the content is poorly presented or fails to provide sufficient information on the subject. Thoroughness of reporting refers to the extent of necessary background, information provided, level of technical detail presented, and substantiation given for statements made.

4.3.5 Timeliness

Timely, up-to-date information is preferred and consideration should only be given to older documents if they make a significant contribution to the subject.

4.3.6 Authority of author, source, sponsor

Some authors and some organisations are established leaders in their fields and have contributed so consistently to the field that virtually anything they produce merits selection. However, the habit of automatically and uncritically accepting everything from these sources should be avoided.

4.3.7 Audience

Preference is given to documents which appeal to the broader audience of the database, however attempts should be made to maintain a comprehensive coverage which will include documents on extremely narrow or specialised topics (ERIC, 1980).

4.3.8 Availability

The degree to which a document is readily available from sources can affect the selection decision, if the database producer does not provide or cooperate in a document backup service. It is frustrating to the user to obtain a citation for a document which is not readily available. This is particularly pertinent for unpublished papers and those having only local or specialised distribution. Theses also fall into this category although more tertiary institutions are providing access to these documents through micropublication.

5. COOPERATIVE ACQUISITION ARRANGEMENTS

One practical means of ensuring comprehensiveness in the database is the cooperative contribution arrangement. Usually this involves a group of organisations sharing the selection/indexing tasks, with one organisation assuming a central coordinating role. In this way the central database producer can gain valuable assistance with input, and avoid the responsibility and expense of acquiring all the relevant documents.

Such schemes can work well at both international and national levels. Examples are the IRRD system, sponsored by OECD, to which centres in 20 countries contribute, and such specialised national enterprises as AESIS (Tellis, 1978), AEI (Findlay, 1983) and ARI (Bays, 1978; Quinn, 1981). Other systems coordinate through subject orientated centres such as ERIC which operate in the United States with sixteen Clearinghouses.

In such arrangements the central coordinating body usually assumes most of the workload but contributions from other centres mean that the indexing load is shared, acquisition costs are spread, and the appropriate material is more readily identified.

There are a number of ways in which the identification/acquisition/selection tasks may be divided among contributors: by subject, the approach adopted by the Clearinghouses contributing to the ERIC database; by place of imprint, in the IRRD system each member country is responsible for abstracting its own publications; or by allocating different serial titles to each centre.

Cooperative arrangements impose on the central organisation the responsibility to maintain quality and consistency, to monitor contributors' input, and to edit it when necessary. For example, ERIC defines its overall field of education for use in the selection criteria as a combination of the Clearinghouse scope of interest statements which are detailed statements.

Procedures are established for negotiations between Clearinghouses concerning documents will fall within the scope of more than one centre. Documents which are extremely broad or basic in their coverage tend to be assigned to the broader, non-subject orientated Clearinghouses. A central acquisition section monitors collection activities in the Clearinghouses, and maintains a listing of their titles received within the network (ERIC, 1981).

Certain checks are necessary. These include an authority file for corporate names, a thesaurus for subject indexing, detailed indexing guidelines, and a method of ensuring all parts of serial publications are scanned. Communication, in the form of newsletters and regular training meetings, between the central organisation and contributors is vital.

6. RESEARCH IN PROGRESS AND DIRECTORY INFORMATION

Descriptions of research in progress, if systematically collected and presented, are an important information resource for researchers and for those seeking contact with them. Research in progress information identifies sources of subject expertise; provides access to data or potential sources of data well in advance of formal publication; fosters contact between professionals; encourages interchange of ideas; and enables duplication of effort to be identified.

For these reasons research in progress information is sometimes included in bibliographic databases, for example IRRD.

The usual method of acquiring research in progress or directory information is to survey organisations working in the relevant subject area. A mechanism for updating this information at regular intervals is necessary. The general conduct of national research in progress surveys is outlined in OECD 1982 and details of the procedures followed in one country, Australia, are given by Quinn (1983).

Some of the problems associated with acquiring project or directory information are: difficulty in identifying all appropriate organisations; poor response rate; and supply of inadequate detail by the research organisation. Some organisations, such as those with poor publishing procedures, also have very poor records of their own research projects.

7. CONCLUSION

Clearly defined objectives provide a framework within which the database producer operates. Selection principles relate the nature and scope of the documents or information included to these objectives and to the needs of the user. The value and integrity of the database depends on its continuous and thorough coverage of material satisfying the selection criteria. Promulgation of the objectives and selection policy to the user will help him to make most effective use of the database.

REFERENCES

American Psychological Association. 1981. *PsychINFO psychological abstracts information services users reference manual.* Arlington, Va, American Psychological Corporation.

Bays, M. 1978. 'The Australian road index: a co-operative venture'. *Australian Special Libraries News* 12(1): 34-37.

Chall, M. and Wurzel, D. 1977. *Sociological abstracts user's reference manual.* San Diego, Sociological Abstract.

ERIC (Educational Resources Information Center). 1980. *ERIC processing manual. Section 3: selection.* Washington, DC, ERIC.

Findlay, M. 1983. 'Australian education index'. In Peguero, G. (Ed.), *Australian clearing-house and data bases: towards a national policy.* Melbourne, Footscray Institute of Technology, pp. 102-111.

Lay, M. G. 1979. 'The ARRB information system'. *Australian Road Research Board Technical Manual ATM No. 7.* Vermon South, ARRB.

OECD Road Research Programme. 1982. *International road research documentation (IRRD) working rules.* 4th ed. Paris, OECD.

Quinn, S. 1981. 'Reference services of the Australian Road Research Board: co-operative aspects'. *Australian Road Research Board Internal Report AIR 809-1.* Melbourne, ARRB.

Quinn, S. 1983. 'Documentation of Australian road research projects'. *Australian Road Research Board Internal Report AIR 810-2.* Melbourne, ARRB.

Tellis, D. A. 1978. 'The Australian earth sciences information systems (AESIS) a co-operative national venture'. *Australian Special Libraries News* 12(1): 37-43.

11. The future

Peter Judge

1. Introduction
2. Technical developments
   2.1 Microprocessors
   2.2 Memories
   2.3 Text processing
   2.4 Communications
   2.5 Electronic publishing
3. The future market
4. Conclusion
Further reading

1. INTRODUCTION

In this book we have shown that databases can be developed for a variety of purposes: archiving; sorting and typesetting to produce a printed publication; and provision of a source of current information which can be interrogated online. For all these applications the rapid developments in computers, communications and text processing ('word processing') are highly relevant, and making the tasks easier day by day. They are also bringing down the costs. Already, the possibility exists of undertaking database activities on microcomputers which would have been almost unthinkable five years ago. This means that small databases are now more easily accessible for applications which a few years ago would have been dismissed as uneconomic. It also means that existing databases can become more ambitious in terms of size, detail of content and audience ('the market').

There is a temptation, given ways of doing something better through new technology, simply to try to do the *same* thing, only better. But 'better' may not be good enough; with changes of this kind occurring in both the

SMALL SCALE DATABASES
ISBN 0 12 391970 3

technical possibilities and the economics of the operations, there is an opportunity to take a fresh look at the objectives and the market for the information which is being put into the database. Moreover, these changes are taking place at a time when across the world the old definitions of professional activity are being questioned and redrawn. 'Librarians' and 'information workers' are broadening their horizons, overlapping with each others' functions, and becoming increasingly involved in related areas such as computer technology, records management, management and administrative information systems, and so on. We are seeing advertisements for 'Information Managers' whose job descriptions cover an ever increasing breadth of field. Clearly, when planning or replanning a database, close attention must be paid to this trend. The changes going on around us are providing a new context for our databases, and we need to recognise how this will affect our activities in order to direct them most effectively.

It is fair to say that almost anything we can imagine is technically possible. Increasingly, it is becoming economically possible, as well. However, the one great constraint in forward planning is likely to be the users—our 'market'. The processes of innovation have traditionally been influenced by 'technology push' and 'market pull'. More often, it is a market *pressure* rather than a *pull* which decides whether the more imaginative applications of new technology can be applied in practice. Users have been brought up in traditional ways, and their interest is in the information from the database, not in the technical virtuosity of the database or its producer. If that virtuosity can be shown to provide better or cheaper information, the potential users' interest will hopefully be captured. But they will also need to be convinced that it is an *easier* way of doing things. If users are to search the database online, the system will need to be an extremely *friendly* one.

It has been cynically pointed out that most so-called 'friendly' systems are anything but. Protocols and command language are skills which have to be acquired, and users (particularly, but not exclusively, older users) can be very resistant to learning such new skills. Depending on the kind and size of the database it may be possible to build large numbers of prompts into the search procedure, so that untutored users are helped from query to query, and can obtain the information they require with only the minimum of effort to learn new tricks. However, such a 'menu' driven search system is generally extravagant in the time that the user is connected to the system, so that it is more expensive than a database management system using simple flexible commands. Its slowness also means that the more experienced user can be thoroughly frustrated by having to wade through the menu to find the information, rather than going straight to it.

As things stand at present, there seem to be limited options for somebody developing a database who wants to appeal to an audience of widely differing skills. The database can be designed to please the unskilled majority of the potential users, at the risk of boring the others (and increasing their costs). The system can be complicated by providing two paths, although for a small database this may be an unjustifiable extravagance. Users can be put through training courses, although user training seems at variance with the concept of 'friendliness' and in any case is speedily forgotten by most users unless it is constantly practised. With an eye to the long term, the database can be offered to a limited online basis at present while looking to the future when better professional training in universities and schools will ensure a high degree of computer literacy on the part of all potential users. Of all aspects of the future, this educational implication will perhaps be the most far reaching, the most exciting, and the one which most often tends to be overlooked.

In the pages which follow, I will look at some of the technical and market developments which should influence planning for future databases. All of these developments are with us already to various extents, so you may think that 'future' is perhaps a misnomer. However, with such wide differences of sophistication in database activities in different parts of the world, and even within a particular country, what may seem 'old hat' to one user may be 'blue sky' to another. The future is a moving target with fuzzy boundaries. We can only identify an area of the technical horizon to aim at, and plan our activities to move in that general direction. But with the rate of technical change as rapid as it is, yesterday's blue sky is already old hat; today *is* the future—you are standing in it!

2. TECHNICAL DEVELOPMENTS

2.1 Microprocessors

Small powerful computers—and indeed, large powerful computers, to say nothing of wrist watches, robots and rockets—depend on the enormously complex circuitry now possible in tiny slices of semiconductor material, commonly referred to as silicon chips. The costs of computing have come down dramatically as a result of this kind of development, by about 20–30% per annum. Obviously the processes of miniaturisation and cost reduction must slow down at some stage, or we shall eventually have fob sized mainframe computers and inexpensive memories at the atomic scale, but in the immediate future it appears that these trends will continue, and the 'personal computer' is currently selling in millions in both developed and developing countries.

2.2 Memories

We have grown accustomed to computer memories on magnetic tape or magnetic discs. Recent developments have improved memory capabilities by factors of up to a 1000, bringing down the costs proportionately. In small computers this has been associated with the change from floppy discs to Winchester discs. The latter have sealed head/disc assemblies which enable greater precision and hence greater information densities, so, for a given size of disc, much more information can be held. Disc storage units the size of shoe boxes can store the equivalent of five complete sets of the Encyclopaedia Britannica.

However, other systems of storage are also coming into operation. One of these, similar in principle to the new compact discs which are revolutionising the high fidelity reproduction of music, is the optical video disc. Optical video discs are currently being used in the United States as high quality substitutes for video cassettes. They record an hour's colour TV program on their two surfaces, encoding the information in a series of tiny pits burnt into a metal film by laser, and subsequently read back by another laser of lower power. Rotating at 1800 rpm, a 12 inch video disc carries the equivalent of 54 000 TV frames, each of them separately addressable. Each frame is carried on one spiral of the disc, 315 000 pits to each track. The disc is sandwiched between two layers of plastic and is proof against scratches, dirt or wear. Indeed, the first demonstration disc that I saw had been completely cracked from edge to edge on one side, but still played perfectly without any interference or noticeable degradation of quality.

By making more efficient use of the information in these minute pits, much greater information densities are possible. Digital optical discs, such as those put out by Laserdata in the United States, offer one million pages of text on a 12 inch disc. Storage costs plummet: $4 per million characters on a computer magnetic disc pack, but only 2¢ per million on a Laserdata Data Disc, and hardware a fraction the price of computer hardware to do a comparable job of retrieving the information.

2.3 Text processing

The office word processor is only the tip of a very large iceberg. Linking a memory to a typewriter enables rapid production of letters or reports with multiple drafts and content and layout exactly as intended. However, the coded information in that memory can also be transmitted across the globe or used to compose type for publication. In the first case we have the basis for an electronic mail system; in the second for the dramatic revolution in printing technology which we have seen over the past decade.

When Gutenburg invented the art of printing by moveable type in the mid fifteenth century (as we now know, long after the same development in China), he began the process which has led to our information revolution. A skilled hand compositor, setting 2000 characters per hour, would take 22 hours to set a page of a newspaper. The development of the linotype machine increased the speed by a factor of five, and punched-tape casting was nearly three times faster again. However, computer fed photocomposition can now set eight million characters per hour (a page of newspaper in 15 seconds) and there seems every likelihood that this can be increased in future by a factor of four. Herein lie the seeds of a paradox: much of our electronic development has in it the germ of a 'paperless society', but at present much of it seems dedicated to the outpouring of printed paper.

This is certainly true in most offices. In large organisations now, word processing units linked to the firm's computer network enable letters or reports to be printed very rapidly, often at remote locations, encouraging discussion of texts at successive draft stages in a way which could never have happened before. In theory, discussion of the text could take place via the telephone, while looking at the image of the text on a VDU. In practice, the text is usually printed out, so that handwritten corrections can be made and sent back to the originating office, perhaps by facsimile transmission via the telephone network. Where individual typewriters are not linked to the computer in this way, it is possible to transfer their output to the computer by the use of OCR. This enables any typewriter which can be equipped with a golf ball or daisy wheel of an appropriate typeface (often called 'OCRB') to be read into the computer system at speeds in excess of 150 characters a second. Ink jet and laser printers can work at much the same speed, or faster up to 1000 characters a second, so that once material is entered into the computerised text processing centre via OCR its output can be extremely rapid.

Electronic mail services, of the kinds indicated above, have been shown to increase the flow of paper rather than reduce it; even if not working on successive drafts of the text, a copy of each message is usually required 'for the record', and not all of those interested in a particular message may have the appropriate equipment to receive it, so that they need paper too. The forecast is that the so-called paper-based electronic mail systems will at least initially generate a vastly increased number of pieces of paper: 21 billion paper messages by electronic mail in 1992 compared with only 4 million in 1982. However, the key feature of these developments, and of computer-fed photocomposition for publishing, is that for a time at least the message is coded in an electronic memory. This provides the basis for further processing, including electronic translation or electronic conferencing. It also provides the basis for on demand publication, which in the longer term may replace a proportion of the printed publications which we now see.

There is one warning associated with the development of electronic storage devices for archiving. Where there is access to the computer store by online users, these users must not have the right to make changes to the store without the supervision of the database manager. A database updated online leaves no record of what was there before, unless such a record is deliberately programmed into the system. Future archivists may therefore find a diminishing volume of material for their conservation or study.

2.4 Communications

Currently we are seeing a shift from analogue to digital modes of transmission in all types of communications: voice, facsimile, telephone, computer to computer links, and so on. There are two factors here which are enormously supportive of information retrieval and sharing activities. One factor is technical, typified by digitising or packet-switching. In this, each message is broken into pieces which are fired down a communications channel, together with a stream of pieces of other messages, so identified that at the other end they can be reconstituted back into the original messages and delivered separately. This means that large numbers of messages can be sent simultaneously down a single channel. The other factor is distance-independent pricing, which means that the originator of the message pays according to the quantity of information he is transmitting rather than the distance he is transmitting it.

An advantage of the newer ways of communicating is access to increased bandwidth, which may be important in transmitting images as well as coded text. Communication by satellite may seem little different from communication by wire. Our international telephone calls go via a mixture of copper wires, satellites and broadcast repeaters without us knowing or caring much about the route used (although the great distances introduced by satellites sometimes mean that our conversations are curiously punctuated by long pauses between question and answer). Optical fibres offer enormous channel capacity; a single optical fibre the width of a human hair can carry 800 simultaneous telephone conversations, or transmit 1400 books an hour in digital form. The same fibre, driven by a pulsed laser, is potentially capable of speeds 100 million times faster than that, transmitting one billion books per second down one fibre! Such figures may seem absurd, but emphasise what a tiny fraction of the power of modern communications technology we are so far exploiting.

Dependent on the degree to which local telephone and communication tariffs reflect the technical capabilities of these new communication channels, and so attract new business on economic as well as technical grounds, there are a number of implications for database working which may be important in planning systems. Packet-switching, if associated with a tariff which is distance-independent and is based on the amount transmitted rather than the connect-time, may mean that we can afford to spend (or encourage our users to spend) more time online thinking about the most efficient way of retrieving the exact information we or they require from the database. It also enables us to move material relatively inexpensively around the local network or across the globe. This may encourage us to deposit (or sell) parts of our database into the systems of our regular users, or to acquire parts of other, complementary databases into our own and keep both parts permanently in the memory of our system. This transfer, of parts of databases for subsequent local use, is known as 'down-loading'. Used wisely, down-loading into our database may be a way of rapidly enhancing the value of that database to users, at relatively little cost to ourselves. Down-loading from our database may be an effective way of marketing part of our product, but with the disadvantage that, once absorbed into another database, the anonymity of the records may mean that visibility of our product is lost. It is also a form of electronic publication, and responds to one of the problems raised earlier, that of obtaining the full text of the documents to which our attention has been drawn by a bibliographic database. However down-loading does raise new kinds of copyright and tariff problems.

2.5 Electronic publishing

Most technical publications are currently suffering a steady decline in sales variously estimated at 2–5% per annum. This decline follows a period of sustained growth when almost everything that was published could be sure of reaching a sales level high enough for the publisher to at least break even.

The decline is due to a number of factors. One factor is the vicious circle that the rise in publishing costs which has priced the major technical journals out of the hands of the individual buyer, has brought about diminished print runs, which in turn put unit costs even higher. In scholarly books, the average print run has dropped in the last ten years from around 2400 to well below 1000—for example 600–700. Another factor is the economic pressure on libraries, which are cutting back on purchases of non-essential publications, which they hope to cover through interlibrary loans. Another factor is the invention of the plain paper copier, which has made the explosion of interlibrary loans possible; an estimated 60 million to 100 million loans in the United States of America alone! In the case of abstracts journals, another is online working which has increased the global cost of bibliographic access to literature, but reduced the cost to the individual to a level which seems relatively trivial compared with the cost of subscribing to the paper copy. (The number of Chemical Abstracts subscribers not renewing each year has doubled since it went online.)

In this situation, what can the traditional publisher do? He can become more efficient: computer-assisted production control, editing and typesetting are fast becoming normal. He can improve the product, generally by making it bigger, and put the price up by an even greater amount than his customers would have swallowed otherwise. He can try through copyright action to recover the losses he incurs from theft by photocopying.

Losses by photocopying are likely to increase rather than diminish. Major libraries everywhere are streamlining their machinery both to provide and to request and receive photocopies of separate papers for their readers. The British Library Lending Division deals with two million requests a year from the United Kingdom, and a further half million from over 100 overseas countries. It is collaborating with the European Commission to explore even more efficient ways of transmitting material electronically via satellite, preferably using the digital text produced by the big publishers during their computer-assisted typesetting.

While some publishers would see these developments as a legalised international conspiracy to commit massive piracy, others are exploring new ways of putting text onto the market through these electronic means, so obtaining some return from the supply of separate articles rather than the whole journal. A part of the problem is that the text produced for typesetting purposes and held in a computer memory is at present not compatible with ways of holding graphics in computer memory; this is particularly true for halftones. Halftones can be transmitted electronically with high quality (as is done by all newspapers which produce distant edition, for example) but this is done by a scanning mechanism similar to that of television, which is not compatible with the digitised text available for searching or other processing. Electronic books and journals are being produced, at least experimentally, in most of the developed countries of the world, and are already worth over $3 billion a year. This is less than a tenth of the value of printed information, but it is growing at 25% per annum, more than twicc thc growth rate of print media.

A recent Delphi study suggests that a half of our indexing and abstracting services will be available only in electronic form by the year 2000. The same study, however, forecasts that not even 25% of academic journals will have changed to electronic form until after 2000. On the other hand, 50% of technical reports should be electronic by 1995 and 90% after 2000; for reference books it is projected that 25% will be available in electronic form by 1990 and 50% after 2000. These are impressive figures (if they are realised!) but they imply that there will still be a great deal of information published *on paper* into the foreseeable future. Those of us whose databases depend on paper-based publications for their input or output, can take note of this forecast with either relief or dismay, depending on its implications.

However, there are other implications besides the technically feasible or the economically desirable. We are already finding that some institutions (particularly academic institutions) place arbitrary restrictions on the use of information services in order to keep within budgets, regardless of the fact that alternatives to these databases may be much more costly to the user (although the costs are concealed) and the loss in time and in efficient access to information may have damaging effects on the productivity of research or other activities.

In developing countries this situation is aggravated. Many of the professionals concerned with library and information services in these countries are well aware of what is available and of the potential applications of this technology in their countries. However, they are effectively prevented from providing these services because of the lack of computer hardware and trained operators. In many cases they also lack an effective communications infrastructure within their country, and in most cases they lack the convertible currency needed to pay for the use of overseas databases. Moreover, their potential users—including their governments—have been unaware of the power of these services, so that there is a Catch 22 situation: because they lack the means to be effective, they have been starved of the resources to become effective.

This situation is now beginning to change, there is a realisation that good information services underlie all the processes of economic, social and cultural development. Inasmuch as most modern information services depend on databases, it is an economic necessity that these be well used. But in order that this will happen, there has to be an unpredecented educational effort to bring about a greater degree of *computeracy* in the academic, managerial and government sections of the workforce.

Meanwhile, those of us who are in countries which are at the forefront of technological developments in the field, find ourselves being pulled two ways. The present economics of technical and scientific journal publication require the buyer to take the journal (or conference proceedings) as a *package*. Those papers which are wanted and will be read by the purchaser are probably in the minority, mixed in with a large number of papers which will not be read. This is why the journal has been described as 'a gigantic confidence trick'. Although in the beginning it was a device to ensure the wide dissemination of new knowledge, it has become a marketing device to ensure the profitability of journal publication by the subsidy of the large number of articles which will *not be read* (at least, not by any one purchaser) by the few which *will be read*. However, this is what scientists are used to.

If we look at an electronic publication, it has two grave disadvantages, for both the publisher and the author. It enables the purchaser to buy only those papers which are in demand. The concept of the 'package' is lost and inevitably the price of the single article must rise to a new economic level.

Also, there is another Catch 22 situation: good scientific papers will not be submitted to an electronic journal (let alone to a 'centre' for providing separate articles electronically) until it is widely recognised and carries the same prestige as the present printed journals, which will not happen until those good papers are submitted... Whatever happens, the authors of the second and third rung papers will not benefit in an electronic journal from association with the authors of the first rung papers, as they do in the printed journal by having their papers discovered and read by serendipity.

In spite of these disadvantages of the electronic journal, is it fair to say that the traditional ink on paper scholarly publication is obsolescent? If we do not put a time scale on it, it may well be, and this could influence how we plan to publish and market our database. There are two strong market pulls acting in the same direction as the electronic push:

i. The squeeze on library budgets world-wide coincides with an increased demand for information from libraries and the paper copies can barely keep up with this demand.
ii. Planning is underway in many parts of the globe for improved documentation delivery services and shared resources, based on electronic storage, transmission and display.

The pressure for electronic-assisted storage, retrieval and transfer may lead to more parallel publishing of scholarly journals (print-on-paper and electronic publication simultaneously, or with a short time difference to maintain sales of print-on-paper). This is especially likely once the problem of delivering high quality graphics with computer-searchable text is resolved and this becomes an economic reality.

From parallel publishing to the fast delivery of separate articles which only achieve paper form (if at all) at a local document delivery centre, is a very short step. High speed printers can already provide paper copy from computer input at extraordinary speeds (for example the Xerox 9700 Laser Beam Printer at two A4 pages a second). The bookshop or library of the future may be a computer catalogue or index, from which the full text of the journal article or book which is required can be called up and then printed and bound 'on demand' while the customer waits. At two pages a second, a three hundred page book could be produced in two and a half minutes!

This is the *technical* possibility. Will the user accept it?

3. THE FUTURE MARKET

In the last section I have looked at those technical developments which may make the database producers' task easier in sharing information, and in obtaining books and journal articles which his bibliographic database has identified as relevant to the user's need. But, do we have any indications of whether the user will be demanding this kind of service, or whether, when offered this service, the user will be prepared to pay an economic price to receive it?

The short answer has to be, '*no*'! Even after 20 years of online systems, existing information services are grossly under-utilised. It has been pointed out that the 4 million to 5 million online searches performed on (mainly) bibliographic databases in the United States, represents an average of only two searches a year for each of the technically qualified individuals who might be in the market for such services. In most other developed countries, the average usage rate is probably only half that. It should probably be at least 25 times that. What is missing so far?

It has been pointed out that millions of drill bits are sold every year in the world, although nobody wants drill bits, they want holes. In much the same way, information services are being offered, or in a few cases aggressively marketed, around the world when nobody wants a *service*, what they want, is the *information*. One of the problems faced by producers of databases is that their systems may be seen by users as counterproductive, for two reasons. On the one hand, it is thought that the systems are an obstacle between the user and the information he is seeking. On the other, it is thought that so much information will be retrieved that the user will be swamped by it, 'information overload'. A part of the marketing or educational task is to convince users that an information system is a means of selecting a *smaller* quantity of high quality information than they would usually be presented with, from a much *larger* quantity of information than they would normally have access to. These concepts of information *selectivity* and *reduction* cannot be overemphasised.

At present, users are also brainwashed by the circumstances of their education and training. In universities and schools, ferreting on the library shelves, or making efficient use of the library catalogue or of the printed indexes is seen as a part of the training of future professionals. Most of them, once qualified, thankfully leave all this behind and survive on the knowledge that they have acquired at university, supplemented by reading a few journals or books which they believe are sufficient to maintain their knowledge of their field. This is true in universities and technical schools even at the postgraduate level, where the library is often reluctant to make the use of electronic databases widely available because of the perceived cost involved. It is far cheaper, in budgetary terms, to let users spend a day browsing along the library shelves, or peering in abstracts journals, than to give them ten minutes on a computerised database. In consequence, even in the special circumstances where the database has been produced in-house and is therefore effectively free of marginal cost for increased use, these habits of thinking persist and users are intimidated on the grounds of the supposed cost. If the service is offered online for users to do the searching personally, rather than as a service where the searches are performed by the database operators, there may be a variety of other intimidating factors.

Not least of these is the fact that in most countries of the world, it is unusual for professionals to have even the experience of using a typewriter. In consequence, a keyboard of any kind is something which is strange and intimidating, and if access to information requires performing these unaccustomed rituals, the user will prefer to go elsewhere.

This situation is changing with the changing nature of education in most countries. On the one hand, it is more common these days for students to type their assignments, so that they are at least familiar with the typewriter. On the other hand, more schools are now providing some training on computers, so that the computer is itself a familiar object in an educational setting. It is also, of course, an increasingly familiar object in the home setting, even if it being largely used for playing Star Wars and Donkey Kong!

For these reasons, it is likely that the market is in fact changing and becoming more amenable to the idea of searching information by computer. Incidentally, it is also becoming more amenable to the concept that information is a commodity which has a value and which must be paid for.

None of this reduces the requirement on the part of a database operator to *market* the database (as part of an information service) and to ensure the continued visibility of that database as in integral part of the organisation's mainstream activities.

One of the criticisms made of current information systems is that the relativity low level of use reflects a lack of sensitivity on the part of system designers or operators to the users' actual needs. For this reason database producers need to be continuously conscious of and sensitive to market requirements and their changing nature in the future.

One of the disadvantages of the marketing process is that it requires the database producer to identify the particular group of people (the 'market segment') to whom the database is directed. That group of people may be only the database producer, recording material for personal or archival reasons; it may be the readers of a publication, if the database is a step on the road towards the printing process; or it may be a group of users in-house, national or international. In each case the same question arises 'Who (and how many) are the users?'.

On the answer to this question depends all of the next stages, because all future planning must be directed towards satisfying that perceived demand. If the answer is dishonest, or wildly wrong, the economics of the whole operation will be wrong. In a commercial situation, a market projection will be drawn up for a number of years surrounding the first introduction of the new product. The forecasting element here, the *future market* as the product and its sales (or use) develop, will condition the amount of effort put into the database, and the cut off point after which a decision has to be taken to continue it or not.

The purpose of this final section is to emphasise the importance of those market forecasts, in relation to the new technical and economic possibilities which are opening up. You will find it relatively easy, in the technical literature, to identify the technical developments which can be helpful in the development of your particular database. You will find it much more difficult to pin down the trends in the market place and in users' habits or their readiness to accept the kind of service which you wish to offer through your database. To some extent you will have to make these forecasts yourself, in your own organisation by discussion with your potential users and finding out what features in your service will make it more acceptable to them.

4. CONCLUSION

I said earlier 'this *is* the future—you're standing in it'. The developments which have been discussed in this chapter are here already, and awaiting application. None of this is blue sky. However, all of it is new and all of it is constantly new and changing in any specific situation, such as the one in which you find yourself. In this state of flux, bear in mind that forecasting the future is not only impossible but pointless; what we have to do is to identify a future which we want to be part of, and plan how to get there. Good luck!

FURTHER READING

Journals

Communication Technology Impact
Monitor
Newsidic

Glossary

ACER Australian Council for Educational Research.
ACI Australian Consolidated Industries.
AEI Australian Education Index.
AESIS Austraiian Earth Sciences Information System.
AMDEL Australian Mineral Development Laboratories.
AMF Australian Mineral Foundation.
ARI Australian Road Index.
ASFIS Aquatic Services and Fisheries Information System.
AUSINET Australian Information Network (ACI Computer Services).
AUSMARC Large scale database of the National Library of Australia.
AWRC Australian Water Resources Council.
BMR Bureau of Mineral Resources.
BP British Petroleum.
CAB Commonwealth Agricultural Bureau.
CAI Computer Aided Instruction.
CILES Central Information, Library and Editorial Section (CSIRO).
CODEN Unique number identifying journal titles (similar to ISSN)
CPM Critical Path Method.
CRRERIS Commonwealth Regional Renewable Energy Resources Information System.
CSIRO Commonwealth Scientific Industrial Research Organization.
CSIRONET Bibliographic database operated by CSIRO.
DBMS Database management systems.
DIALOG Lockheed Corporation online data retrieval system.
EEC European Economic Community.
ELHILL Computer software used by US National Library of Medicine on MEDLINE.
ERIC Educational Resources Information Center.
ESRISAT Earth Science and Related Information-Selected Annotated Titles.
EUREKA Experimental information retrieval software package.
FOCUS A 4GL.
GFMS General File Maintenance System (CSIRO).
4GL Fourth Generation Language.
IRRD International Road Research Documentation.
ISBN International Standard Book Number.

ISSN International Standard Serial Number.
KWIC Key Word In Context.
KWOC Key Word Out of Context.
LC Library of Congress.
LCMARC Large scale database of the Library of Congress.
LCSH Library of Congress Subject Headings.
LISA Library and Information Science Abstracts.
MARC MAchine-Readable Catalogue.
MEDLARS MEDical Literature Analysis and Retrieval System.
MEDLINE MEDLARS online.
NLA National Library of Australia.
OCR Optical Character Recognition.
OCRB Typeface able to be read by OCR.
OECD Organization for Economic Cooperation and Development.
ORBIT Retrieval software used by Orbit Information Services.
OSTI Office for Scientific and Technical Information.
PERT Program Evaluation and Review Technique.
PRECIS PREserved Context Index System.
SADME South Australian Department of Mines and Energy.
SIRE Syracuse Information Retrieval Experiment (software).
STAIRS Information retrieval software package.
STATUS Information retrieval software package.
SYN STAIRS command for synonym retrieval.
VDU Visual display unit.

Index

A
Abbreviations 143
AESIS 78, 83, 85–89
AND logic 159–160, 162
AUSINET 78, 148
Australian Marine Research in Progress 14
Australian Thesaurus of Earth Sciences and Related Terms 85
Authority files 141, 145
AWRC 78

B
Batch processing 140
Bibliographic databases 1, 2, 38, 41–42, 45, 77–81
Bibliographic records 3
Boolean logic 159, 161
Bradford distribution 91

C
Chained files 46
Citation data 144
Clientele *see* Users
Clustered files 46–47
Commercial databases 49, 53
Computed access files 46
Computer hardware 10, 11
Computer software 8, 9, 10, 11, 151
Computers
  processors 60–62
  character sets 61
  communication 63, 70
  input devices 62–64
  mainframes 59–71 *passim.*
  microcomputers 59–71 *passim.*
  minicomputers 59–71 *passim.*
  output devices 66–67
  processors 60–62
  purchasing decisions 71
  response time 61
  storage units 60, 64–66, 67–68
  system capacity 61
Computing networks
  CSIRONET 84
  CSIRO, CILES 86
Control data 142, 145
Copyright 114–115
Cost benefit ratio 91–92
Cost benefits 84, 89–96
Cost determinants 33, 34
Cost effectiveness 89–94
Costs
  cataloguing 84
  databases, development 81–85
  data entry 87
  data preparation 87
  data processing 83–87
  earth sciences information 87–89
  management overheads 83, 89
Costs and benefits 99–100 *passim.*
  recovery and charging 113–114
Current awareness services 83
  earth sciences, Australia 85
  ESRISAT 85, 86

D
Data amendment 29, 30
Data editing 142, 143
Data entry media 27
Data entry systems 27
Data fields 18, 29
Data integrity 40
DBMS software 44–45
Data structures 5

Data validation 26, 27, 28, 29, 40, 145
Database creators 6
Database design 13, 14, 148
Database evaluation 13
Database management systems 2, 3, 4
Database updating 19, 26, 27, 28, 29, 30
Databases
  design, flexibility 74
  distributed 68
  factors affecting 74
Decision making process
  elements in 74–75
  steps in 75–77
Dedicated systems 69
Descriptive data 142, 143–144
DIALOG 147, 150, 157, 160
Directories 17
Disc storage
  backup 65–66
  fixed discs 64–65
  floppy discs 64, 65, 68, 69
Document handling 140–141
Document location 144
Document recording 141
Down-loading 187
Duplicate checking 40

E
Earth sciences information 83
Economic efficiency 33, 34
Editorial standards 139, 142–145
ELHILL 158
Environmental considerations
  air conditioning 70
  ancillary storage 70
  cabling 70
  lighting 70
  noise 67, 70
Error messages 29, 145
ESRISAT 83, 85
EUREKA 161
Evaluation of software 51–54
Exhaustivity 151

F
Fields and subfields 4, 5, 9 (Fig.)
Formatext 84
Free text retrieval 149, 150
Friendly systems 183
Future trends in
  communications 186–187
  memories 184
  microprocessors 183
  text processing 184–186
  the market for information 190–193

G
Geoscience information *see* Earth sciences information
Geoscience *see* Earth sciences
Goals *see* Objectives
Graphic output 66–67

H
Hard copy products 32, 33
Hardware selection 27, 34
Homographs 152, 153

I
Index terms 148, 149, 150
Indexed sequential files 47
Indexing and indexes 6, 19, 32, 33, 148, 149, 150, 151, 161, 162
Information services
  earth sciences, costs 81–89
  evaluation 89–94
Information systems
  design of 79–81
  elements in 77
  models 78–79
Inverted files 46
Item identifiers 18, 27, 28, 29

J–K–L
Joysticks 62
Keyboards 62
LCSH 150, 155
Legal responsibilities 115–116
Library of Congress Subject Headings *see* LCSH
Light pens 62

M–N
Machine readable catalogue *see* MARC
Magnetic tape 64
Maintenance 142
MARC 2, 3, 4, 5
Marketing 111
Monographs 141
Mouse 62
Natural language 154

O
Objectives
  elements in formulation 76
Offline storage 67–68
Online information retrieval 151–155
Online retrieval 17, 19, 28, 29, 31
Online retrieval systems 30, 31, 32
Online searching 143
Online storage 67–68
Operating system 44

Optical character recognition 62
Optical fibres 186
Optical video discs 184
ORBIT 147, 150, 158
OR logic 159–160, 162
Output production 32, 33

P
'Paperless society' 185
Plotters 66–67
PRECIS 7, 160
Precision 13, 159–161
Printers 63–64, 66
Programming languages 44
Proofreading 29, 30, 142

R
Recall 13, 157–159
Reference databases *see* Bibliographic databases
Relevance assessment 143
Renewable energy information
  CRRERIS 81
Research-in-progress databases 17, 18, 19, 28
Resolution of logical records 2
Resources for information provision 77

S
Search protocols 161, 162, 163
Search strategies 161, 162, 163
Searching
  natural language 39
  relevance 39–40
Sequential files 45–46
Serial documents 141
Service bureau 51
Shared systems 68–69
SIRE 161
Software
  cost consideration 56
  definition 38
  development 50–51
  for microcomputers 55
  packages 48–49
  qualitative aspects 38–40
  quantitative aspects 40–41
  security 53–54
Software selection 30, 31, 33, 34
Specificity 150, 151
Staff numbers and kind 105–106
  sharing 107
STAIRS 147, 150, 157
STATUS 150, 157
STREAMLINE 78
  software
    Formatext 84
    GFMS 86
Subject indexing 149, 150, 151
Synonyms 153, 157
Syntactic devices 160–161

T
Target information 77
Term term relationships 152
Textual databases
  characteristics 41–43
  software 43
Thesauri
  earth sciences 85
  development costs 91
Training 54, 55
Turnkey systems 47–48
Typesetting 33

U
Unit costs 83–84, 89
User manual 110
  feed-back 111, 112, 113
User needs 143
User services provision 30, 31, 32
Users 77

V
VDU (visual display unit) 62–64, 66, 67
Vocabulary control 12, 152–157

W
Water information
  STREAMLINE 78
  WATR 78
Weighting 161
Wordforms 158

6 7 8 9 0 1 2 3 4 5
A B C D E F G H I J